"As an adoptive parent of the 1960s, reading *A Life Let Go* by Patricia Florin was both painful and illuminating. Painful because it brought to the fore the experience of birth mothers exiled to a life of not knowing what had happened to their offspring... Illuminating because Florin explores both her own and other birth mothers' experiences... This is must reading for adoptive parents.... It is also important reading for the children of both closed and open adoptions...."

> ~ Herbert Long, Th.D.; Diplomate, Process Oriented
> Psychology; Former Dean of Students and Peabody
> Lecturer, Harvard Divinity School; Adjunct Faculty,
> Marylhurst University

"What is it like to be imprisoned by a secret? In *A Life Let Go*, Patricia Florin recounts in heartbreaking detail how she was forced to become a shadow in her own home after becoming pregnant as a young, melancholy teen. Although she surrenders her child to adoption and returns to her previous routine, the experience casts a shadow over her entire life. She yearns to know what became of her daughter, but the closed adoption bars her from knowing anything—not even her name. When her daughter comes looking for her years later, Florin must confront the secrets she has endured and reconcile the past to reunite her family. Throughout her journey, she finds comfort in a circle of women who have surrendered children to adoption and skillfully weaves their stories together in this memoir of loss, recovery, and the enduring power of love."

> ~ Janet Oelklaus, NW California Representative
> American Adoption Congress

A LIFE LET GO

A Memoir and Five Birth Mother Stories of Closed Adoption

Long Journey Home Press
Williams, Oregon

A Life Let Go:
A Memoir and Five Birth Mother Stories of Closed Adoption

Long Journey Home Press
Williams, Oregon
www.patriciaflorin.info

Cover by Chris Molé Design

Second edition: 2018

ISBN 978-0-9965823-0-8

Manufactured in the United States of America

10 9 8 7 6 5 4 3 2 1

When you make a decision, that decision is based on your age, your life experience, your knowledge, your wisdom, your childhood and the influence of those around you. At the moment you make that decision, you have no other choice.

~ Rollo May, existential psychotherapist, at adoption conference in Boston in 1987, as quoted by Joe Soll, LCSW

For Andrea

CONTENTS

PREFACE   iii

1 HIDDEN, Patricia's Story   1

2 THE CIRCLE   91

3 NEW BEGINNINGS, Nancy's Story   97

4 ANIMA, Evelyn's Story   133

5 EXPOSED, Marti's Story   179

6 WOUNDED REBEL, Dena's Story   207

7 THE DECISION, Kate's Story   239

8 FULL CIRCLE   281

9 THE GIFT   289

FURTHER READINGS   293

ACKNOWLEDGMENTS   295

Most of the names in my own story are real. In the other stories, the names of the women and their families and, in some cases, their geographical locations have been changed.

PREFACE

1972

I was sixteen years old and pregnant. My family hoped to protect my reputation by keeping the pregnancy secret, so I was hidden inside our home. Afterward, I did not talk of the birth. Where the baby was placed was a secret even I did not know.

When the grief and fear of being found out knocked on my heart, I also hid from them. I took to bed and lay motionless until they gave up and left.

On October 28, 1988 I received one of those phone calls that divides life into *before* and *after*. My daughter was looking for me, and I began the work of undoing the shame that burdened my life and learning to be in the world without relying on secrets.

While doing this work, I found invaluable friends in other women who had lost a baby in adoption. Their insights and stories helped me to see what I could not on my own. Their influence was so vital that I wanted to include some of their stories in this book.

It is my deep desire that women who have faced this "decision" and all its consequences will find in these stories support and comfort. The more I think about the women still dealing with their feelings alone and in secret, the more compelled I feel to reach out to them. This book is a reminder to them that they are not alone. It is also my hope that adoptees reading these stories will gain some understanding of their own birth mothers, and that the parents who adopted them who have not yet done so will be able to acknowledge and welcome the bond that connects us all.

Some Terms

Birth mother. A woman who gives birth to a child and relinquishes that child for adoption. Sometimes called *natural mother* or *first mother.*

Closed adoption. In closed adoption there is no contact between the birth family and the adoptive family. In most cases, they never meet. The adoptive family is usually chosen by an agency social worker, although private adoptions, where a lawyer or physician makes the arrangements, still occur. Searching for birth family is seen by many as breaking confidentiality.

Open adoption. In open adoption birth parents meet and often choose adoptive parents for their child. The birth family and adoptive family may develop a lifelong relationship, ranging from exchanging occasional pictures to the birth family being invited to the adoptee's birthdays and special events. Although these terms are negotiated, they are not legally binding in all states.

Sealed records. The legal wall between adoptees and birth families was intended to be unbreachable without a court order. In most states adoptees have two birth certificates: one with the adoptive parents' names and a second, legally sealed certificate with the birth parents' names. As the number of people searching for birth family increased, and as many adoptees exerted pressure to have access to their own birth records, several states have changed their laws to make the original birth certificate, an invaluable search instrument, available to adoptees.

1

HIDDEN – Patricia's Story

For four and a half months I was the shadow looking out the upstairs windows of our home. Our city, a suburb of Chicago, was known for its nice homes and conservative values. Our religion, Catholicism, was known for its clear rules and lines of authority. Our family, well, it was known for its size—Dad, Mom, Grandma, and eight kids—and our boisterous ways. We were also known for our Sunday dinners, taken in the dining room, guests welcome, and the penny-ante poker game afterward.

It was a Sunday evening in March 1972, and at sixteen, I was in my last month of pregnancy. So while Sunday dinner played out downstairs, I hid in my brother's room. As long as I was stuck up there, I was supposed to be answering essay questions for a take-home history test.

The rest of the house had smooth plaster walls, crown moldings, and thick carpeting. This room was different, less hospitable. The walls, white stucco crags that crumbled in places, brought to mind an old-world prison. Across from the desk was a short door that led to the attic. We kids had been warned never to go in there for fear of breaking through the floor. I had seen inside there once: bare joists and rafters slanting down to meet the roofline of the story below, a few boxes of who knew what, and the monster house ventilator that banged furiously when it was windy, like that night. This room, although probably ade-

1

quate for my eighteen-year-old brother's sensibilities, was my least favorite. However, its strategic advantage was its two doors, one leading to my parents' bedroom and the other to the opposite end of the hallway. If I heard someone come too close to one side of the room, I would sneak out the other side and around to one of the three other rooms. And, in case I was spotted anyway, I wore a large poncho.

The wind eased up, and I heard voices and laughter coming from downstairs. They were having a good time. I heard footsteps on the stairs. With mild panic, I stood, fluffed the large poncho around my middle, and readied myself to sneak out one of the two doors.

"It's just me," my brother Ed said as he came to one of the doors. "Mom sent dinner." He came in with a plate piled with food. I sat down again, and he handed me the plate. Roast beef, mashed potatoes, and green beans simmered in bacon grease for five hours.

Our relationship always had been a battle, sometimes physical. He always won those. The verbal ones, well, no one won. So it was strange to sit in his room, and also that he was being so nice to me.

"How long do you think they'll be here?" I asked.

"Usual I guess. Why?"

"I'm having trouble with this homework."

"You can't be a senior if you don't pass history." He left.

A year ahead of me in school, he was full of advice. And a lot of things had to happen before I could be a senior, including having a baby and giving it up without anyone besides some family finding out.

How had I let this happen? I knew girls got pregnant, but I remember thinking: *Not me.* I trusted Mother Nature knew better than to let someone who was fifteen conceive.

2

Where I met the father of the baby the previous year was something else the family was keeping secret.

As my fifteenth birthday had approached, a darkness swept over me. It was as if something had punched a hole in my psyche and was pulling all feeling out of me until the only thing left was despair. I stopped caring about schoolwork, stopped talking to people except to answer questions, started reading books like *I Never Promised You a Rose Garden* and *The Bell Jar*. My grades slipped. Whenever I didn't have to be in school, I was in bed indulging dark thoughts: *I'm not supposed to be here; nobody cares and nothing matters.*

I remember walking into my own surprise birthday party, depressed, and not terribly surprised. I wore a bulky, rust-colored sweater and brown pants. I went down the stairs to my friend Kathi's rec room—party central—where a Beatles' song played and friends who hardly said hello to me at school greeted me with shouts of "Surprise!" and "Happy birthday!" Another couple of hours to fake my way through. It occurred to me that I should have just killed myself the day before and saved today's effort and the potential discomfort for the party goers who might look back and wonder what was wrong with me that they hadn't noticed. But none of them looked comfortable in the skin they wore either. We kids followed one another around in hopes of bumping into the right way of being in the world—what were we supposed to do and how were we supposed to do it? It was as if the instruction manual for moving into adulthood was written on air and we were expected to find the right spots to breathe it in to know what to do next.

* * *

Nineteen sixty-nine brought Woodstock. Because I was only thirteen and living halfway across the country, it barely made it onto

my radar. But protestors in the form of Students for a Demo-
cratic Society and hippies with their colorful, loving messages
showed up even in our tucked-away suburb. Part of me craved
what I saw as a casting away of rules in order to be true to one-
self. Another part of me was terrified at the idea. All of me was
fascinated. And the moon landing... I sat with Kathi's family in
their den and we all watched on TV as a human touched another
celestial body. And the musical *Hair*, I knew the lyrics by heart
and sang them with gusto, although the lyrics of track two were
beyond my vocabulary. Something wild in me responded to this
soundtrack about pleasure and rebellion and fighting for the
freedom to be unique. That year my heart was full of hope and
promise.

But by 1970 the world was making less sense to me. I saw
that most of the people taking hallucinogens and telling us it
was the way to enlightenment couldn't seem to take care of
themselves. Young men were dying in Vietnam because their
birthdays fell on the wrong day and they were drafted. Demon-
strators at Kent State were shot. I started to recognize contradic-
tions between what authority said and what authority did, and I
lost confidence in those who ran things. An insane, power-brutal
world was cracking my childhood image of the way the world
was supposed to be—open, honest, respectful.

At my high school, Immaculate Conception, the nuns had
modernized their habits—less veil, more hair, coiffed and
sprayed, and panty-hosed legs below the knee. (Their shoes
were still ugly black clunks.) More lay people were teaching.
Our uniform skirts were allowed to come above the knee by an
inch or two. Even then I recognized that these were baby steps as
voices cried out against conformity, racism, and sexism. People
were dragging one another into the streets, shouting, waving
angry banners. Some streets burned with anger.

Our own suburb wasn't on fire, but individuals were. Families on the street broke up—infidelity and alcohol. A sham world was cracking.

In my own home, although we said we loved one another, and enjoyed being together, violence had woven itself into the fabric of our family. My siblings and I argued, screamed insults, pulled hair, and threw punches, shoes, hairbrushes, and dishes. Mom didn't know what to do with us, and Dad was rarely witness because we were careful not to let loose when he was home; it might release his own violence. My image of our happy family was cracking.

I sought comfort in church. When I took the host, I waited to feel the presence of the Almighty, but I felt no uplift, no inspiration, no touch of mystery. I listened to the nun playing Bach on the organ during communion. I had stopped taking piano lessons, because of the nun who had smacked my hands when I had played a piece of music too fast. Here reverent, there violent. Cracking.

I was cracking. I mentally flogged myself for being inadequate to cope with the world. Over the years teachers had told my mom that I was a sensitive child. I never heard them suggest ways to manage it.

After the surprise birthday party, every minute felt like a desolate hour. I took one step, then the next, and the next. If joy had been presented to me with fireworks and flowers, I could not have seen it. Despair reached its bony fingers into my chest and squeezed: *Quit. It doesn't get better, only longer.*

I stole twenty painkillers, Darvon, left at the house by my sister's boyfriend. I decided I would take them to school, swallow them there, then hide behind some bushes at the library. A stranger would find me, a janitor or landscaper.

I tried to imagine the afterlife. Would everything go white? Black? Empty foreverness? Could I bear it? Would there be a *me* to bear it, or would my consciousness end? What did it mean to give up consciousness? Would God be there? Would he punish me? How? What was worse—this despair, or some unimaginable punishment? What would death feel like? A blank? No thinking?

I put the pills in a tissue in my purse. I felt lighter now that there was a plan.

Back-up plan: If I changed my mind after taking the pills, I would tell a teacher. It couldn't be a nun, not about suicide, considered a mortal sin by the Catholic Church. They would ask questions for which I had no answers, probably drag me before a priest, blame my lack of faith—and we would get nowhere. Most of the other teachers were men, and Mr. G., the biology teacher, was able to reach kids better than the other teachers. I decided that if I chickened out I would go tell him.

The final bell rang. Metal lockers banged, oversized wood doors swung on their brass hinges again and again as my classmates raced out of the four-story brick fortress. I went into the bathroom, opened my purse, and took out the pink tissue with the twenty Darvon. Afraid of gagging, I took out only four, filled my hand with water, swallowed. The plastic capsules caught in my throat. I put my purse under my arm and used both hands to cup more water, and swallowed it all down. I kept popping capsules in my mouth and chasing them down with water from my hands until the pink tissue was empty.

I wondered how long it would take. I wasn't feeling different yet. I opened and closed my hands. They still worked. Maybe, while I could still walk, I should head across the street to the public library so I could hide under the bushes.

I walked down the hall toward the door when my stomach wretched. Was that the pills or fear? Death? Now that I had done it, I did not feel headed to freedom. What if I was wrong? About everything?

I ran up three flights of stairs to Mr. G's room. He looked up from his grade book. I felt awful that I was about to pull him into this ugly desperation.

"I took pills. Too many."

He looked stunned, then blinked. I figured options must be running through his mind. "We'll go to the hospital," he said. "And call your parents."

Oh no... Now I would have to face them, look them in the eye, let them see that I didn't want this life they gave me. Maybe I could still run, hide.

Mr. G. took me by the arm and walked me out of the building.

In the emergency room, throwing up, I saw two and three of everything. Mom, shoulders slumped, looked as if she was giving up too. Dad looked agitated and confused as he held the pan under my chin while I threw up again and again.

Mr. G. came into the room and said he heard I was going to be okay. Dad gave the pan to Mom and went to thank Mr. G.

I was admitted for the night to keep IV fluids going. They asked that one of my parents stay and keep an eye on me. Mom slept in the chair in the corner.

Mom and Dad did not ask me why I had done it. I could not have explained it if they had. I knew without their telling me that my taking the pills had to be kept a secret so I wouldn't be publicly pegged as a mental case.

It was legally required that I see a psychiatrist, and the hospital referred my parents to one who specialized in the treatment of adolescents. The psychiatrist asked me questions: Why do you think you did this? Are you unhappy at home? I would stare at my hands in my lap and stay silent. As hard as I tried, I could find no words to explain. Nothing made sense. I knew only that waking up and going through the day had become so exhausting that I didn't want to do it anymore, but I was too afraid to die. My despair deepened.

After four weeks of meetings, the psychiatrist told me about the hospital, a private psychiatric hospital that had an adolescent program. He thought I could get the help I needed there. He told my parents. They asked if that was what I wanted. I recognized that I was profoundly stuck and needed something drastic, so I nodded: yes.

Over the next few days Mom reminded me that I didn't have to go. "I know," I told her.

Confused and terrified, three days after Christmas 1970 I entered the hospital.

For the first three days I was to be observed in the second-most secure ward. After the humiliating ordeal of having two women examine me naked, back and front, to check for bruises, and mark their piece of paper, I was placed in a room at the end of the hall with a depressed, middle-aged woman. I never left the bed except to go to the bathroom. She stayed in bed and kept her back to me. We didn't speak. I wondered if she was what I would become.

I stopped eating.

I was then moved to a room across from the nurses' station. No roommate. My first night in that room, with only the light from the hallway shining in, I saw someone enter. Terrified, I quietly slid my glasses off the table and put them on. A shadow, a short, stooped woman wearing a nightgown, walked past my bed. Was she coming to hurt me? What was her mental problem? She walked over to the corner of the room. Then I heard a noise. She was peeing. My heart beat in my ears and I tried to quiet it so I could hear the shuffle of her feet across the floor. Someone else came into the room, whispered to her, "Sheila, Sheila, not here," and steered her back out into the hall. No one came to mop up the urine. The poor woman probably had dementia, but back then I didn't understand such things, and I didn't sleep for fear she would come back.

After three days I was moved to the adolescent ward, also a locked ward. It was New Year's Eve and most of the kids had gone home on passes. In the rec room, I sat next to the nurses' station and watched other kids talk and laugh. The lights were low and someone had put on the album *Tommy* by The Who. When the song "See Me, Feel Me" came on, my skin crawled. This was a mistake. I didn't belong here. But it was almost eleven at night in the dead of winter. I would not give in and call my parents. And no one here threatened me. For the most part, they left me alone.

One girl came up and demanded to know why I was there.

"Depressed," I answered.

"Huh. I'm here for drugs. Toni's here because she's pregnant *and* does drugs." And she went on to tell me the reasons other patients were there. Most of the patients were kids with drug problems or chronic run-aways. There was a charming car thief, sixteen years old, who already had fourteen thefts on his record. Frankie was a paranoid schizophrenic who grunted instead of talked. I didn't know what to make of it all except to add it to the chaos.

The ward was staffed by hip, young social workers who "rapped" with us about our problems. Boys' rooms were down one hallway, girls' down the other, and the nurses' station in between. We shared two to a room, two rooms to a bathroom.

Most of the time I roomed with Annie, a suicidal adoptee. We had the same birthday.

Every weekday morning we attended high school-level classes in another part of the building. Afternoons were for therapy sessions, occupational therapy crafts, and sometimes a field trip on the El into Chicago to see a movie, the first R-rated ones I had been allowed to see. Even today as I look back, I do not see that anything therapeutic was being accomplished for me. But at least I was in the company of other social outliers, those of us who were not normal, and I could let go of pretending that life was working for me.

That was where I met Alex, who was also fifteen. His father had abandoned their family, and his mother was mentally ill and unable to care for her seven children. The children became wards of the state and were placed in different foster homes. Alex, the oldest, had been sent to this hospital to learn to control his anger. When I met him, he had been living there twelve months and seemed comfortable with the set-up, as if it was his home. Looking back, the hospital probably offered him predictability and support.

He was kind to me and had a great sense of humor. Most important, he looked me in the eye and told me he loved me. He said it easily and often. All of a sudden, I felt seen. The only privacy we had was the corner of the separate TV room. Chairs against one wall, TV in the corner, we huddled in the opposite corner and used the half-closed door to hide behind while we kissed, touched, crushed our clothed bodies together. My body woke up, showed me something more powerful than this depression, more powerful than my loneliness and confusion, more immediate than prayer. Maybe this was my prayer, my plea for life to begin again. As my body responded, my mind shut down except for the niggling thought: *I'm sinning.* But this was too compelling for me to stop. More than all the therapy, his warm affection comforted me.

In spite of his reputation for having a violent temper, Alex never directed his anger at me. I saw him get violent only once. Some other boys on the ward were teasing a defenseless patient, the paranoid schizophrenic boy who made grunting sounds instead of speaking. When Alex saw them teasing this boy, he started yelling, picked up a round table three feet in diameter, lifted it over his head, and threw it against the wall to draw their attention. I saw it as an expression of righteous anger, not self-indulgent. Three male workers came running out and climbed on Alex to subdue him. They took him back to his room and injected him with Thorazine. For a day and a half he lay in his bed and looked unconscious. And I felt like I had lost my connection to the world. I kept walking past his room, peeking in at his sleeping body, and selfishly wondered if I would ever be loved again.

My worst time at the hospital came five weeks in, when I was put in the intensive care unit. My fault. I had swiped a butter knife from the cafeteria. I thought I could use it to unscrew my ground floor bedroom window. Then I and three others could escape, maybe run the many miles in the early February night to my married sister's house. She had just enough moxie and questioning of authority that maybe we could count on her to move us to the next place, head us out West or something. But although I wanted freedom and made plans, the truth was, I was never serious about the escape. Even as the four of us planned and giggled about it, I had enough sense to know we wouldn't make it in the outside world. The freedom I craved did not have to do with freedom from the hospital. It had to do with freedom from despair. Taking the knife was an act of rebellion, an act of empowerment, and a way I could thumb my nose at the world.

Another patient, one who was not in on the escape plan, had caught wind of it and snitched on us. After dinner one night, three of the staff came into my room, emptied my drawers and closet and searched for more contraband. (I had none.) I had to take off my clothes again in front of two female staff to see if I was hiding anything else. They couldn't know that I wasn't serious about escaping, and my regular shrink, who probably would have believed me, was on vacation. Another shrink, one known for his no-nonsense methods with adolescents, was in charge of me until mine got back. He sent me to the intensive care unit. The three others involved were put on restriction: no leaving the ward—not for class, not to walk outside, and their meals would be brought to the ward, where they were served with plastic utensils.

ICU was on the second floor with a double-entry, double-lock system. Someone was always watching the main room from the security-glassed nurses' station. Across from the main area were ten rooms, maybe seven by seven, one person to a room. The doors, which opened from the outside, had a one-foot-square observation window. The only furniture in the room was a shallow bed with rough white sheets, a wool blanket, and a small pillow. It was bolted to the floor. A large window overlooked the paved basketball court one story below. Until I was let out of my room in the morning, I would sit on the tile floor and scrape frost off the window.

We each had assigned drawers in the common area. A staff member would escort us over and unlock the drawer so we could choose our clothes for the day. Staying in pajamas was not an option, except for one elderly woman who stayed in a bathrobe and sat in the corner. I changed in the one bathroom we all shared.

Two rooms in the center were always locked. One of the other patients whispered to me that they were the padded rooms and in one was a murderer and in the other a rapist. When it was mealtime, we watched as they brought in two big guys to stand guard while someone unlocked the door and another brought in a tray of food. I heard them talk to whoever was in there, but couldn't make out the words. And I never learned the real reason they were there.

There was little talking. I don't remember if talking was discouraged or if we just didn't feel like it. I certainly didn't. On my first day there, I was given a schedule page marked in fifteen-minute increments and asked to fill in all the times between breakfast and bedtime. Most of my time was allotted for schoolwork, which was sent up from the adolescent ward. At nine in the morning we played medicine ball. As depressed as I was, I wanted to laugh at the ridiculousness of a bunch of spiritless people standing in a circle under the caged fluorescent light and the supervision of hospital personnel as we politely tossed that heavy brown sack of a ball to one another. The TV was on for a short time each evening. Patients were allowed off the ward only for shrink appointments, and always with an escort.

That stark, narrow ward lit by dim tubes of ceiling lights was a container for insanity. Normal people came and went, most only as far as the nurses' station. I would look up from where I sat at the long communal table doing homework and see them looking back at us. Usually they just talked to the staff. When they left, a staff member buzzed them out, the doors clanged open to the next set of doors, then snapped shut and locked, securing our isolation.

Sometimes someone yelled out, which brought staff running to shush them. Cigarette lighters, in the possession of staff members only, flicked on to light the only break in the tension: another cigarette. I started smoking three packs a day. In the evening I filled out my schedule for the next day.

I knew this was where the craziest people were sent, but I didn't feel crazy. Maybe that meant I really was. Part of me knew something profound was off inside of me, something that hadn't been located, named, understood. Still, I believed my being here was all just a mistake.

Fortunately, after four days my regular doctor returned and placed me back on the adolescent ward.

Three months into my hospitalization, our family's insurance coverage ran out, and I was released. After the self-contained world of the hospital, the real world loomed more terrifying and unpredictable than before. My only defense was to shrink myself into a small package. At school I passed other students in the halls without catching anyone's eye. If someone asked why I had been gone, I would follow Mom's instructions and say that I had had mono. I studied to occupy my mind, and wondered when this prison sentence was going to be over. And what would be next? I couldn't fathom a future. I still flirted with death thoughts, but knew I didn't have it in me to kill myself. There was only one other choice—wait it out.

After I left the hospital, Alex and I talked on the phone almost every day. He was to stay there another few months, then they would release him to a foster home. Neither of us could drive yet, but every few weeks he would take a bus to see me, or one of my parents would drive me to see him, and we would spend the day together. We were two scared kids hanging onto each other and exploring each other's bodies whenever we could find a secluded spot in nature where we could remove some of our clothes. We felt safe in each other's company, even as we played the risky game of sexual intimacy.

14

Mom had never talked to me about sex and how babies were made. It wasn't that she was reluctant to. She had just lost track of which of her children she had talked to about it. But information about sex was readily available in 1971. A maintenance man at the hospital who had befriended Alex had given him a booklet that explained a woman's ovulation cycle, and we both read it. Alex even got condoms, which we didn't bother to use. In my naiveté, I thought biology itself would not allow conception in someone so young and clearly unable to handle it. Besides, we had had intercourse only three times.

When my period, which had never been late, was three days overdue, I was terror-stricken. Alex had been released from the hospital and into foster care, and I did not know how to reach him. So I confided in Kathi. Her face mirrored the panic I felt. Neither of us knew what to do.

I decided to wait. Maybe my period would just come. Meanwhile, cigarettes started to nauseate me, so I quit smoking.

The first time Alex called me, I told him. By then it had been over a week. All I remember of the conversation was that he got quiet and I didn't feel any better for having told him. He called again a week later. Still no period. He lived twenty miles away at this point and did not have driver's license, much less a car. Visits weren't possible. Phone calls were difficult for him to arrange.

In August, after I missed my second period, he stopped calling. I wasn't surprised, or even terribly upset. Just scared, and lonely. In the small world of the hospital, my feelings for him had made sense to me. He had reached through my gray depression and brought me back to something closer to normal. He was a nice guy, but maybe we were meant only to be hospital friends, and now that circumstances had put space between us, the feelings weren't compelling enough. He had to have sensed it. When he stopped calling me, I was angry that he could walk

15

away from the pregnancy, and I couldn't. But even that anger was mild. Panic had such a tight hold on me that there wasn't room left for much else.

Something was happening in my body that I tried to deny with every breath. I did not, and could not, see it as new life growing, only as trouble. In the middle of the night, when everyone else was asleep (the only private time when you shared a bed with a sister), I would admit to myself that I was probably pregnant. I cried into pillows and made deals with God: *If you make this go away, I'll always believe in you and I'll always be good.* Kathi knew of a contact where I could get an abortion, illegal at the time, but I was too afraid to break the law and possibly risk my life. So I started my junior year of high school in late August naively believing that things would just work out somehow.

On an October afternoon, Mom pulled me out of the stupor I had holed up in for four months. That day when I got home from school, she told me to go to my room because she wanted to talk to me. I sat on the edge of the bed. With a heavy sigh, she sat in the chair by the windows. She usually sat leaning forward, with her forearm on her knee, a position I later learned helped her breathe through her later-diagnosed emphysema. This time she leaned back and rested her arms on the chair, and turned her penetrating gaze on me. "Last night your father got a phone call."

I met her gaze and waited.

"It was Alex's doctor."

Alex's old shrink from the hospital.

"Alex told him you are pregnant. Are you?" Right to the point.

"I don't know."

She sucked air through clenched teeth. "When was your last period?"

"June." I didn't want to have this conversation.

"Do you have to urinate a lot?"

"I don't know. What's a lot?"

"Are your breasts sore?"

Her questions were pounding on my denial. "I don't know."

More and more frustrated with my answers, this mild woman who thought of her children as gifts from God and who had never raised her voice in anger to me, spewed out, "I'd like to sew you up and cut him off!"

I was stunned. A shockwave snapped my confidence in her love for me.

We sat in silence. Mom looked out the window. I, shocked and shamed, stared at the floor.

"I'll find a doctor," she said at last. "We'll make an appointment." We couldn't see our regular family doctor about this because someone we knew might find out. "Who else knows?"

"Just Kathi."

We found a doctor a few towns over who specialized in teen problems. He was the first person to speak to me as if I were an adult. After he questioned and examined me, he told me that yes, I was pregnant. He sounded practically cheery about it. He asked if I wanted Mom to be part of our discussion. I knew I needed guidance and that she would be making decisions with me, so I agreed. Once she was in the room, he told her I was about four-and-a-half months along and in good health. I was just shy of my sixteenth birthday and she was worried I would have physical complications because I was so young. He told her it was unlikely, that if I was old enough to conceive, I was old enough to have a healthy pregnancy. He then asked if I would be keeping the baby. For the first time I grasped there would be another human being involved. I looked to Mom for an answer.

"No," she said.

"You'll be giving the baby up for adoption, then?" the doctor asked.

"Yes," she said. She asked if he could recommend someone for us to talk to that could arrange things.

I listened while they talked about my future and the future of this other being. I couldn't fathom there was a person inside my body, a person that would have to come out. I just wanted to disappear.

We had to figure out what to do when I started showing. Back then, an unmarried pregnant woman was seen as immoral and often subjected to ridicule and the family either sent her away or hid her. I believed my entire family would be subjected to social shunning and the baby would be in for a lifetime of ridicule. And those who associated with these women and children and their families risked tainting themselves and their own social standing. We had to keep my pregnancy hidden. Afterward, if I were discreet about the pregnancy, I would have the life I was supposed to, that is, marry a good man and raise his children. That was the thinking.

When two social workers from the state came to our house, one asked if I wanted to go to a home for unwed mothers. I had already gone away the year before and did not want to be in another institution. If I had to have this frightening experience, I wanted to stay where everything was familiar. I told her no.

We had a large circle of family and friends, and thinking back, I'm still not sure how it was decided who would be told about the pregnancy. The four other siblings still living at home were told. Two of my sisters were engaged and their fiancés were always around, so they were told. My married older sister and her husband were told. Their house would be my back-up hiding place if our house got too crowded for me to hide. For some reason I still don't know, my two oldest brothers and their families were not told, which is why I had to hide upstairs when they were over for dinner. Grandma, who had lived with us for almost twenty years, was not told. She was in her eighties and getting senile and increasingly self-involved. Mom figured she wouldn't notice. I was not to tell any of my other friends. So, only five siblings, two fiancés, my parents, Alex, and my friend Kathi knew, and all of us understood it was to be kept secret.

By Thanksgiving, when I was not quite five months along, my belly had grown large enough that I was self-conscious, and decided it was time to hide. Mom and Dad had already talked to the school principal, paid the rest of the year's tuition in advance, and arranged for me to do schoolwork from home once I went into hiding. My brother Ed, a senior, would check in with my teachers every day to pick up and drop off assignments. Finishing junior year on time depended on how well I did my work.

At first I liked staying home. In the mornings after Dad left for work and the other kids left for school or work, Mom and Grandma would do housework. I would sleep until nine or ten, then roll out of bed, make myself some breakfast, and check out the school assignments. Whenever the kitchen table wasn't set for a meal, my typewriter was set up in the middle of it and my papers strewn around. Friday was my German shepherd and constant companion.

Two months later, my sister Anne lost her secretarial job. While I felt bad for her, her being home meant I had company. When she wasn't looking for work, I invited her to distract me from homework by doing crossword puzzles and word games. We would sit at the kitchen table and challenge each other in word games. When the phone rang Anne and I would whisper or write down what we wanted to say so the person on the phone wouldn't know I was there and not at school.

I hated the three o'clock hour. That was when Ed returned from school with new assignments for me. Also, my younger sister, Marie, came home. Sometimes their friends would drop by, so I had to pay attention to who was coming in the front and back doors of the house in case it was someone who wasn't supposed to know. If it was, I went to my bedroom and closed the door. Because Marie and I shared a room, it wasn't always safe to hide there, in case she brought a friend home, so I went upstairs to Mom and Dad's bedroom. I watched TV and kept an eye out the front window to see when people left. Mom helped me keep track of the comings and goings, and would send one of my sisters or my brother to tell me when the coast was clear.

I quickly learned all the ways I could be seen: walking along the upstairs hall, getting trapped in the kitchen breakfast nook when someone came in the back door, or by someone standing at the glass-paned front door. That happened once. A Saturday afternoon late in the pregnancy my older brother Joe and his wife May came by unexpectedly. I was sitting in the chair directly across from the front door. I could not get out of the room without being seen. So I camouflaged my swollen belly by putting my feet on the chair and draping the poncho over my bent knees to create a tent. They came in and stopped to talk to me. I struggled to sound casual. Mom walked in. Her eyes got big as she took in the situation. She invited Joe and May into the kitchen to talk while she prepared dinner. With no chance I could make it past the kitchen door to go upstairs without them seeing me, I stayed in the chair with my knees bent. They stayed only half-an-hour. When they left, I stood and stretched, and Mom and I shared a nervous laugh.

Late night was my favorite time. My older sisters were usually out with their fiancés, and the others had gone to bed. With Friday at my feet, I would do homework at the kitchen table.

I left the house only to see the doctor. As long as we were out, Mom would stop at the grocery store afterward. In the beginning I went in with her, but I stopped after seeing one of my classmates in the store. With nothing to do but wait in the car, I would scrunch into the seat and look out the windshield at the store's wall, study how the rows of bricks matched up, watch light glint off grocery carts, listen to cars starting up and shutting down and the sound of tires on gritty winter pavement. My passive body stiffened in the cold. I told myself I was learning patience.

The sharp sound of the key sliding into the trunk lock always jarred me, as if I were being unlocked. I would let out a sigh of relief as Mom got in. She set her purse on the seat next to her, stuck the key in the ignition, checked the mirrors, and backed out. Soon, motion and different views out the windows of the car would revive a bit of me.

Although I wasn't locked up, every moment of every day was dictated by the threat of discovery, and as the pregnancy advanced, the more restricted and cautious my moves had to be. That winter the house felt smaller. Beyond the bare branches of the tall elms, I could see only bits of the white winter sky. Four months passed, and my belly grew. Whenever I started to ask myself what was going to happen, what labor would feel like, what would happen to my body, what would happen to my life afterward, I put myself off, slipping deeper into surreal denial.

In February I got a letter from Alex saying he had been moved to another foster home. He apologized for not calling and asked how I was. My first reaction was: He hasn't forgotten me and he is owning his part in this. My second reaction was anger more fully realized than before. How dare he try to get in touch now! Why didn't he call when I was alone and scared and needed him? I thought of how he had told his shrink, who called my parents at Alex's request. I realized that even though Alex didn't call me, it must have been eating at him, and that had been his way of being responsible. Now he wrote asking how he could help.

He couldn't. He was sixteen and in school. Mom asked if I wanted to marry him. Actually she said, "You don't want to marry him, do you?" The truth was something about my feelings for him felt off. Besides, breaking from him permanently would stand me in better stead with my parents, and would bring that chapter of my life to a close.

I wrote back, two words scrawled in black across a sheet of orange stationery: Buzz off! And yes, I feel guilty about that now. He was trying to do right.

I was in the last month of pregnancy that Sunday night in March as I sat in my brother Ed's room and waited out company by answering essay questions for history. Restlessness was getting the best of me.

After nine o'clock, Ed finally came into the room again. "They're gone," he said. "I want my room back."

I handed him my test paper. "Mr. Andrews wants it tomorrow." He took it from me and put it with his own school papers.

I grabbed my books, papers, and the empty dinner plate. I had been stuck up there for five hours. Stiff, I worked my way along the dark hallway and down the stairs, stepping to the side on the third stair from the bottom, which had a loose board under the carpet. I strained to identify the voices coming from the other room. Just because he had said it was safe didn't mean he was right. Maybe a visitor had lingered in the bathroom and was now standing in the kitchen. Holding my books and plate in front of me, I poked my head into the dining room. No one there. I peeked into the kitchen.

"Hi, honey." Mom's voice. "Everyone's gone."

At sixty-two, Mom had been raising the eight of us for the last thirty-one years. I was seventh in the birth order. Marie, the youngest, was fourteen. The three oldest had married, moved out, and had kids of their own.

People liked to be around Mom. She was wise, quick-witted, and gentle. She made sure we were dressed and fed, got us to school, checked that we did our homework, hugged us often. When I look through my memories of her, I see several expressions: a woman who looked overwhelmed, often amused, at times bewildered, and always exhausted. I suspect it was not the life she had imagined for herself.

She had attended Northwestern University, dropped out a year and a half later, and went on to study drama and speech. During the Great Depression, to supplement her income teaching children elocution, she worked as a waitress. That's where she met my dad, three years younger and a recent transplant from Alabama. He worked as a meat carver and went on to open his own cafeteria, then a donut shop. Later he ran cafes and counter eateries at O'Hare airport and the downtown train station. After they married, it took seven years and a few miscarriages before they finally had a child, a boy, in 1941. A year and a half later, another boy. Three years later, a girl. After a five-year break, my mom turned forty-one, and over the next seven years they had five more children. By the time I came along, they had been married twenty-one years.

Between Dad's Southern sensibilities and Mom's Catholic devotion, rules in our home were well defined: Respect your elders and all authorities; do what you're told; be truthful; go to church; come to dinner promptly and with your hair brushed and hands washed; do not interrupt Dad. Actually, we weren't supposed to interrupt anyone else either, but that became nearly impossible to enforce.

An only child herself, Mom had an unrealistic sense of how siblings behaved. She thought we would be readymade playmates and didn't understand why we fought. But fight we did. Then, as kids do, the next day, or the next hour, we would be playing Monopoly or cards. We were a mystery to her. We were a mystery to ourselves.

After a dreary winter, the first warm spring day finally came. Being able to smell the wet earth and feel a warm breeze on my skin always felt like freedom to me. But I was trapped in the house. I was lying in bed, crying, and Dad came in and asked what was wrong. I explained that I just wanted to go *out*. He suggested we get a milkshake.

"But what if someone sees me?"

"We'll make sure they don't."

He went into McDonald's and came out with two milkshakes made green in honor of St. Patrick's Day, and we sipped on them as we took a long drive in the country. I rolled down the window to feel the wind on my face and to soak up the fragrant, warm air. Dad drove until I asked him to turn around because my bladder was reaching its limit.

He was known for being impatient, short-tempered, but the anger was rare these days, as if he had settled into himself and into the responsibilities of a large family. He helped relatives and friends with money or advice when asked. He kept company with relatives in the nursing home. This was a good man, a kind man, as long as he didn't lose his patience. And I found his patience with me during this time to be extraordinary. He never yelled at me, never lectured me, never asked me why. He just held my hand when I put it out for him.

We had no shower in the house, only a tub, and when I took a bath, I couldn't avoid my round, hard, red-striped belly. When I lay back, my breasts looked like mountains and my belly like a half-globe. On its own, it would move, roll, stretch the skin, and I would watch in disbelief. Another human being was living inside of me. What was that poking out, a foot? a hand? a knee? Where was the head? I was convinced this baby was a girl. And I wasn't worried about her welfare, because it was all arranged: She would be born, then taken to another family, and she would never know the difference. Still, I felt like I was failing her somehow, and I found myself whispering to her, "I'm so sorry."

The thought of childbirth terrified me. Like most girls, I had heard horror stories. I asked Mom how I would know I was in labor. Smiling a little, she said, "Don't worry, you'll know." I wanted more information and didn't understand why she didn't give it to me. Looking back, I think she had a simple system for filing her experiences: past that was funny, past that was thank-God-that's-over-with, and present what's-on-my-plate-now. She was not the kind of person to examine and sift through an experience so she could describe it. I tried to envision what I thought women in childbirth felt. Sharp, searing pain? Dull ache? Dull ache, then sharp, searing pain? Where exactly would I feel it? Could I handle it? Would I die? I reassured myself that millions of women had had babies and had done just fine.

At three thirty on Good Friday afternoon, I was walking through the dining room when a broad pressure on my lower back, like two large hands pressing into me, caught my attention. I stopped and leaned over the heavy table as the pressure intensified, forced its way around to the front and came to a point at my lower abdomen, shoving its way down. Oh. So *this* was it. Mom was right. I knew. And if it had been in my power to pick a bad time to go into labor, this would have been it. That night my sister Louise was hosting a wedding shower at our house for her friend and a couple dozen guests were expected. I was already planning on hiding upstairs, but for the first time, I felt imposed upon. I wanted Louise to un-invite these people, but I said nothing.

Looking concerned and irritated, Mom sent me upstairs. My dad, brother, and younger sister would keep me company while Mom and Louise ran the party. Mom doubted I would have to go to the hospital for several hours yet. She said first babies took longer.

Upstairs, I turned on the TV, but I couldn't follow it. I was too excited. All my worry about the pain of labor had come to nothing. The contractions were steady but slow, uncomfortable but bearable. I just wished those strangers weren't downstairs. On his shift to keep me company, my brother said he thought it would be funny if the baby was born the next day—April Fools'. Dad helped time the pains, wrote down the minutes apart, and encouraged me to squeeze his hand if it hurt too much. My sister Marie was so eager to help that if I had sent her to boil sheets, I think she would have tried.

By midnight the party guests had left, and Mom said I could come down to the kitchen, where she and my two other sisters were cleaning up. About every ten or twelve minutes I had another labor pain. In between, we nervously joked. By two o'clock, almost eleven hours after labor had started, Mom was concerned it wasn't progressing and had me call the doctor. I thought she should do it, since she was my parent. She gave me a stern look, dialed, and handed me the phone. I told the woman on the phone I was a patient of theirs and thought I was in labor. She told me to go to the hospital so they could check me.

My sister's fiancé (another wedding coming up) drove Mom and me to the hospital. My dad had to work the next day, so he stayed home to sleep.

Over the last several office visits the doctor had explained, in detail, the procedures they would follow during labor and delivery. So when the nurse gave me an enema and shaved my pubic hair, I wasn't surprised, just humiliated. She was an older woman with a crackly voice. Her tone was bitter, almost hostile, each time she spoke to me. At one point she brought in a paper for me to sign.

"What is this?" I asked.

"Authorization for circumcision," she snapped.

"What?"

Clearly annoyed, she said, "I don't believe it," and left the room. A few minutes later she came back in with my mom. She showed Mom the paper and said, "Please explain this to her."

Mom looked at the paper and then at me. "Do you understand what circumcision is?"

Oh, *that's* what they were talking about. "Yes," I said. I didn't see why I had to sign permission for a circumcision when I was convinced I was having a girl, but I signed it anyway.

Mom stayed with me the rest of the night. The light in the room was dim, and she fell asleep sitting in a chair with the top half of her body draped across the bed, her head resting on her crossed arms. The labor pains eased. When I wasn't watching the clock, I watched her. She had been up twenty hours, a busy twenty hours. She worked so hard and wasn't in the best of health. She smoked a lot and her breathing was shallow, stiff. I felt guilty for keeping her up.

Eventually I napped too, waking up to a pink dawn peeking through the blinds. April Fools' Day.

Mom went home at eight that morning. In that room with the lights off and the blinds drawn so I could rest between contractions, I felt detached from the rest of the world and tried not to be frightened. I kept thinking something must be wrong because labor was taking so long. I wondered if the nurses had forgotten I was there and thought about climbing out of bed to go look for someone. Before I would get up the nerve, a nurse would check on me. My oldest sister, Catherine, called in the middle of the day to see how I was and asked if I wanted her to come. "No, don't come. I'm fine," I told her. Besides, I was sure Mom and Dad would come back when Dad got home from work. What I didn't say was that I thought this was fair penance for my sin of having sex before marriage and for being generally screwed up. I see now that I hoped this would earn me forgiveness and a clear way forward.

At five o'clock that evening came a reprieve, as Dad in his overcoat and fedora and Mom in her long coat, dress, and heels, came in the room.

Dad turned on the light. "How's it going, Patrutski?"

"Fine. Except I'm hungry." I hadn't had anything to eat since labor had started more than twenty-four hours before.

Dad asked the nurse, a different one now, to find me some dinner. I told them the labor was still mild. They decided to go home for their own dinner and come back later.

Back to penance, this time with the light on.

A nurse brought in a hamburger and French fries. I ate half the burger, then felt a more intense pain. Seemed labor just needed a little food to get things moving. Dad came back at eight, and he and I timed pains. In between, he thought of things for us to talk about, small talk, jokes from *Reader's Digest*. When my eyes closed, he got quiet. The pains slowed down again. At ten o'clock he went home to rest, promising he would come back when I called for him.

At eleven labor got strong. The doctor said he was going to give me a cervical block to numb the cervix, and the nurse called my parents. Dad came back.

"Just squeeze my hand when it hurts," he said.

I wanted to show I was tough and willing to suffer the full consequences of my choices, so I made up my mind not to make noise.

The more intense the contractions, the more alien everything became. I felt like I had stumbled into the back rooms of a human being factory. Cold, shiny instruments, needles, gowned workers, bright lights punching through shadowy places, voices echoing in the hallway, the swishing of women's pantyhose.

At four in the morning the doctor gave me a second cervical block. It did not relieve the pain in my abdomen and back.

I couldn't think of the past, or what life would be like after this. I couldn't even think of the baby. My entire world was the metal rail I held onto, the blue wall behind that, Dad's warm hand over mine, and my insides wrenching. I had not seen pictures of labor and birth, and did not want to know what was going on. I just wanted it to be over.

An hour later two gowned people came in with a gurney and wheeled me into the delivery room. The nurse put my legs in stirrups and draped a white sheet over them. A cloth hung between my top half and bottom half, blocking me from seeing beyond my chest. How silly of them to think that was necessary, I thought, as I stared at the white ceiling and the round lights in large, metal, reflective pans. So *this* was where it was going to finally happen.

A black mask was placed over my mouth and nose. "I want you to count backward from a hundred, Patricia," said a male voice.

I tilted my head back and saw someone in a white gown, mask, cap, and glasses.

"We're going to give you gas now. Everything is fine. One hundred…"

"…Ninety-nine, ninety-eight…." Darkness.

Hoarse yelling. Something solid and soft slipping out of me. What was that? And why was someone yelling?

"It's all right. Everything's okay," the doctor said. "That's just the placenta coming out."

I realized that I was the one yelling.

"It's a girl," he said. He sounded excited.

My next thoughts were: Of course it's a girl. What's a placenta?

"Would you like to see her?" he asked.

I thought I wouldn't be allowed to. He was not my regular doctor, so maybe he didn't know any better.

"Yes," I said quietly. Would I get away with this? Would I get in trouble?

The nurse appeared with a baby wrapped in a blanket. The baby's skin was red and wrinkled, and her hair was dark. I smiled and went to touch her head, but felt my hand pulled up short. My arms had been strapped down at the wrist. The other nurse came over and unbuckled the strap.

I reached up and touched the baby's head. It felt wrong, sticky. I pulled away my hand. Blood. Why? Was something wrong? I looked at the nurse for her reaction. She didn't seem to think anything of it. I guessed the blood was from the birth, and normal. I put my hand back on the baby's head. This being was *real.* I kept my hand there, thought to her: *Don't ever forget me. Never forget. Never forget.*

"Okay," the nurse said. She waited another moment.

I heard her say, "We've got to go," and I withdrew my hand. She pulled the baby to her and turned. I lifted my head to watch as they left the room. I let my head fall back down. "What time is it?" I asked.

"The time of birth is five-fourteen a.m.," the doctor answered from somewhere beyond the sheet curtain. "I'm almost finished stitching you up."

I had never had stitches before. Odd, somebody was doing something to my body and I was just lying there.

I looked out the window and again saw warm pink seeping into the sky. Easter Sunday, April 2, 1972.

To keep from being seen on the maternity ward, I was taken to a medical ward. I had no roommate.

Relief breathed through me. Excitement chased it down. Look what happened... I did it! It's over! My heart felt as if it were pumping enough blood to run a marathon. I couldn't sleep. Mid-morning I called Kathi to tell her that the baby was a girl. Early that afternoon, Mom, who was cooking Easter dinner for over twenty, left Dad to monitor things at home so she could get away to check up on me. Two of my sisters, Catherine and Louise, came with her. Louise brought me a gift, an African violet.

Once again I lay alone in a hospital room. Because the physical ordeal was over, I thought I would fall asleep, but so much excitement, and perhaps adrenalin, coursed through my body that it was almost as if I had forgotten how.

I couldn't help but think of my family back at the house. Easter Sunday dinner was probably finished. I imagined the cross-talking, the clatter of dishes being washed and put away, the sound of hands slapping at the table in friendly frustration as poker chips were raked up by the winner, my oldest brother playing the piano, and my little nieces and nephews squealing as they chased one another. And somewhere in this hospital was a new baby.

A nurse came in. Dark blond hair, white uniform, plain features. Nothing about her really stood out. She asked how "we" were doing.

"Fine," I answered.

She walked over to the cabinet next to my bed, pulled out the bag of goodies they gave to each patient, and took out lotion. "Would you like me to massage your back?"

I was surprised. I didn't know nurses did that. And I had never had a massage before. How much of my body, my ugly changed body, would she have to see?

"I can warm the lotion. It should relax you."

Now that she was closer, I could see her eyes. Such kindness there, and my body craved relaxation. "Okay."

"I'll be right back."

She returned with the warm lotion and asked me to turn on my stomach. She waited while I adjusted my underwear and pads, then she untied the back of my gown and pulled up the sheets to cover the bottom half of me.

I was rethinking my decision. I had had enough of being prodded, poked, lifted, examined, assessed. As if sensing my skittishness, she started up at my shoulders. Taut with battle, I tried to keep myself from pulling away. She massaged them until they gave in to her touch. She massaged circles down my spine; applied slow, firm pressure across my aching lower back.

Up again to the shoulders and down to the lower back. I welled up in tears as months of tension were drawn out of my body.

Fifteen minutes later, she closed my gown. I rolled onto my back and looked at her. I saw her as an angel of kindness. She pulled the blanket up, turned the light low. "Rest."

For the first time in days, I slept.

The hospital social worker said I could give the baby a name and that it would be her legal name for a while. I had assumed I wouldn't have any say. This was a tremendous privilege. I wanted her name to be perfect. When I woke in the middle of the night, I tried out names. Another pink dawn stretched into the sky, and I knew her name: April Dawn. Beauty and hope.

Late the next morning, the hospital social worker had papers for me to sign. He and two others, witnesses, stood at the foot of my bed as he passed me the first one: authorization for the hospital to provide medical treatment for April. Nothing was wrong, he said, standard procedure. I'm not sure, but I think the second paper authorized the state to take temporary custody of April so they could place her in a home.

Giving birth had presented me with a sudden and weighty responsibility. Just two days before I had signed my first legal paper, the authorization for circumcision in case the baby was a boy. I knew in my heart that would come to nothing, so signing it didn't faze me. But *this...* this would set in motion the baby's future. I looked at the papers, tried make sense of the words. I couldn't. But giving her up had been the agreement all along. I couldn't start questioning it now. Besides, my signature would let the adults extract us both from trouble. In the end, it was the only thing I could do for the baby, and for myself.

I did what we all expected. I signed.

The next day I was going home. The hospital social worker came in again. He asked if I wanted to see the baby before I went home. I couldn't believe my good fortune, and tried to sound collected. "Yes."

"I'll take you to the nursery, but we'll have to use the wheelchair. Hospital policy."

When we got there, the social worker gestured, and a nurse wheeled over the plastic bassinet with a tag that said "Baby Girl Watson." I stood and looked through the nursery window. She was asleep. Her skin had lost its redness, and her hair was lighter. She was really here. And she was going to have a life I would never know about. I wanted her to wake up so I could look into her eyes and burn an impression of who she was into my memory. I waited. She slept. It felt as if a veil were being drawn between us. I couldn't feel her presence. Just a sleeping baby, almost like a doll.

The social worker, standing behind me, asked if I was ready to leave. I nodded, stepped back into the wheelchair, and he took me back to my room. I dressed to leave the hospital, feeling cheated by the veil, but mostly numb.

Mom and I pulled away from the hospital. The "ordeal" was over. The hiding could stop. I had expected to feel light, free, but I did not. I held tight to the African violet.

* * *

The next morning I woke to pain. My breasts felt hot, rock hard, and as if they were in a vise. The front of my nightgown was soaked. I was frightened something was terribly wrong. I called Mom into my room and showed her the front of my gown. She asked if they had given me a shot after the baby was born.

"I remember them saying something about a shot to dry up the milk," I answered. To me, dry meant dry, and empty, not full and hot and wet. "So why is this happening?"

She said it was normal and she would buy breast pads at the store. An hour later, girded with breast pads as well as sanitary pads, I was stiff and uncomfortable. My breasts were swollen and lumpy, my belly was a floppy sack, the episiotomy stitches stung. This was a different body.

The next day, three days after April was born, Mrs. Barry, the social worker from the state, came over to the house with more papers for me to sign. We were alone in the living room. I sat in a soft chair while she stood and handed me papers one at a time. The first paper stated that I was under no duress to sign. I looked up at her and said, "No duress? Are you kidding?" She patiently explained that the statement meant no one was forcing me to sign the papers. I knew different and recognized the sad truth of it. I felt forced by the society in which I lived; by my youth, inexperience, and financial dependence; by my family and our religion; and mostly by my shame. Of course I was under duress. I signed.

The other paper was the actual relinquishment of my baby, April Dawn, for adoption. The ramifications of signing this paper were not only too complex for me to sort out, but too deep to feel. I told myself: Don't think, just sign.

After I signed she let me know that the family adopting April was Roman Catholic, the father had dark hair and was of Italian descent, and the mother had blond hair and was of Irish descent. They had had one biological child who died, and had one adopted son four years old. I felt relieved that she would have two parents who were ready for her, a brother, a whole family. And I felt like a traitor because I had just made sure she would

35

never know the family she came from. This adoption was closed. No contact between the parties. Ever.

Then Mrs. Barry told me that the state had just passed a law that birth fathers also had to agree to adoptions, so Alex had to sign the papers. She said April would stay in a foster home until they found him and he signed.

A wave of nausea washed over me. I knew Alex would sign the papers. But they had to *find* him? They were his guardians too. Shouldn't they know where he was? Had I really just signed custody of my baby over to them?

When I asked her about it, Mrs. Barry explained that his case was handled by another office and she was waiting to hear from them, no need to worry.

But I did. April was not going straight to her new home, but to another stranger's home. So, who were *these* people? When I asked, she told me they were an experienced foster family who had taken care of many babies. I had already signed the papers, so I didn't think I had any say in the matter.

Mrs. Barry assured me that April would be fine. She then told me that the adoptive family planned to move out of state after the adoption. My heart sank. I knew I wasn't allowed to know who the family was, but I was holding a secret hope that some day I would spot them, see a dad with dark hair and a mom with light hair who had a boy four years older than his little sister, who definitely looked familiar. And I could study her face, see her open eyes, smile at her. The social work network believed it was better to keep the birth family separate from the adoptive family so the child would have no confusion. I never questioned it. They were the experts. Who was I to know?

She asked if I had any other questions. I felt myself freezing up. "No." She left. I went into my room, lay on the bed, and waited for sadness to come, grief to overwhelm me, tears.

Nothing. Just cold emptiness. Mom came in and sat on the bed next to me, held my hand in both of hers. "Time heals all wounds." Was I wounded? I couldn't feel it.

My sister Louise walked by my room, asked what was going on. Mom told her I had just signed the papers. Louise, in her typically pragmatic way, said, "I can't imagine what that feels like." Neither could I.

When feelings of sadness, happiness, or anger arose, they ran into a wall of heavy numbness that kept me on a tight emotional tether. Others mistook me for being a calm person when really I was walled off. This so-called calmness and, sometimes, panic that my secret would be discovered were all that manifested. But at least I was functioning, and that was enough. More, in fact, than I had been in a couple of years. And as if by silent agreement, no one asked how I was feeling. My sense of it is that we all understood it was treacherous territory and not bringing it up was a kindness to keep from pushing me back into that dark forest. Although I couldn't understand it then, now I see the numbness for the blessing it brought: First, survive. Maybe later I could feel.

The front steps of our house became my perch. I sat on the cold concrete and lifted my face to the sky, let the breeze blow over me, took in the new buds on the elm trees, smelled the moist earth ready to burst. I didn't care how chilly those steps got, I stayed. When a car came down our street, panic still gripped my stomach and I had to fight the urge to run and hide. I made myself stay and silently dare to be seen.

Mom said I could have visitors now. Although I had talked to Kathi on the phone a few times, I hadn't seen her since before Christmas. She asked if she could tell Peggy, our classmate. Peggy was caring and kind, and not the type to trade in juicy gossip for a social foothold. Still, if we told Peggy, would she tell someone else? Although April was, I hoped, out of harm's way, I still had to keep her birth secret, for my sake and the sake of my family. Yet bumping into that hard necessity was a powerful urge to come clean. Maybe telling the truth to one other person would give me some relief. Maybe it would lighten the heaviness that kept me flat. If I couldn't trust Peggy, then I couldn't trust anyone. Kathi told her, and they came to see me.

The three of us sat on the steps outside. They filled me in on what was going on at school. Then I said to Peggy, "I know you know." She looked at me, her blue eyes full of compassion. She said she was sorry I had to go through that. The relief didn't follow. She said that it must have been hard. I shrugged, because I didn't know what to say. Truth was, it didn't really feel hard, not yet, and I didn't want them to see I wasn't feeling the grief one would imagine. They might get the wrong idea, think I was indifferent, when what I really was, was frozen.

We moved on to talking about the upcoming senior year, classes we were going to take. They talked about the colleges they were considering. Marquette University, University of Illinois, DePaul University, Notre Dame. Two of my brothers had graduated from Loyola, another was headed to Illinois Benedictine, and a sister to Mundelein. Anything not named Immaculate Conception sounded exotic to me, like Egypt or Tahiti. I leaned back, looked at the cathedral of elm trees, and listened. College, life after high school, I couldn't imagine it.

Before they left I had to ask. "Do you think anyone at school suspects?" They both shook their heads. I wanted to believe them, so I did.

And finally, I could stay downstairs for Sunday dinner. My oldest brothers and sisters-in-law thought they hadn't seen me in the last three and a half months because I was such a busy, social

38

teenager. After surprised hellos, I avoided eye contact, skirted around questions, helped out in the kitchen, watched my nieces and nephews. The oldest was eight years old, and the youngest, three. They chased one another around the living room, dining room, and downstairs bedrooms. I had been an aunt since I was eight years old. These kids were like bonus siblings.

As we ate dinner, I took in the comfort of all being together again. People passing food, arms at angles while hands moved forks from plates to mouths. Bodies and faces put to the sounds of clanking, talking, and laughter I had been listening to from upstairs.

As much as I loved being able to go outside again, I mysteriously found myself drawn back to my bedroom, where I stared out the window. Over the winter I had studied that old maple tree, traced my eyes over the broad trunk's woody furrows. I knew this room, too. Two dressers, an old wooden desk, tan pressboard ceiling with brown lines that looked like ladders that hooked together the pink walls. Sometimes I stared so long at the ceiling that it felt like my body was rising up to it. Somehow I recognized that I was flirting with an emotional state as dangerous as the depression.

I wanted to be less trouble to the family. So I helped Mom deep clean the house for my sister Anne's wedding, got fitted for a bridesmaid dress, finished some school assignments. I had taken Driver's Ed the previous September and hadn't driven since. Dad took me out to practice. Then, after two wobbly tries at the DMV, I got my license. Suddenly I was driving to the store to pick up things Mom forgot or chauffeuring my younger sister, Marie.

Mom asked if I was ready to return to school. Not yet, I told her. The thought of being so visible frightened me. I was not ready to face most of the people I had been hiding from—the kids and teachers at school. She agreed to let me stay home for the five weeks left in the school year. I had fallen behind in assignments, so I worked to catch up. Trigonometry, however, was going under, even though the instructor had sent home a seven-page handwritten explanation of what the book was trying to get across. I would have to take an incomplete or repeat it next year.

In June I went back to the hospital where April was born and asked the social worker who had handled my case to help me get hired there as a candy striper, that I wanted to be of use. Except I didn't tell him my entire reason for wanting to volunteer: I wanted to be in the place where I had last seen her. It was as close as I could get to putting myself in her presence. I hoped a word from him would get me past the red tape of the approval process.

It worked. A few days later I was wearing a red-and-white-striped pinafore and white blouse and working at the snack bar. I couldn't get the hang of working the soda machine, the slushy machine, or the ice dispenser without splashing the counter, myself, and the floor, and I was dangerously tentative with the coffeepots. It was a disastrous assignment, and not at all what I had had in mind. They reassigned me to the book cart. Pushing the heavy cart, I made my way around door frames, visitor chairs, and beds. I learned to check the rooms first, to see if the patients were conscious. I would whisper, "Book?" I usually got a shake of the head. If there was no answer, I waited what I hoped was the proper amount of time before backing myself and the cart out of the room. Then I discovered the pediatric ward, and found a good fit reading picture books to kids.

When I wasn't struggling with the logistics of the work, I asked myself if I could feel her presence. The answer was always *no*. I saw that if I wanted to move forward in life, I would have to turn elsewhere.

In August, wanting to get paid to work, Kathi and I scoured job openings in our area. She got a part-time job at a nursing home and I was hired as a cashier at a discount store. I was good at it. That was something at least.

The social worker had said April's family was Catholic. She had also said they were moving out of state. Hoping she had lied about that, at Sunday Mass whenever I heard a baby cry, I looked around for the family. What color was the mother's hair? The father's? Was there a four-year-old boy with them?

Then, heavy with secrets, I returned for my senior year of high school.

The dreaded first day of school. I wriggled into pantyhose, slid into my pleated, green-gray plaid uniform skirt, and tucked in my white button-up blouse. (We were not allowed to let our blouses hang out.) I cloaked myself in a long, navy sweater vest. A couple of weeks before, I had gotten my hair permed for the first time. My straight brown hair was now an unfortunate frizz because the beautician had left the solution on too long. I had also bought a new pair of glasses—modern, rectangle-shaped, silver-rimmed. Going back to school would break through the last pieces of the cocoon of isolation.

We had a small senior class, a little over a hundred students. Kathi, my anchor all through school, had gone off to college a year early. Maybe I would see Peggy, although we hadn't seen each other since that afternoon last spring. I hadn't reconnected with anyone else. All I knew to do was to smile and move like a pawn.

I had gotten my schedule and books a couple of days before, so it wasn't my first time in the building that year, but this time it was fully loaded and operational. The noise—slamming of metal lockers, shout-talking, hundreds of footfalls on tile—shot through me as I rushed to find my new locker. I hurried to my first class: accounting.

On seeing me, a couple of kids asked where I had been. ("Sick. Mono.") The rest said hi as if it had been only the summer that had passed since I had last been there. Two years in a row I had disappeared from school for months. Maybe it made me weird, or mysterious. Or maybe they knew the truth and were too polite to ask. Or maybe it wasn't important enough to them to be curious. Whatever the reason, I was relieved.

Following accounting was political science, English, lunch, then chemistry and psychology, with religion and P.E. on alternate days. My P.E. clothes still fit, but stretchmarks ran up and down my abdomen. When changing clothes, I was careful to face the lockers and not to expose more than arms, legs, and back. We were never forced to take showers, so I didn't. During lunch some of us walked across the street to the park where we could smoke, a habit I had picked up again after the pregnancy. We talked about classes, jobs, events, and deadlines, nothing too personal.

Each day was like pushing through the thick air of a huge lie, and everything I did felt heavy. Put on the uniform, carry books up and down the crowded staircases and hallways, sit at desks and pass time in class. All to appear normal and get the diploma. The first rule of hiding: Hide the fact that you're hiding.

The month of April neared, and a dark, quiet panic arose. Her first birthday was coming up. I believed the date should not have meaning to me anymore. I certainly didn't have a right to feel this bad; I had given her up, she was not my child, and wherever she was, she was probably well cared for and happy. I walked through two weeks of panicky shame. Sadness rose and tried to take hold. I would not allow it; I was afraid it would level me.

On April 2, her birthday, it was as if I were living in two times—one where I went to school and pretended to be like my classmates and the other where I relived moments from the day of her birth and questions that wouldn't stop: Where was she? Was she okay? Who was taking care of her? I looked around at my classmates and wanted to tell them how significant the day was, that it marked a year since a new being had come into the world. I finished the school day torn, then went home to bed.

No one there mentioned her birthday, and I was relieved (What would I say about it anyway? How was I supposed to feel? What was I supposed to say?) and at the same time I was put out that April was not being acknowledged. I also understood that this had to be the way of things with an illegitimate child. I was powerless to change it.

The next day the sadness stabilized and the darkness and panic lifted. One year now. My inner turmoil was hushed again.

As high school came to a close, the big question was: What next? College—how? I had no money, no transportation, no guidance. Work—what? I was still seventeen and the only work I had done was as a typist, a cashier, and a candy striper. In August my oldest brother, a manager at a health insurance company, helped me get a job there as a statistical clerk. Monday through Friday I took the train downtown and sat at a metal desk in line with several others, all of us reconciling tables of numbers. After work I took the bus back to the train station, the train back to the suburbs, where I smoked and watched TV.

Sometimes I walked instead of taking the bus. Amid cement, steel, and glass giants, I felt excited. They represented sophistication and adventure. I knew I wasn't ready for what they offered. I settled for reminding myself that I was gathering experience that, maybe, someday would mean something. I would stop on the bridge and look down into the green-brown Chicago River, amazed it survived being penned-in and molded by buildings. Or had it? Muck and suds gathered at the embankments. Sometimes I headed over to State Street and window shopped. Once I bought something, a daring flowered halter top and matching blouse. I stopped in Marshall Field's, pretended to shop. I went into different cafés, bought myself Cokes, watched people pass by. Every time I did something new, I congratulated myself for not succumbing to the urge to hide among the crowds. Breaking routine sparked in me something vital, some part of me that was still excited about life trying to make its way through.

Dad also commuted, and we took the same trains to and from the city. We sat together and shared a newspaper. Back home I ate dinner with the others, then either went to my room to read and fall asleep, or sat myself in the breakfast nook in front of the new mini, black-and-white TV and watched sitcoms. What full lives the characters seemed to have.

One Saturday in September Kathi called to tell me that Alex was at her house. He had gone there because he didn't think my parents would allow him to see me. I felt as if my head had been shoved underwater. The mental hospital, the sex, which I still thought of as shameful, the pregnancy, the fear, the hiding, the baby—his return threw me back into it all. I told her no, I wouldn't see him.

She called back to say he wouldn't take no for an answer. Her voice rose enough that I decided the only way out was to go over there and see what he had to say.

He was waiting beside his car. Not sure if it was a good idea, I got in because I didn't want to expose Kathi's family to further drama. He asked where the nearest park was, so we could talk. Sitting next to him, the shame, the fear, and the sadness I had been trying to forget distorted my vision.

"How are you?" he asked.

I gave him a tight "Okay."

We didn't talk until we got to the park. He pulled in back of the rock museum and its sparkling gray-white wall. I'm not sure whose idea it was to sit there instead of somewhere else in that lush park I knew so well. Probably mine. Hiding seemed the natural thing to do when we were together.

I stared at the wall while Alex told me about his life since the hospital. He had graduated from high school, and the state, as his guardian, had set him up with a job and an apartment, and he had managed to buy the used car we were sitting in. He said he lived over an hour away and was doing some kind of maintenance work. He was thinking about going into the Air Force and becoming an airplane mechanic. Then he apologized for not calling me.

I stayed quiet. Twenty months had passed since I had sent him the "buzz off" letter. Why now? And why after I had asked him to stay away? Finally, he came out with it.

"I think we should get back together," he said.

My first thought was that this would be a mistake. Not only would my parents not support it, but more important, my feelings didn't. There was too much shame for me to get past. Then I remembered how he had pulled me out of the depths of depression with his affection and kindness. I realized that he wasn't ready to give up on me. Loneliness reminded me that I had had no other offers.

"We could get back together and maybe we could find her," he said.

Find who? The baby? That was crazy. My mind imagined us seeing her, a year and a half old now, in a stroller being pushed by her mother. Alex and I would be standing behind yet another building and watching them.

"What would we do if we found her?" I asked.

"We'd run away to another part of the country."

I knew it wasn't possible, or even right. I looked at him, his hazel eyes behind thick glasses, and shook my head.

"I know, it's not realistic," he admitted. "But it helps to think we could. The way things are, we'll never know what happened to her."

"I know."

We let it drop.

But we shared a grief. That, his kindness, and the promise of his companionship pulled on me to see him again. Because we both worked during the week, I in the city and he an hour and a half in the other direction, we agreed to meet on our next day off, a week later. Then he dropped me off a block from home. I didn't tell my parents.

The next Saturday I met him at the end of the block, got into his car, and we drove to his apartment. He was proud to have his own place, and I was happy for him. Against many odds, he was making a life for himself. That Saturday we blended grief with friendship and tentative sex. (I was terrified of getting pregnant, and agreed to sex only because it was the right time in my cycle not to get pregnant. Still, no condoms.)

Then he asked me to marry him. Why did I feel panic? When someone asks you to marry him, shouldn't you feel exultant?

"My parents won't approve," I said. "And I can't marry anybody. I'm not even eighteen yet."

"We'll wait until your birthday, then we'll elope."

I said I would think about it. First, I thought, I had to come clean with my parents. Then maybe the rest of what I felt would sort itself out.

When I told them Alex and I were seeing each other again, they looked alarmed, but contained it. Mom said that he and I were from different backgrounds, a disparity that would doom us to unhappiness. I vehemently disagreed. Dad said he appreciated my honesty and accepted that I would do as I wished. I saw that I was disappointing them, and that choked off the relief I had expected to feel.

Alex and I met on two more Saturdays. It was mid-October and my eighteenth birthday was a few weeks away. I thought about eloping with him. Here was the person who had loved me when I was desperate for it. He had a good heart, laughed a lot, worked hard. I examined why I felt panicky about marrying him. Truth was, although I appreciated him, and was beyond grateful to him, I was trying to force a romantic feeling that wasn't there. I knew the most merciful thing to do was to end it.

Because of his history I wondered if I should be concerned about how he would manage his anger. I really doubted it would be a problem, but as a precaution, I asked Kathi to come along, and she brought another friend.

Alex met me at the duck pond on the Northern Illinois University campus. It was nearer to his home. Kathi and her friend stood at a discreet distance while I explained to him that marrying didn't feel right, that he should find someone who loved him as he deserved. Once he was convinced I wasn't going to change my mind, he walked away, got in his car, and drove off. I felt sad, but relieved that, finally, I was honest with myself and him and we could both move on.

Three weeks later, on my eighteenth birthday, I felt the tired-ness of an old woman. My body was stiff, my mind robotic, I went to work alongside thousands of other commuters, ran numbers on the calculator all day, headed home with thousands more, ate dinner, watched TV, and smoked. The holidays came and went.

I felt trapped, confined, stuck in place. I was desperate to get out, to go somewhere, anywhere. But I didn't have a car or enough money to take a trip by train or plane. In February I worked up the nerve to ask my parents to take me on a weekend trip. "Please," I said, "I just have to get out of here." To my surprise, they agreed. This would be the third time I had ever been away from Chicago and its suburbs.

That next Friday night Dad drove Mom, my younger sister Marie, and me to Milwaukee, two hours north, for the weekend. Along the way I couldn't stop staring as we passed houses and neighborhoods and drove along expanses of snow and wild trees. The sky was bigger. I found myself breathing deeper. Then a new city and a Holiday Inn several stories high with an indoor swimming pool. They took Marie and me to an expensive res-taurant, our first, and told us we could order anything on the menu. Then Marie and I swam in the pool.

On Saturday Mom asked if I wanted some time alone. I found myself saying yes. They took Marie to see more of the city, and I had a couple of hours. Finally away from home. As I looked out onto blocks of buildings surrounded by snow, inside me there was a soft snapping, a breaking of my winter's ice.

That little trip, the movement away from familiar scenery, lightened me. Life still held surprises and promise.

In early March, I began to notice this guy standing with the next group over among the morning commuters waiting for the train.

He was hard not to notice. All the other men looked the same: dark suits, starched white shirts, black shoes, overcoats, and clean-shaven. But he wore gray-green-brown pants, a colored shirt, and a tan corduroy jacket with a banana sticking out of the left-hand pocket. His mustache was the only facial hair around. Not my type. One evening while I waited for the train home, I sat in a little diner and sipped on a Coke as I watched the rush of commuters move up the wide ramp toward the trains. There was the tan corduroy jacket. He happened to look over at the diner window. He stepped out of the current of people, walked into the diner, and up to my booth.

"Mind if I join you?"

This diner was one of the places my dad managed, and the people behind the counter knew me. If this guy turned out to be trouble, I could just yell and they would help me out. "Sure."

When he sat across the booth from me, I noticed he had gotten one part of the business uniform right—he wore a tie.

"This is going to sound corny," he started.

One of those thoughts that come out of nowhere dropped on me: *Always be honest with this man, no games.*

He continued, "But I feel like I've known you for a long time."

Too honestly, I said, "Is that the best line you can come up with?"

"I told you it was corny," he shrugged, "but it's true."

He was so earnest, I laughed.

"I'm Steve."

We rode home in the same train car. We laughed, talked, worked the crossword puzzle. I learned he had grown up a mere five blocks away but for the last five years had been in New Mexico for college. Now he worked as an environmental engi-

neer for the EPA. After that, we rode together for every com-
mute, and parted ways in front of my house.

Three weeks later, we went out on our first date—dinner and
a movie. That evening I laughed so hard that I nearly lost my
dinner. It had been a long time since I had felt such levity with
life.

Two days later, I left town for a week. It was to be my first
solo vacation. I had been saving up for months for the plane
ticket to Virginia to see my sister Anne and her husband, John,
who was in the Navy. I had timed the trip to distract myself
from April's second birthday, although I mentioned that to no
one.

Anne and John took me on a tour of Washington, DC. The
cherry blossoms had started to bloom. We drove along the Blue
Ridge Parkway. In the evenings we played cards, got goofy,
laughed. In quiet moments I felt the darkness creep up. I pushed
it back down.

When I returned, Steve and I became nearly inseparable. We
went to downtown restaurants, where I got my first taste of eth-
nic food and tried wines and coffees. Sometimes we played
hooky from work and drove to a lake or a forest preserve. He
was passionate about open spaces, and that awoke in me a
deeper appreciation of nature. He was so at ease with himself
and refreshingly comfortable to be with. Not only did my heart
beat faster when I saw him, but here at last was someone I could
talk to, who managed to get me to open up. But I had not told
him about April, or the mental hospital. If he knew, would he
stop seeing me? One night we were sitting in his car and the
topic of skeletons in the closet came up.

"So," he asked, "how many kids do you have?"

I felt a stab. Why would he ask *that*? Did he already know?
Should I lie? It was time to learn how much I could trust him.

"One."

"Really," he said teasingly. "How old?"

"Two."

He got very still. I waited.

"I was just kidding," he said.

"I'm not."

He leaned back, reached into his pocket for a cigarette, and lit it. I watched him draw in the smoke, blow it out, take another drag. Shit, I thought, he's going to leave me.

"Boy or girl?"

"Girl."

"Where is she?"

"I gave her up. She was adopted."

He was near the end of his cigarette.

"There's more," I said.

He started the car. "Let's go somewhere else and talk."

"My front steps," I suggested.

We drove to my house. Everyone was asleep. Instead of going inside, we sat on the steps out front under the canopy of elm trees lit from beneath by a streetlamp. The cold from the cement seeped into my skin as I told him the whole story. Then I asked him what he thought.

"I don't know what to think," he said.

I asked if he had any skeletons. He told me about his heavy drug use in college, and said it wasn't a problem anymore, that he was done with it.

We sat in silence and smoked.

Then he told me that he saw my skeletons as experiences that had helped shape me, a me he liked. And I told him that as long as he was really clean, I was okay with his skeleton.

I introduced him to my whole family at Sunday dinner. He held his own in the boisterous discussions about politics, kept quiet when the talk turned to the church (he was not Catholic), and gave as good as he got at the post-dinner poker game.

He then took me to his parents' house for a Sunday afternoon backyard picnic. His mom and dad, uncle, and sister. They were a quiet group, talked about science, the environment, the stock market, and sweets.

Three months into the relationship Steve and I still hadn't had sex. He wanted to. So did I, but I was terrified of getting pregnant again. I called my doctor about birth control. Because I smoked, he wouldn't put me on the Pill. He thought IUDs were too dangerous. The only option he gave me was a diaphragm. I couldn't keep one of those around. Mom would probably find it and flip out at my having sex outside of marriage again. So we practiced restraint when we could, and used condoms when we couldn't.

Although we were not officially engaged, he had started to joke about it. "Wanna get married?" he would ask, just being playful, and maybe testing the waters. "Are you asking me?" I would tease. He would smile.

In October, eight months after we met, we took a train to New Mexico and stayed, in separate bedrooms, at his aunt and uncle's. Steve wanted to show me the places where he had spent his college years. He wanted to leave Chicago and hoped this trip would convince me to leave as well.

After a lifetime of trees and buildings so crowded that my point of view was limited to a block, the miles of sagebrush and dry, sandy ground were a shock. I loved the expansive blue sky and the rugged mountains in the distance. But I felt vulnerable, exposed, and knew I couldn't live here. Besides, I wasn't ready to leave my family. He said he couldn't stay in Chicago. Then we made a deal: He would wait for me for five years, then we would move west, but to someplace greener. Somewhere in that promise was the assumption that we would get married.

On my nineteenth birthday, along with a yellow rubber duck, he gave me an engagement ring.

I floated through the days that followed. I felt so loved and wanted by someone whom I loved in the same way, and I had a pretty little diamond ring to prove it.

My parents were happy about the match. Dad even joined the Millionaires Club with the idea that we could have the wedding reception there. The ceremony itself would, of course, be in church. After everything I had put them through in the last four years, and especially because I had had a baby out of wedlock, I was surprised and touched by their offer of a big wedding.

I asked Steve what he wanted. He agreed to have a Catholic ceremony as long as he didn't have to convert. Other than that, he wasn't interested in the arrangements, just wanted me to let him know where to be and what to do. His parents expressed no preferences either. It was up to me.

I thought about a wedding in spring, when things blossomed. Maybe add a new anniversary, one I could celebrate, to the month of April. I saw a small, intimate gathering of a couple of dozen people in our home lit by candlelight on a Friday evening. A piano player and a violin, and a little fancy food. I hoped my dad wouldn't be disappointed.

In the background another drama unfolded. My period was late. It had been due on my birthday. Almost four weeks later, a heaviness woke me in the middle of the night. My breasts were tight and sore. This could *not* be happening again.

When I told Steve it was possible I was pregnant, he asked what we should do. How did *I* know?

The obvious thing was to find out for sure. I wanted to give my doctor some of the blame; he would not give me the Pill or an IUD. But I was too embarrassed to face him. In mid-December, six weeks after my period should have started, I went to Steve's doctor. He had tacked me onto the end of his day, at six in the evening. He checked me and said yes, I was pregnant.

Ensnared again by my own recklessness.

"Do you know what you want to do?" the doctor asked.

"No."

Abortion was legal now, but it wasn't what I wanted to do. No more than I wanted to marry a man just because I was pregnant. For several days I had been thinking that if the doctor confirmed the pregnancy, I would run away to California. Kathi was living there now. She would take me in, and I could get a job and wait for this baby to be born. I was convinced I could give this one up too if I had to. Then I would make sure I never had another baby.

Steve was in the waiting room. He looked nervous. We went out to his red Volkswagen. Once inside, doors closed, he turned to me. "Well?"

I nodded.

He looked stricken. "When?"

"July. Late July."

"Okay."

I told him of my plan to go to California.

He looked at me, studied my face in the light of the streetlamp. "Why would you do that?"

"Because I will always wonder if you married me because I was pregnant."

"But that's not true."

"You *have* to say that."

I saw struggle on his face as he stared out the windshield. Finally, he said, "Remember when we got engaged?"

"Yes."

He turned to me. "We didn't know you were pregnant."

He was right. I had been so panicky that I missed that critical detail. A tinge of hope. Still, I wanted to be sure. "But you'll feel trapped."

"I'm not. I don't."

With all my heart I wanted to believe that.

He said, "How could you trap me when neither of us knew?" He was fighting for us.

One more thing to figure out. "And what should we do about the baby?" I asked.

"We should have it."

Was he in? Whatever it took? Could I trust him?

I thought about how a baby would take a huge chunk of my freedom at a time when I wanted to explore more of the world, return to school, and, well, I didn't know what else yet. And only three years before, I was too young to raise April. What did I have going for me now that I had not then? Then I realized: A lot. I was not a depressed sixteen-year-old and I had developed skills both in the workforce and with people. There was Steve as the father. Not only was he older and educated, but he had a good job and was willing and able to be part of this. And more than anything, I wanted to be with him. Together, we could do this.

I wish I could say I was relieved. And in part, a huge part, the part that would get to live with Steve, I was. But casting a wide shadow over my relief and excitement was shame, shame for having had sex before marriage *again*, for getting pregnant *again*, and for feeling so lost. That shame was smothering my happiness and directing important decisions. Although we were already engaged and both families were happy about it, I wanted more time before telling them I was pregnant. We planned to elope in secret, then call and let them know we'd married. To ease any fallout about the pregnancy, especially from my mom, we'd wait a couple of months before telling them.

We went to a realtor, who helped us find a house to rent in the next town over, we had our blood tests done, and two weeks later we took a Friday off work and got married at the county courthouse.

Steve had had my wedding ring engraved with our initials and the date. During the ceremony, when he struggled to get it on my bloated ring finger, I started giggling. The judge looked at me, seemed to recognize it as nervousness, and continued asking us to repeat after him.

It was not until afterward when a clerk wrote our names in flowery script on the fancy marriage certificate that the full realization of what we had done hit me. Our knot was officially tied. Now I could live with this guy. What happiness!

For a honeymoon we spent two nights in Milwaukee, far enough away to discourage family practical jokers from dropping in once we called home to tell them. That night we called our parents. My dad answered the phone. Since we were engaged anyway, it was only a mild surprise. Still, he asked if I was okay, where we were, and when we would be back. On our return Sunday afternoon, he asked to see the marriage certificate. Anticipating this, Steve had it in hand. While Mom hugged us and told us she was happy for us, Dad read it over. Satisfied we were legally married, he shook Steve's hand and congratulated us.

When we went over to Steve's folks, they were polite and welcoming. I think they were happy about it. If they weren't, they kept that to themselves.

It was back to work Monday morning. Our rented house had a mattress on the floor, an orange crate for a bedside table, no chairs, and Steve's childhood clown lamp. I had brought my clothes, a bookshelf, a typewriter, and a sewing machine. Steve's parents brought us all kinds of rummage sale furniture: couches, end tables, a kitchen table. My folks bought us a color TV. They both threw parties to celebrate. We still had not told them about the baby.

One Saturday afternoon in late February, I braced myself and went to my parents' house to break it to them. Only my mom was home. Surprised and happy to see me, she came into the dim living room, where I stood next to the front door.

Hugging me, she asked, "To what do I owe this pleasure?"

"I have something to tell you."

She stood so that we were face to face.

Uneasy, I met her eyes. "I'm pregnant."

Her shoulders sagged. "When is it due?"

"July."

She lifted her chin and shook her head. "I suspected as much. I never could see you walking down the aisle in white anyway."

She might as well have slapped me.

* * *

In Steve's family, our son, Chris, was the first grandchild. In mine, he was the eighth, on paper anyway. Ninth, if you included April. Everyone but some of my immediate family and the doctor was told this was my first pregnancy.

Labor was much easier, only seven hours, and although numbed from the waist down, I was awake for the entire birth. Then the nurse strapped my arms down. "Please don't," I said. "I promise I won't touch anything. " She said she had to, it was procedure. To keep from panicking, I kept telling myself that this time was different. Then Steve, gowned and masked, came into the room. Yes, this was different.

After Christopher was born, the nurses cleaned him off and put him in a bassinet with a clear plastic hood. They wheeled him away. Soon I was wheeled into the hallway, Steve walking alongside the gurney, and they pulled up the metal and plastic bubble with our son inside, smiled, and left us to bond.

I touched the plastic. "Can't we take this thing off?" I asked Steve.

"I don't think we're supposed to. Besides, I don't see how it works."

So our bonding was limited to watching him sleep.

Not five minutes later the nurse came back.

"Can you take that hood off?" I asked.

She said I shouldn't worry, that I'd get plenty of time with him, as they let the babies stay with the mothers all day, and besides, right now, I was supposed to go to recovery, then get settled in my room for the night. She pushed the plastic bassinette. "I'll take him to the nursery and we'll take care of him."

Although my hands were not strapped down, I had the catheter in and knew my own body needed care. Still, something was off about how they were doing this. I had understood that I wasn't to be given any authority with April, but this time was supposed to be different. Didn't I have a say? Soon we would all be together as a family, if I didn't make crazy-waves. I swallowed my sadness and watched as she wheeled him away.

At nineteen I was the youngest of the four women in the maternity room. Two of us were new moms, and the nurses gave us lessons on how to hold our babies, change their diapers, bathe them, and nurse them.

When I held him, his body reached from my elbow to the end of my arm. He was so *tiny*. Six pounds, thirteen ounces. His skin was satin, his dark hair like feathers. I stuck my finger into his fist, which curled around it. As this bundle of aliveness squirmed, and moved his mouth in his sleep, I was fascinated by his sheer helplessness.

We had to keep him alive, and well, help him learn to talk and walk and find his way in the world. My life had just been signed over to this kid for the next eighteen years. That was the agreement. My own pursuits would have to come second to his. Resentment crept in. I hadn't even figured out what I wanted to be when I grew up. Yes, I wanted a baby; no, I wanted freedom. Back and forth.

He opened his big, dark eyes, searched for focus. I caught his gaze, pulled him to my chest, buried my nose in his hair, his neck. I could not resist. *Okay, kid, we'll do this.*

On my third day in the hospital, a nurse, followed by two nurses-in-training, came in on rounds. When she got to my bed, she looked at me and, for all to hear, said, "I see this is your second baby."

Suddenly I couldn't breathe. Why would she say that? In front of all these people?

"No," I lied, "you're mistaken."

"Your chart said this is your second baby."

I wanted to hit her. Wasn't it in the chart that I'd given her up? "This is my first baby." My heart was pounding with fear and an unexpected release of grief.

An aide poked her, nodded toward the door, and they left the room.

After April was born, my mom and the social workers had made two promises: That time would heal the wound of giving up the baby and that I would have others. Well, now I had another baby, and this one counted as my first. As for the wound, it had been over three years and it was not healing so much as being buried under new events.

My mom was taken with what a beautiful baby Chris was, and later, by his playful personality. He made her laugh. Did she see him as the innocent in all this? Had she forgiven me? Had I proven to her that I was a responsible mother? Whatever the reason, our relationship was easier now. Chris was our bridge.

Steve and I took turns sitting in the recliner with Christopher on our laps, or tucked him between us in the bed, knitting ourselves into a family. I was so worried that I would ruin him that I read up on parenting and subscribed to *Parents* magazine to learn what the experts thought and how successful moms set up their households. On Saturdays I took classes in psychology and management at the community college while Steve stayed with Chris.

When Chris was a year and a half, Steve, unhappy with government work, decided to go back to school to study medical technology. I returned to work, this time as a secretary to a dean at the community college, and we found a former school teacher who wanted to care for other kids while she raised her own.

One night after a long day of work, picking up Chris at the babysitter's, making dinner, and putting him to bed, I grabbed a soda, my cigarettes and ashtray, and melted into the blue bean-bag chair to catch the end of whatever movie was on TV.

The main character, a single young woman, had had a baby and was fighting to keep him. Her family and the social system insisted she was incapable of raising him. Even though she was ostracized, she fought for her child.

Something stirred inside me, something dark, gritty, threatening. Guilt, shame, and grief that I had unconsciously buried were being scraped against. I wanted to get up and turn off the

TV, but the chair held me. My eyes filled with tears. I wanted to cry out loud but thought if I made a noise, let any of the darkness out, something inside me would break. As I watched this mother fight to raise her baby, I thought how I had not been strong enough to fight for my baby. But it had all worked out, right? April was happy, wasn't she? Two adults were raising her. And I had another child, another household, another chance. Everything was in its rightful place, wasn't it?

At the end of the movie, when her child was a year old, the girl gave up and handed him over. *No... No, don't give up,* I thought. But odds were stacked against her. She could not raise a child without support and financial wherewithal.

Steve, who had been studying for a test, came in, stood by me, and looked at the screen. "What are you watching?"

I stayed silent. We watched the last minute of the movie, then he saw I was crying. He reached down and pulled me out of the beanbag chair and into a hug. His arm around my shoulder, he walked me into Chris's room. We stood in the dim light and looked at our sleeping son—peace in the form of a baby.

"This one you get to keep," Steve said.

For the first time in five years, I let tears flow even as I fought not to get lost in them.

Two years later Steve was finishing up his intern year, and Chris was four. It seemed the right time to make good on my promise to move West. We chose the green, mountainous part of southern Oregon, and settled into a small town where Steve landed a job in a hospital lab.

Then we decided to have our second child. We took natural childbirth classes. This time I was an active participant instead of a strapped-down body on a table. The doctor invited me to make decisions—anesthetic or not? (Not. A decision I would rethink

61

today.) Stay in the labor room or go to the delivery room? (Labor room.) Deliver the baby yourself? (I did—a wet, reddish-purple baby boy. We named him Carl.)

When Carl was almost three, I opened a secretarial service and operated it out of our dining room. Clients came over to have work word-processed, edited, or written. Clients ranged from the man who ran a bug exterminator business and drove a VW with a colorful, bouncy plastic insect on top, to a man who worked for Jet Propulsion Labs, to musicians and artists, therapists, entrepreneurs, teachers, and students. This was the beginning of the personal computer age, and I was someone who had the equipment and knew how to get documents finished and out into the electronic world. This got done between chauffeuring, cooking, play dates, and soccer practices. Six years apart in age, the boys were a good contrast; one a brawny practical joker, the other a wiry thinker. Both were active. Lamps were broken.

Our parenting style was what I think of as responsibly casual. We let the boys rearrange the furniture to make forts and gave them wood, hammers, and nails to make a play structure in the backyard. We allowed video games and TV, but made boundaries around them. At the end of most days, I would lie down with them and read stories. We worried about them, about Chris and his unrealistic reporting of his scholastic accomplishments, about Carl's painful shyness. We did everything we could to help them make themselves into confident people who could create the life they wanted. In the full throes of motherhood, I'd never been so challenged, so busy, so happy.

My life was everything I could want: a good man at my side, two fun kids, interesting work that I could arrange around the family's schedule, and all in a place surrounded by mountains and kind people.

From time to time the depression crept back. I never wanted to fall into that abyss again, and I fought it, looked for answers. The first thing I recognized was that although it started with sadness, it was the immobility—emotional, mental, and physical—that sucked life out of me. So whenever depression returned, my response to it started with physical movement. I filled my bookshelves with self-help books as I sought to understand where this was coming from and what do we really know about our true nature. In the end, dealing with it turned out to be a matter of being easier on myself, questioning what I was thinking and believing, and freeing myself from the "story of me." When I experience depression now, which is rare, I treat it as a signal that something within needs tender attention.

Every year beginning in late March I braced myself for April's birthday. I still kept her existence a secret. Her birthday felt like the anniversary of a death, except I figured I didn't deserve to feel sad, because I had made the choice. As I kept silent about it, my body would go stiff. I tried to picture how she looked. I wondered if someone would tell me if she had died.

In the 1980s, reunions between adoptees and birth parents in closed adoptions were a growing phenomenon. As I watched the talk shows out of the corner of my eye, I felt my body buzz, a reminder that something was locked inside of me, something I did not want to meet.

I read Betty Jean Lifton's *Lost and Found, The Adoption Experience*, the first of my readings on adoption. She included a chapter on birth mothers. I had not heard the term before. Not as cold sounding as biological mother. She wrote about the double life of the birth mother, that she feels she is an imposter. She put words to my experience.

Lifton reported that many adoptees in closed adoption live with a darkness, a void in their biological beginnings, and it carries over, usually negatively, into the rest of their lives. If April was struggling, I wanted to be there for her, but I would not look for her; I did not feel I had the right. Besides, what if she did not know she was adopted? On the other hand, if she sought me out, I wanted to be findable. So in 1986, fourteen years after she was born, I tracked down the state agency that had handled the adoption. They told me they had an adoption registry now, that I could fill out the papers and send them in with my signature authorizing the release of my identifying information. That way, if April asked to know, they would tell her.

A couple of months later I received the forms and a letter of instruction. This was the first thing in writing that I had seen about her birth since the relinquishment papers, which I had not received a copy of. The official state letterhead, and the letter addressed to me, made the relinquishment more real. I wanted to be found. I wanted to know how she was, where she was, who she was becoming. As I sat down to fill out the forms — date of birth, place of birth, birth mother's name, birth father's name if known, and up-to-date contact information — the past was being unearthed. Yes, I gave birth to this child. Yes, Alex was the father. Yes, here is where I live now, not quite out in the open, but ready for you to find me and make it happen. Yes, I am willing to accept the consequences, whatever they may be. As I answered questions, I felt like a toddler taking her first steps — alternating between stumbling and racing.

Then I had to get my signature notarized. I took it to the bank and, as the woman read it, I sat across from her and tried to hide my embarrassment. She made no comment, just went about stamping, recording, looking at my ID, and signing. Finished. Beyond relieved, I plastered more than enough postage on the envelope and mailed it.

A week later I called to make sure it had gotten there. It had. The person on the phone assured me that if April registered as well, they would match us up. (What she didn't tell me was that before this could happen, April had to be twenty-one years old, or eighteen years old with parental permission.)

Steve asked if I was ready for her to come knocking on our door. Of course, I told him, it would be wonderful, exactly what I wanted. Besides, she probably would not come looking until she was at least eighteen and out of high school. That gave me another four years to get ready and to figure out how to tell the boys.

Two years later, on October 28, 1988, the boys were both at friends' houses and Steve was at work. I got home from running errands. It was mid-afternoon. The sun streamed in the windows of the dining room and onto my desk. I dropped a bag of groceries on the kitchen counter and noticed the blinking red light on the answering machine. I pushed the play-back button.

"Hi, this is Anne." My sister who still lived in the Chicago area. "I want to talk to you. It's really important that you call me back."

She hardly ever called. What could be so important? Did someone in the family die?

"I'll be out this evening," the message said, "but you can call me at home late. Even as late as midnight."

That didn't sound good. Hoping she hadn't left yet, I called. She answered.

"What's up?" I asked.

"Are you sitting down?"

"No. Why?"

"Because this is big. *Really* big. Sit down."

"Uh-oh."

"No, no, it's not bad."

She told me that her mother-in-law called, said she had read a personal ad in the local paper, just above the prayer to St. Jude.

Why was she telling me this?

"It said: *Looking for Patricia Watson, biological mother of April Dawn born on April 2, 1972...*"

Heat engulfed me. I started to hyperventilate, then choke.

"Are you okay?" she asked.

It took me a moment, but I managed a "Yes." I couldn't wait to hear more, so I got my breathing under control and said, "Keep reading."

She gave me the name of the person to contact, said the family was in Florida.

"The phone number, tell me," I whispered. I was shaking so hard, I had trouble writing.

"This is so wonderful!" Anne said. She sounded ecstatic.

"I can't talk. Call you later."

Oh my god, oh my god, *oh my god...* A hurricane of emotions: Thrilled they wanted to find me! Relief: The wait was over. A moment of panic: Was she okay? Fear: I didn't know what this would mean. What if it turned out horribly? And more fear: The life I had been living was over now. There was no going back. I would have to tell everyone that I had been lying all this time.

There was a knock at the door. My three o'clock appointment.

As I walked across the room to answer the door, I could not feel my body. I watched myself lock down. Inner numbness returned. I had never noticed myself doing that before.

Somehow I listened to what my client needed, even took notes, then walked her to the door, the whole time acutely aware that a bomb was ticking.

Alone again, it was as if I became two people. One of me paced back and forth, frantically clamoring, *What should I do? I don't know what to do!* The other me sat down at my desk, deliberately picked up the phone, and tried to dial the number I had written down. I watched as my trembling fingers stumbled over the buttons. Then I waited. Four rings, and a click: "This is Tressie. We're not home right now, but leave a message and we'll call you back."

The frantic me was silently hollering *Oh no! Now what?* The calm part took over. "Hi. I'm answering your ad in the paper." Then I added what I thought would get their attention: my name. I left my phone number.

I took both of my selves outside and lit a cigarette, hoping to calm down. Shaking, I could breathe only enough to inhale the smoke. Her family had found me. Something inside me was ripping open. My eyes couldn't focus. I was going to have to tell everyone, let them know what a liar I had been. But I would *know*, I would *know* what happened to her.

Then a horrible thought: What if I had dialed the wrong number? I immediately stomped out the cigarette and raced back inside. This time I triple checked every number as my trembling hand pushed the buttons.

"Hello?"

"Uh… Hi. I am, uh, answering your ad in the paper... My name is Patricia Watson."

"You're kidding!"

"No."

The woman turned out to be the same Tressie as in the message. I had dialed correctly the first time. She had just gotten home. She was April's adoptive mother. To confirm I was the person they were looking for, she asked me questions about April's birth, details that weren't in the ad—time of birth, attending physician, my age and the birth father's age at the time.

"No," she said, "her birth parents were nineteen."

"Well, I was sixteen."

"Oh, wait! That's right!" Then she explained that when they adopted April, the state had told them that the birth father had been nineteen and studying to be a doctor and the birth mother was also nineteen and studying to be a nurse. It was not until they started searching that they learned the truth.

My answers matched.

She asked me what I wanted to know about her.

"What's her name?" I wanted her *real* name, the one she knew herself as, the one everyone called her.

"Andrea Sue," her mother said. "She's a wonderful girl. You should be real proud of her. Beautiful. Smart. She's a junior in high school. Gets good grades."

I could not wrap my head around the fact that I was talking to this woman, to April's... Andrea's mother. My disbelief was so large, I couldn't feel.

Tressie gave me Andrea's height, weight, hair color, eye color, temperament. "She was real shy as a kid," she said.

Was shyness genetic?

"But I think she's outgrown it."

"That's good," I said.

"Her father's name is John. We've been looking for you for two years."

"Two years?" I wondered how that could be when I had registered with the state and told them to release my information.

"Andrea wanted to look, but I was reluctant. Nothing personal," she said. "We just didn't know what we would find. So I went to a search group. I saw that this was going to happen whether I helped or not, so I wanted to be here for her."

"I'm glad." Inside me, walls were crumbling.

Tressie explained that they had started their search with the state. Because Andrea was not yet eighteen, the reunion registry could not check their files to see if there was a match. So Tressie conducted her own search.

In 1972, when the social worker had said I could name the baby, and I had decided to name her April Dawn, I remember hesitating over the blank for her last name. Isn't it customary to give the father's last name? But he wasn't there, he hadn't carried her in his body, and we had no legal relationship. In the back of my mind, a small thought had whispered: Give her your name. So I had written in "Watson." I was told that April Dawn Watson would be the baby's legal name for one year, at which time her adoption would become final and her adoptive parents would change her name.

When Tressie told the social worker at the adoption office they were looking for me, the social worker pointed out to her that my last name was on the adoption papers. On the petition to the court, little baby April Dawn Watson and the Department of Children and Family Services were listed as the defendants. With a few more surreptitious hints from the social worker, Tressie pieced together my first name. Whenever they took a trip from their Florida home back to their former home, south of the Chicago area, Tressie looked in phone books and started calling around, trying to find me. Then someone suggested they place an ad in the newspaper of the town where Andrea was born.

Just then Steve walked in the door, noticed I was on the phone and crying. He looked at me with questioning eyes. While Tressie continued to talk, I wrote, "April!" He looked at his calendar watch, which must have read October. Then it dawned on him what I meant. He put his arms around my shoulders as I listened to Tressie.

69

Finally I told her I couldn't talk anymore because my husband had just come in and I needed to tell him.

"Sure," said Tressie. "Andrea will be home later this evening. We'll tell her we found you. I'm sure she'll want to call."

"Thank you!"

I stood, wrapped my arms around Steve's neck, and sobbed. The wait was over.

That night Steve took the boys out while I waited for the phone call. As soon as they left, even as relief washed through me, seventeen years of stockpiled emotions erupted in madness. The wreck of who I had been back then resurfaced, waiting to be reconciled.

By this time I was lying sideways on the bed, staring through wet eyes at the white wall, which turned into a movie screen showing places, people, and events long past. The depression, the mental hospital, Alex, Mom, now dead three years. I saw myself in the hospital nursery, looking through the window. Only this time it was different. I could *see her face*.

And I wept.

I saw Alex on a train traveling through a field of yellow flowers. In my mind I told him, "April is back." I wondered if she would want to find him too. What should I tell her about him? About us? About where we met?

The phone rang. My heart leapt.

Not Andrea, but my dad. Anne had told him, as well as my siblings who knew about April. Dad asked how I felt about her finding me. When I told him I was happy about it, he said he was glad. I did not ask if he would be disturbed if I did not hide anymore. It did not even come up during this conversation. We both said we were sorry Mom wasn't alive to see this day.

That was a white lie on my part. I suspect April finding me would have been more complicated if Mom were alive. My sense of it was that Mom would have been hesitant about the exposure, worried about repercussions. Two of my sisters disagreed. They believed that because this happened within three days of the anniversary of her death, it was a sign that she had engineered this reunion from beyond the grave. I have no such certainty of anything beyond the grave, or of my mother's ability to change her thinking on this issue. I knew her as a kind woman with a deep heart who would do everything within her power to protect her family. As she escorted me through that secret pregnancy, she was protecting us all. The hard looks she shot my way live with me still. It was clear that she was angry with me, and for more than bringing into the world a life I was ill-prepared to care for. I think she was angry that I had put the family in this position, and probably for committing the sin of having sex before marriage. They were the looks of a mother to a daughter for being sexually careless.

I look back and see the dark circles under her eyes, her legs roped with varicose veins, and her smile slower to surface. At sixty-two, she not only had been raising the last five of her eight kids, but she was developing emphysema. As well as being in mortal fear for her family's moral standing, this woman was tired. Had she grieved over the loss of her eighth grandchild? She never shared that with me, but I cannot imagine she wouldn't have.

It was getting late. Nine o'clock Pacific time, midnight in Florida, and Andrea still hadn't called. Did they tell her? Maybe this was all a mistake. Maybe I was the wrong person after all. Or maybe she was angry with me and didn't want to talk to me. Maybe her parents didn't trust me and wouldn't let her call.

71

My siblings who knew called to check in, see how it was going. We kept the conversations brief.

Because of the three-hour time difference, I gave up hope that I would hear from her that night.

The next day, as I made breakfast for the boys, the flashbacks continued. I was getting more and more nervous that I hadn't heard from her. After Steve took them out for a soccer game, I sat at the computer and typed furiously, pouring out thoughts and feelings. Then, the phone rang.

"Is this Pat?" an adult female voice asked.

"Yes."

"This is Andrea."

We both started to cry.

Struggling to collect myself, I asked, "What is it you want to know most?"

"That you thought about me," she answered, her voice quavering.

We cried harder. I finally managed to answer, "That I thought about you? Of course I thought about you! How could I forget!"

I didn't know what to say next. Do you have a good life? Do you like your parents? I resorted to the detachment of rational psychological studies. "I read somewhere it's common for adoptees to feel angry with their birth parents for giving them up. I understand if you're angry."

"I'm not angry. Not at all. I've had a good life."

It was a short conversation. I struggled to come up with safe things to talk about. Mostly we cried. Afterward, I threw myself on the bed and sobbed. Finally, now that I knew she was alive and well cared for, and that we would probably continue to have contact, it was safe to release the numbness that had rooted when I looked at her through the nursery window, safe to let grief and regret break through.

One phone call and everything had to change. In exchange for the relief of having contact with Andrea, embarrassment and awkwardness awaited me. How was I going to tell family and friends, admit that I was not the person they knew, that I had been holding out on them? After years worrying about what people would think, how could I convince myself that it was okay to tell them? Then I knew: One person at a time.

First, our sons. How would this change our family? Would they lose trust in us? In me? We started with Chris, our happy-go-lucky thirteen-year-old.

He sat at the counter and watched while Steve and I cooked a spaghetti dinner. "We have to talk to you about something," I said. Then I told him that he had an older sister, born to me when I was sixteen, and she lived in Florida and had contacted me.

He looked at Steve, who nodded.

Chris had developed a healthy skepticism. "You guys are kidding me."

We both shook our heads, and he understood it to be the truth.

"Does that mean I'm not the oldest?" he asked.

"Of course you're the oldest," I said. "That doesn't change. You're just not my firstborn."

Then, when he understood Steve was not the father, he bristled. "Who's the guy?"

"Nobody you know," I told him.

We asked him not to tell his brother, to let us tell him.

He went to his room, closed the door. I figured it was going to be okay. He needed time.

I worried about how to break it to seven-year-old Carl, a sensitive, methodical kid who was easily frustrated when things did not make sense to him. I waited another day, to gather nerve and put together an explanation I hoped would make sense to him.

After dinner that next evening Carl and I sat on the couch, and I read him a story. Fortunately, it was a book we had read many times before and my mind did not have to follow along. When I finished reading, I said I had to tell him something. The words I'd practiced came out carefully.

"A long time ago, before you were born, before I knew your dad…." I told him the rest and finished with, "She's sixteen years old now and lives in Florida."

He hopped off the couch and started pacing.

"What's going on, Carl? What are you thinking?"

"I don't know." He paced and said, "Why didn't you tell me?"

"I just did."

"Before."

"It wasn't the right time."

He looked angry, but when I asked him about it, he claimed he wasn't. I suspect he felt duped, hurt we hadn't trusted him with this before.

* * *

I had to tell my brothers who were married and no longer living at home when Andrea was born. I was nervous. Why *hadn't* we told them before? Was Mom's decision only a matter of the fewer who knew the easier it would be to keep the secret, or was there more to it? Maybe she worried they would harshly disapprove of her parenting. As well as of me.

Because they were much older than I—twelve and fourteen years—they had always stood as authorities in my life. When my parents appeared to be nearly worn-out, these brothers had stepped in and taken us younger kids to the beach and muse-ums. They had tried to ease our way into the larger world with guidance and references. So now, with apprehension at having let them down, I called each of them.

They listened, told me they were glad she had found me. My oldest brother offered to send her the family tree he had been working on, and my other brother said he would like to meet her, especially since he lived close to her. For two guys who typically directed the conversation, both sounded oddly sub-dued. Was it shock? Had seventeen years of society's growing acceptance of unwed mothers and non-traditional families sof-tened them? Were they wondering, as had I, how close our fam-ily really was if this could have been kept from them? Or were they torn between feeling betrayed and wanting to be support-ive?

Maybe my mom thought one of them would have wanted to raise the baby along with his own children. I remembered when my sister Catherine told me that she had offered to raise April. This was two years after April's birth and the first I had heard of it. There had been another option? I was stunned. Confused and carefully angry, I confronted Mom, whose illness was develop-ing. Why hadn't she asked me? She said she thought I could not have made a clear decision at the time, and besides, Catherine and I would have argued over how to raise the baby and who her "real" mother was. I disagreed with that assessment. But I could not argue with her final point: Catherine's marriage was unstable. (Two years later it ended in divorce.) Because getting upset agitated Mom's troubled breathing, I dropped it. Besides, I reasoned, just because I was the biological mother did not mean I could have made a better decision at the time; I was a de-pressed sixteen-year-old who could see no further than her own misery.

After Andrea found me, a few times I asked my dad what the thinking was in the decision not to tell my brothers. His response was always, "We did the best we knew how." Since my mom's death, I have talked to her in my head many times, written her letters, told her how I wished she had been gentler with me during that time. I apologized to her for having plunged us all into such a painful situation. I imagined introducing her to Andrea, and pictured the three of us in our family dining room, joking as we set the table for dinner. It took a long time, but in my heart, my mom and I have made a sweet, forgiving peace.

Next, I had to tell Steve's parents. I worried they would want to kick me out of the family. Too afraid to call and talk in person, I wrote them a letter about Andrea, her birth, and that she had found me. A few days later they called, and told me they were excited for me that she had found me. With them, everything was all right. How could I have doubted those good people?

Then it was time to come out to friends and neighbors, and it needed to be soon. Carl wanted to tell his class during sharing time in school, but before then I wanted a chance to tell people my own way. A hard, protective shell had grown over me where Andrea was concerned, and I didn't know how to crack it open and talk freely about it. As it worked out, it started telling itself.

Mari, a dear friend, my yoga instructor, and a client of mine, was just leaving, having given me the work she needed me to do. "So," she asked, "what's new?"

Oh god. "Well," I started, "a big thing happened."

"You won the lottery?"

"No," I said, and smiled, because, well, I sort of did.

"But something good, right?"

"Yes." How was I supposed to say this? …Just start talking, I guess. "A long time ago, sixteen years ago, I had a daughter. She found me. She's okay."

Her jaw dropped. "Oh my god! That's wonderful!" She engulfed me in a hug.

It is wonderful, isn't it? I thought. Why did I feel so scared?

"Tell me! Tell me how it happened, how she found you!"

As I told her, shame still held me in its grip and I couldn't look her in the eye. I was going to have to fight for every inch of myself that I wanted to take back. I thought someone should develop "my birth daughter/son found me" announcement cards.

I continued to tell friends, who reacted with surprise and tenderness. The few negative reactions I had were not the big blow I had feared. I did not feel humiliated, shamed, or even angry about it. Instead, I watched myself detach from them with a swift matter-of-factness that surprised me. I realized two things—their negative reactions were not a result of something I had done, but a result of their own thinking; and my shame came from inside. That was where I would have to address the hold it had on me.

Slowly, I was learning to live with the truth, and as uncomfortable and clumsy as the process was, it brought tremendous relief as years of fear were exposed and starting to dislodge.

In December, six weeks after my first phone conversation with Andrea, we all—Steve, Chris, Carl, and I—went to Florida to meet her and her family. This was possible in part because Steve had told the people at work about Andrea's finding me, and when they realized a training would be held where she and her family lived, they chose him to attend, hoping that by paying for his travel it would be easier for the rest of us to go. So we arranged that Steve would go there, and once his training was over, he would meet Andrea and her family at the airport, and together they would wait to meet the boys and me.

For the three weeks between the time we bought our plane tickets and when we left, I felt like a prisoner about to be released—thrilled, and scared out my wits. Of course I wanted to meet Andrea, but the thought of the actual meeting frightened me. I would probably lose emotional control, in public. For someone who had kept herself tightly contained for so long, it was a terrifying thought. Even as I fretted, I tried to continue my work and home routines. I became aware of an inner source of strength, a gentle force, carrying me through.

When it was at last time for us to leave, a striking calmness came over me. The logistics of leaving the dogs at a new kennel (and writing down its location), the one-day drive to the airport, navigating my way to Kathi's house for an overnight stay (she had moved to the Portland area and was able to be a part of this), leaving the car at an unfamiliar airport (and writing down where it was parked), and riding three planes was remarkably smooth. It wasn't until the last plane that excitement and terror started to get the best of me. I kept looking at the flight attendant, wondered if I should tell her; maybe she could give me something that would hold me together once I got there.

As I walked across the tarmac, Florida's humidity closed in. My legs felt as if they would buckle under the weight. Chris and Carl were in front of me, following the stream of passengers. I was trying to keep them in sight so they wouldn't get lost in the crowd, but the closer we got to the terminal, the more I lost my ability to focus on them.

When we entered the brightly lit building, I heard Chris say, "I see Dad." He and Carl rushed off. I saw Steve about twenty-five feet away. His eyes met mine for a flash before he focused on the boys heading toward him. We had agreed a few days before that he would hang onto them while whatever was going to happen happened.

My eyes then moved to the right. Next to Steve was a short, blond woman, probably Tressie, Andrea's mom. In front of them was a teenage girl. Tressie nudged her softly in my direction. My legs moved me toward her. Long brown hair and glasses. Yes. And crying. Yes. That must be her. She stretched out her arms to me.

We sank into each other's bodies. My face was buried in her hair. She smelled like roses, hairspray, and cigarette smoke. I softly stroked her hair with one hand while I hugged her with the other. Crying, we began to rock. I melted into hot tears and white light.

A flash of light. Her mom was taking pictures.

We pulled apart reluctantly and both used our sleeves to wipe our wet faces.

Another flash.

I looked at her. She had been looking at me under her sleeve. Our eyes met. Staring back at me was the truth: She was *real*. I looked away, and we laughed nervously.

Steve guided the boys over to Andrea so they could introduce themselves, and her mother introduced herself to me. Her nasal Chicago *A's* sounded like home. I smiled and looked at her eyes. Hazel and clear.

Tressie drove Andrea, Chris, and me in her car, and Steve drove our rental car with Carl riding shotgun. We would meet at the Denny's by our motel. Chris sat in front with Tressie, and I sat in the back next to Andrea. About two minutes into the ride, she reached up and playfully tugged Chris's hair. "Hey, Mom," he said in his best tattle-tale whine, "she's picking on me already!" He could be counted on for comic relief.

79

The next few days were fairy-tale wonderful. We were invited to their home, where I met Andrea's father, John, and her brother, George. She showed me her bedroom, her prom dresses, her Barbie collection, pictures of when she was growing up, some of which Tressie gave me to keep. We all helped decorate their Christmas tree.

Andrea hung out with us for three days. Seeing my three offspring at the beach, playing and joking together, filled me with a sense of completion, and as she jumped waves with Chris and Carl, I couldn't keep my eyes off this full-grown young woman in a pink bikini. Open and cheerful, she completely engaged me with her beauty, her affection, and the invitation to get to know her. When I looked into her eyes, sat next to her in the car, our arms and legs touching, heard her laugh, I was filled with wonder. She was no longer a dream.

The boys thought it was great having an older sister who could drive. She pulled up to the motel in her pale yellow Camaro, and they all begged us to let her take them for a ride. When they returned, Chris's and Carl's grins told me everything was more than okay. They then sprawled on the beds in the motel room. Andrea pulled out some new *MadLibs* books, and choosing nouns, verbs, adjectives, and adverbs, we made humorous stories. Their sibling-ship was coming together.

* * *

That afternoon when Andrea and I were picking our way over oil-slicked sunbathers on the beach, she asked me about her birth father. I braced myself. It would have to come out, of course, but a little at a time. I wanted the family to get to know me, and trust me, before I told the whole story.

"His name is Alex. We were fifteen when we met."

"Just high school kids, huh?"

"Yes."

"How did you meet?"

How could I tell this sixteen-year-old that her birth father and I met in a mental institution? I could lose her before we had gotten a chance to know each other. I needed time before I told her.

"Oh, we were just hanging around the same place at the same time." Nerves lit up my stomach. "I noticed him, and he was very kind to me."

"Do I look like him?"

It didn't matter if I was uncomfortable; these answers belonged to her.

"He was tall," I said, "over six feet, slender, dark hair, gray eyes. Your eyes remind me of his. If you want to look for him, I'll give you what information I can."

She told me she didn't want to look right now. Maybe later. Then she told me about herself, her childhood, her family, and her friends. We talked about God and religion, thunderstorms, playing the piano, and school. When we ran into people she knew, she introduced me as her birth mom.

On our second morning there Tressie took me out to breakfast. She told me about their search for me and Andrea's need to know me. Tressie also defined what she thought our roles should be—she and John would do the parenting and I would be the birth mother who was like an aunt or older friend. I agreed, grateful for the clear guidelines for a way to relate to Andrea without interfering in her parents' relationship with her. Tressie then told me, smiling, that it was nothing personal but she was glad I lived three thousand miles away. I understood what she meant. Distance made boundaries easier to honor. What struck me were her courage and her honesty. I liked this woman.

In conversations with Andrea and her mom, we discovered that we had all been lied to by the adoption agency. The social worker had told me that Andrea's family was going to move out of state after the adoption. They had no plans to move. They didn't move to Florida until eight years later. And what we had already discovered, that the agency had told Tressie and John that Andrea's birth father and I were nineteen and in college. Because of this misinformation Andrea had wondered how we could have chosen to work on our careers instead of raising her. She had considered searching for me earlier, but worried that if I didn't care enough then, I wouldn't care enough now. When she learned that we had been only sixteen, she realized that Alex and I had not made that kind of choice, and she felt more comfortable about searching.

Now that we were reunited, I thought there would be no more pain, so I was surprised when it was so difficult to say good-bye to Andrea at the end of our visit. We were in the parking lot of our motel. Steve and the boys teased with her, said good-bye, and walked over to Denny's for breakfast. I stood and looked at her as she sat in her car.

"Thank you for finding me," I said.

"Thank you for coming," she said.

I didn't want this to end. Neither, I suspect, did she.

"Call me any time you want," I said. "Day or night."

"Thanks."

"And you can come visit us."

"Yes!"

There was no more delaying this parting.

"Better get to school," I said.

"I know."

We hugged through the window. "Good-bye, Andrea," I whispered in her hair. Had she gotten out of the car, I don't think I could have let her go.

She swallowed hard. "Bye." She turned to drive. Through the parking lot, onto the street... disappeared into traffic. It felt like something was ripped from my body. I didn't understand why I should feel so bereft. I turned and walked to Denny's to find Steve and the boys.

A couple of hours later, when the plane lifted from the ground, that feeling left on its own. Then I was able to relax and revisit the excitement and joy I felt spending time with her. Back home, my days were underscored with a light happiness. Occasionally my time sense still vacillated between present and past. Andrea and I spoke on the phone every week. Sometimes I talked to Tressie. We exchanged Christmas gifts and cards. We all treaded slowly and carefully along the learning curve of this new relationship.

A couple of months after the reunion, Steve and I were alone in the car on our way to the store. He said he had something to ask me. By his tone, I suspected it would be an inconvenience.

"Trust me, this isn't easy for me," he said.

I started to wonder if I had missed something obvious, that I would be one of those women who is blindsided by her husband asking for a divorce. "Just say it!"

"Okay, okay." He paused. "I want us to have another baby."

A baby?

He went on, saying how we already had two and that should be enough, but—

"Why?" I asked.

"I can't explain why, just that I feel strongly about it."

Chris was thirteen and in eighth grade. Carl was seven and in first. For the first time in more than thirteen years I had a few daylight hours to use as I wished. Not only that, but I could set a work schedule that did not interfere with evening family time. Did I want to give up that long-awaited flexibility for yet another six or seven years? Then I had an *uh-oh* memory.

Steve and I had decided a couple of years before that our family was complete and we were finished having children. Occasionally I thought about that decision, and it felt right. A few months before, however, an odd doubt had crept in. So I resolved that if Steve ever asked to have another child, then I would know it was meant to be. It felt like a pact with the universe, one I was confident would not be tested. After all, how often does a man with two children ask his wife to have another? Now my marker was being called in. Maybe, I thought, this child was meant to be. Two days after Steve brought it up, I told him yes.

It was not until this latest pregnancy that I realized how reserved I had been when expecting Chris and Carl. I think having Andrea back in my life made it possible for me to feel differently this time, to be completely enchanted with this being's presence in my body. On Christmas Day, our daughter, Haley Noelle, was born.

Neighbors put up an "It's a Girl!" banner across our front porch. The boys made comments about gaining two sisters in one year. We called Andrea from the hospital, and she was excited to have a new sister. Steve's folks, who had lost their daughter, age thirty-seven, in a car accident three years before, held the baby as if she was an answer to a prayer. Steve held her like a china doll. When I was alone with Haley, I would take her to the recliner and prop her up on my legs so I could stare at her. Often I silently cried. A loss was being amended.

A year and a half after our reunion, Andrea asked about Alex. She said she was ready to find him. Certainly she and her parents deserved to know the rest of the story, but I thought if anything could jeopardize my continued relationship with her, it was this. I could only hope that by now they knew me well enough that even though I had been in a mental hospital, they could trust me.

Only Steve, my siblings, and a couple of friends knew about my hospitalization. Being hospitalized was proof that I was someone who could, and had, fallen outside of normal, and I had kept it a secret because I wanted to be thought of as normal. Not only was I embarrassed, but I was afraid that Andrea and her family would pull away from me, and that other parents wouldn't let their children play with my children. Now that secret would have to be exposed as well, whatever the outcome.

I thought Tressie should decide whether or not Andrea, who had just turned eighteen, was ready to know. So I called Tressie and told her. She did not sound upset or concerned. As with everything else, she took it in stride. She said she thought Andrea was ready to know but that I should be the one to tell her.

As I waited for Andrea to come to the phone, my insides were in turmoil.

When she got on the phone, I said I wanted to tell her the story of Alex and me, how we met, and that it was a difficult story to tell. I let that sit for a moment as my heart pounded out a panic that maybe she wouldn't want to know me anymore and this would be our last conversation. Then I told her about my depression and about Alex's problems with anger. I told her we met in the mental hospital. I held my breath.

She sounded mildly surprised, but it did not seem to be the big deal I feared. I understood that again the issue I had to confront was not rejection from outside, but my own shame, my own rejection of what had transpired.

Andrea and I talked on the phone regularly. She came out to Oregon, saw the mountains, put her hand in the other ocean, and got to know us all better. We had gone back there as well. Then, in October 1991, three years after we had met at the airport in Florida, she would be getting married, and we were invited.

Steve, Chris, Carl, Haley, and I headed to Illinois, where Andrea's parents now lived and the wedding would be held. My father and stepmother, Eva, were also invited, as were my older brother Joe and older sister Catherine and their families. Dad, Eva, and Joe had all met Andrea, but Catherine, the sister who had offered to raise her, would see her for first time in a wedding gown.

Another wedding guest would be Alex. Tressie had found him a few months before. They had written and spoken on the phone. He lived in Texas with his wife and their four children. Andrea invited him and his family to her wedding, but only Alex would be able to make the trip.

Eighteen years had passed since I had seen him. I was nervous. And I was curious how his life had turned out, but I didn't want to upset Steve by appearing too curious. To Steve, Alex was not just an old boyfriend, but the only other man I'd had sex with, and we'd had a child. Now that child was getting married.

Seeing Andrea again was momentous in itself, but this occasion came with loads of other emotional fodder: Seeing her get married! Hoping her fiancé, Scott, was going to be a good husband. Being the not-really-mother of the bride. Meeting Andrea's family and friends while trying not to feel like a circus freak. (There's the birth mother!) Seeing Alex again. Steve meeting Alex. Then there was my father and brother meeting Alex—I had forgotten to tell them he would be there. So, with an odd mixture of joy and trepidation, I attended her wedding.

My sister Anne babysat Haley as Steve, our boys, and I rode to the wedding with my sister Catherine and her husband and son. We had started piling out of the car in the parking lot when I caught sight of a tall man getting out of his car. I watched him walk to the building. His gait was familiar. Alex. My mind plunged into memories. Oh god, today this would all be so public. And had he been sitting in his car waiting for us to arrive? What did that mean?

He got to the door before we did and held it open. I looked up at him. He was smiling. I saw a man who did not share my shame, seemed undaunted by the opinions of others, and was happy to be there. Where I had burdened myself with shame, he seemed to have none. I looked away and managed an awkward hello as I headed up the stairs.

I looked at Steve in front of me. His back was rigid. Once upstairs, Alex and Steve traded names, shook hands, then Steve steered the kids away. Alex reintroduced himself to my brother Joe, who then reintroduced him to my father, now seventy-nine. Dad had not felt kindly toward Alex in the past, and I waited for the fireworks or the biting comment. But everyone was amiable. Maybe time had eased some bad feelings, or maybe they were all being polite.

The day before, Alex had met Andrea and her family for the first time. She later told me their meeting was more tentative. I am sure the timing of that first meeting, one day before the wedding, probably did not help.

Now John and Tressie walked over to us and welcomed us all. Occasionally someone came up to me and asked if I was the birth mother. When I said yes, some responded with: "I just knew it! You look like her!" I wondered if Alex was getting the same reactions.

My stomach was in knots. And I needed to breathe. So I kept making hasty trips to the bathroom. On one of them my sister Catherine followed me in and asked if I was okay. Truth was, I didn't know. One minute I was elated and the next I was a bundle of nerves.

One thing was for sure: I could not get my fill of Andrea. Before the ceremony Tressie had searched me out and told me Andrea wanted to see me. In the bridal waiting room Andrea hugged me so tightly, so sweetly, I had to fight back tears, which she helped me do by lifting up her gown and showing me her shoes: purple high-top sneakers.

During the ceremony we sat midway back on the bride's side. Alex, who perhaps did not realize there was a bride's side and a groom's side, sat across the aisle. My brother Joe and sister Catherine sat with him. Later they told me he had looked a little lost and they thought he could use the company.

At one point during the ceremony as I looked around at the guests, it occurred to me that if I had not engaged in careless sex one afternoon twenty years before, none of us would be sitting here. In that moment, I deeply understood that there is no such thing as an isolated act. This particular act had looped and wrapped and folded in on itself and other acts, pushed forward, pulled a hidden past into the present, and placed it in front of me as if to say: Now isn't this a fine moment. Who knew?

Later at the reception, I saw Steve and Alex talking. Steve's five-foot-eight-inch stocky frame and Alex's six-foot-four slender one reminded me of Abbot and Costello. Steve looked uneasy. Alex was relaxed. Later Steve told me that if there was any unfinished business I had with Alex, go ahead and take care of it, just don't dance with him. I knew it took courage for him to make space for Alex, and I told him thanks but nothing was unfinished.

However, Alex approached me. We talked, although not about the past. He did most of the talking, filling me in on the highlights of his last eighteen years. He told me he had a son from a short first marriage. This was his second marriage and they had been together over ten years and had four children. He showed me pictures of his wife and kids. He told me that he worked as a motorcycle mechanic, liked to act and paint, and had dedicated his life to God. He said he was happy. I was glad. After such a rough start, he had put together a fulfilling life for himself.

For me, the high point of the wedding was when I worked my way down the reception line after the ceremony. My sister Catherine and I joked about how to introduce ourselves. "I'll just say I'm the birth aunt," she said. I told her it sounded like something that's supposed to be exterminated. We laughed and moved along the line.

Then I came to John, Andrea's adoptive father. Thick salt-and-pepper hair, beard to match, he looked dapper in his tuxedo. His brown eyes sparkled with pride. When I reached out my hand to shake his, he startled me by grasping me in a tight hug. He started to cry, and whispered, "Thank you. Thank you."

For the first time, I felt something new about all this: a sense of dignity.

* * *

It has been over forty years since Andrea was born. She has been a great gift. Not only do I get to enjoy her gracious, happy presence, but her birth and her return gave me a chance to right myself, twice. The first time, after my initial depression, I believe having given birth and knowing that she was out there took suicide off the table; the legacy of such an act would have delivered to her a blow she should not have to bear. The second time was when she found me and I could bring the past to light and relieve myself of the burden of shame.

Back then, the shame, the hiding, the lies told by me, my family, the social workers—all made sense. Pregnancy outside of marriage was so stigmatized that we had to fight for our survival within the community. I find the difference in social attitudes today amazing, and hopeful. Dignity has been restored to pregnancy, and women now have genuine options that can be explored openly.

But my own healing took decades. An integral part of that was the support group that I belonged to: The Circle.

2

THE CIRCLE

Society is so different today. Having and raising a child without first being married has become an acceptable part of our national social fabric. Until the last decades of the twentieth century, however, being unmarried and pregnant plunged a woman and her family into a dark age. Post World War II, the social and economic consequences of not conforming to national expectations about family were harsh. The national consciousness believed itself to be beating back the forces of Communism and Socialism. Also, the society was fighting against the threats of the Beat Generation and the sexual revolution as they butted up against what were believed to be our national ideals.

Ann Fessler explains in her book *The Girls Who Went Away:*

> The nuclear family — typified by a male bread-winner and a wife who stayed home and devoted herself to the needs of her husband and children — was held up not only as the ideal, but the patriotic endeavor. Men and women who did not conform to this model "risked being perceived as perverted, immoral, un-patriotic, and pathological" (May, *Homeward Bound*, 1988). The belief being espoused was

that the strength of the country depended [on
the population adhering to this model].[1]

And even as sexual attitudes and practices gradually loos-
ened, the social consequences of "getting caught" by way of a
pregnancy did not. Public humiliation, social ostracism, and
even losing one's job threatened the women and their families.

During that time, if a single woman became pregnant, particularly a white woman,[2] she either hid inside a quick marriage
(usually to the birth father), or she went to "visit relatives" —
often a maternity home—to give birth and immediately give up
her baby in secret. To protect herself, her child, and her family
from social stigma, she signed papers to relinquish the baby to
an agency, a lawyer, or a physician for placement with another
family. She would never know the identity of the adoptive family and would never see or hear from that child again. This

---

[1] Ann Fessler, *The Girls Who Went Away, The Hidden History of Women
Who Surrendered Children for Adoption in the Decades Before* Roe v. Wade
(New York, Penguin, 2006), 111.

[2] Kathy S. Stolley, "Statistics on Adoption in the United States," *The
Future of Children ADOPTION* (Vol. 3, No. 1, Spring 1993, p. 32). Stolley
reports that the relinquishment rate among white women giving birth
premaritally fluctuated from a high of 19 percent before 1973 to just
over 3 percent in the late 1980s. Among black women, the relinquishment rate has been consistently low, at 2 percent (p. 32).

The Child Welfare Information Gateway reports that since the mid-
1970s, "Among never-married women, relinquishment by Black
women has remained very low — declining from 1.5 percent to nearly 0
percent, while relinquishment by White women has declined sharply,
from nearly 20 percent to less than 2 percent" ("Voluntary Relinquishment for Adoption," https://www.childwelfare.gov/pubs/s_place.cfm
pub. 2005, accessed 10/20/14).

And, according to Rickie Solinger in *Wake Up Little Susie* (as quoted
in Susan Wadia-Ells' *The Adoption Reader,* p. x), black women were ex-
cluded from white-only maternity homes.

would be, she was told, not only in her best interest, but in the best interests of her child and of the birth and adoptive families.

Although most women who relinquished a child for adoption were single and had never been married, six percent of women who made this choice were married.[3] Birth control was less reliable and abortion was illegal, so if the birth parents were unable to raise the child, a closed adoption was a couple's last option. In light of the tremendous social pressure for a married couple to raise their children, most of them kept the birth and adoption a secret.

The hallmark of closed adoptions was privacy. The birth family and adoptive family did not even know each other's names. In most states, the adoptee's original birth certificate became a sealed record. This system meant that relinquished offspring were forced to endure the consequences of not knowing their birth families. As they reached adulthood, many adoptees who knew they were adopted asked questions: Who did I come from? Why did they give me up? Who do I look like? Do I have brothers and sisters? What medical problems do I need to watch out for? The grown children stood in their curiosity and fear and asked their birth mothers to show themselves.

As birth mothers, we understood we would never be allowed to know what happened to our offspring. It is tempting to say we made this choice out of love for the child. That may be true, in part. But it is also true that we had no other options. The choice in the culture of that time was clear: either keep the child and become pariahs, or give up the child and keep quiet about it.

---

[3] Stolley (p. 32) reports that according to the 1982 National Survey of Family Growth (NSFG), six percent of the women who relinquished a child to adoption were married at the time and another 6 percent had been previously married.

So we relinquished our babies to a system incubated in a culture of fear, shame, and, perhaps most unfortunately, in the mistaken belief that babies do not experience a sense of loss. Social workers, lawyers, and doctors arranged for new parents while we turned back to our lives and, telling few what we had done, waited to heal whatever we could allow ourselves to feel.

Most of us were told that we would move on and forget. I never could, nor could the other birth mothers I have met. Even those who exiled the pain and loss to the recesses of their past found that the past refused to be buried. Still, we rarely spoke of that part of our lives

I always had a deep desire to meet other birth mothers. What had happened to them? Was what I had experienced typical? How did they manage the secrecy and silence? In the early 1990s, Nancy, one of the women who tells her story in this book, wanted to start a support group. She placed a public service announcement, which I heard. Together with a few other women, we co-founded a group for birth mothers, adoptees, and adoptive parents. When we were deciding what to call it, Suzanne, a birth mother who was part Native American and part Irish Catholic, said that when she lost her daughter to adoption she felt that her spiritual circle—the core of who she was—had broken. As a result, she felt a split within herself. We all felt this split, a loss of continuity, and a diminishment of ourselves as women, mothers, and human beings. We named our group The Circle.

I would have been lost without these women. They, and the many others who came to the group over the eleven years we met, knew what it was to be involved in the secrecy of closed adoption. When we birth mothers met, we told our stories, explored them, and mined them for the truth. We laughed and cried. We even held a retreat in the mountains, where we tried to take mental journeys back to certain points in our past and return with wisdom. No social workers or therapists were invited. We had to do this for ourselves.

So much of my healing has come from hearing the other women's stories that I have chosen five of their stories to share alongside my own. They cover the time period from 1959 to 1983. In some of the stories the birth mother may sound remote or distant. Detachment is an effective means of emotional survival and very much a part of the journey. Each woman tape-recorded her story, sometimes prompted by questions from me, and each chose a title to represent her experience. As I rearranged the transcripts for chronology and space, it was my goal to stay as true to their voices as I could and present their stories without comment. After much discussion with the women I interviewed, I did change their names and the names of their families, and in some cases their geographical locations, to protect their privacy. Most of the names in my own story are real, including those of my immediate family, my birth daughter, and her adoptive parents. In writing my own story, I had the advantage of time to dig into my past again and again. That produced a longer, more detailed narrative than the others'.

The other stories are:

Nancy, lost and wandering in her early twenties, was anxious to win the approval of her family by doing the "right thing" when she became pregnant.

Evelyn and her husband, married only a short time before she became pregnant, did not feel ready to be parents.

Marti, the married mother of two young children, was unable to take on the care of another child at that time in her life.

Dena was a rebellious teenager who turned to drugs. When she learned she was pregnant, she married the abusive birth father but was subsequently forced by circumstances and family to relinquish her baby.

Kate, a young, unmarried woman from a loving family, was ready to raise her baby but was talked into adoption by a social worker.

A later chapter in this book tells of a meeting I went to with several adoptive parents and an adoptee. I was reluctant to go because I thought of adoptive parents as the altruistic heroes to the birth mothers' women-of-shame. I knew this was wrong, but a loud, angry part of my heart screamed it anyway. The honesty and vulnerability shown at that meeting stay with me today. I made my peace with adoptive parents.

I no longer hide, physically or emotionally, from what took place. Nor do the other women in this book. We have been found, some by our offspring and others by opening our hearts. And, if we've been lucky, both.

3

After Andrea found me in 1988, I sought contact with other birth mothers who had been through reunion. Most birth mothers were still keeping their secret. I heard about a local adoption rights group and called them. A woman told me the group was now defunct and offered her advice: Reunion in adoption is an emotional roller coaster, better call a doctor and get some tranquilizers. My thought was that these feelings had been buried for seventeen years; it was time to let them out. I craved the company of other birth mothers, to hear what it had been like for them, to put our stories up against one another's and see what we had in common. Almost three years passed before I saw a public service announcement on TV: Looking for birth mothers to join a support group.

Maybe it was the habit of hiding. Maybe it was fear of looking other birth mothers in the eye and seeing wounds and untruths that I had not yet acknowledged in myself. Whatever the reason, in spite of my excitement, it took me a few days to get up the nerve to call. The woman who had posted it was Nancy. I was the only person to respond to the announcement. She and I agreed to meet at a local restaurant.

In her thirties, Nancy was solid and stocky, built to take life head-on. We were cautious at first, but it wasn't long before our excitement at meeting each other, and Nancy's natural gregariousness, brought down our defenses and we were gabbing like old childhood friends. Not only did her open, easy manner and plain-spoken honesty pull me in, but I admired how she used humor to deal with her pain. Before I met her, I had never been able to laugh about giving up a child for adoption. She helped me unload my own burden, take it apart and look at it, and even laugh about the extraordinary lengths I had taken to hide. She was a warm fire in a cold neighborhood.

When I heard her story, then worked with her on telling it, I couldn't help but wonder at the contradiction between the strong, funny woman I was coming to know and the yes-woman she claimed to have been when she relinquished her child in the early 1980s. She debunked for me the story I used to tell myself that if I had only been older when Andrea was born, or if it had happened even a decade later, I would have had more choices. Maybe not. Many of us came to pregnancy naïve, ill-informed, and with dark beliefs about ourselves and about the inevitable financial deprivation and moral stain our children would inherit. Although many women did find a way to raise their offspring in a single-parent household, for those still battling societal expectations, not even the added choices and freedoms of the 1980s could help.

I had thought the '80s had brought enough openness, acceptance, and support for single mothers, that women were no longer being manipulated or coerced into relinquishing their children. In many places that was true, but not everywhere. Still thriving was the belief that women could not—or should not—raise children alone. Along with that stood the assumption that those children would be teased and bullied. Women were still being herded into homes for unwed mothers, bitterly known among some birth mothers as baby factories. Built into such models is a direct conflict of interest when advising pregnant women—the homes make money when an adoption is accomplished. Because Nancy had been in such a home, I asked her to go into detail about that part of her experience.

Only a few years after Nancy relinquished her son, she took a long look at herself and the choices she had made. She dipped into still-fresh grief without the consolation of knowing where he was and if he was all right. Her strength came through for her.

NEW BEGINNINGS – Nancy's Story

I was a receptionist in a nursing home. Randy was a maintenance man. I dated the maintenance man before him too. What can I say, I love a handy man. That was in 1982. But this really begins a few years before I met him.

In 1980 I was nineteen and living with Mom and Henry, my step-dad, in Oregon. When I moved ten miles away to go to secretarial school, I got into drugs, pot mostly, and started sleeping around. I was failing and unhappy. So when my cousin called and asked me to come live with them in New Mexico, I packed up all my stuff and sold my car. My aunt and uncle had a plane ticket waiting for me at the airport. It was a wonderful opportunity, a fresh start.

They had a working ranch with longhorn Texas cattle. I did indoor maid work—cleaning, kitchen, basic stuff. And I got paid for it. In summer their two kids came home from college and brought friends who needed work. Then come fall everybody went back to wherever they came from. After the kids left to go back to school, I moved to be closer to this guy I'd been seeing. Quentin, my first love. He was four years younger than I was. I fell just head-over-heels.

I was working at a bank at the time. It wasn't long before the bank politely asked me to leave. I was not a very good teller.

Then Quentin and I broke up. Things were falling apart.

This side of the family was Baptist, very Baptist. Did the Sunday morning, Sunday night, Wednesday night, Thursday night thing. I thought, when in Rome, do as the Romans do. When I lost my job and broke up with Quentin, I felt like I needed some guidance and I called the minister. We agreed I'd go back to my aunt and uncle's town and he'd meet me at the bus station. So I packed all my stuff, got on the bus, went back, and nobody was at the bus depot. After cruising through town with my luggage and looking for the minister, I found him at the football field. He was coaching, but he wasn't even the coach. He had forgotten about me. I don't remember if he apologized. If he did, it wasn't to my liking.

After that I left his church and went to the Assembly of God. We're talking speaking in tongues. Yeah, buddy. Dancing in the aisles. Maybe eight people would show up at a time. It was wonderful. Never felt more love in my life. It felt like I had found *home*.

I got a job as a waitress at a restaurant. That's about when I met Jerry through a mutual friend. I was twenty-two and he was forty-six, the same age my father was when he died of a heart attack two days before my fourteenth birthday. Not only that, but they had the same first name.

Jerry loved me, paid attention to me, and it wasn't long before I moved in with him. The problem was when he got mad. I would ask what I'd done, and he'd say I had to figure it out for myself, then wouldn't talk to me. We'd been living together for seven months the time he didn't talk to me for an entire week. That's when I packed up and went back to my aunt and uncle's ranch.

A little over a month later I realized I hadn't had a regular period, just spotting. I went to Planned Parenthood and had a pregnancy test. It was inconclusive.

When I was two months along, my grandmother went with me to see a midwife. My grandmother didn't have to say it, but it was clear to me that she disapproved of me having sex. We sat in the waiting room of the dome building with an earthy smell. Then they called my name. I saw the midwife, this hippie looking, natural kind of gal with a little girl of her own. They both walked me into the exam room. My grandmother stood and said, "Well, if she can be in the room, so can I," and she came along.

It didn't have those clean white walls, but I felt safe enough. I popped myself up on the table. As I sat there with my feet in the stirrups I was aware of my grandmother sitting there. We didn't have a lot of open conversations. We had the grandmother-granddaughter relationship, lived in the same house (my aunt and uncle's), and most of our interaction was going to church together. We didn't talk about my being pregnant, but a lot of judgmental feelings came from that household, and I was embarrassed, self-conscious.

The midwife wasn't sure if I was pregnant. She said my uterus was swollen and soft. And we knew that my period was over seven weeks late. So I was probably pregnant.

I was excited. This pregnancy was *mine* and I was hoping it was the start of something positive for me. I saw it as bringing me out of adolescence and giving me a chance to grow up, to be an adult, something no one expected me to do. And I wanted people to be excited for me. If the baby was a boy, I would name him after my father, and if it was a girl, a female version of his name. I even asked two friends to be godparents. I was so consumed and excited by the immediateness of being pregnant that I didn't think about what it would take to raise a child. I remember falling asleep at night, rubbing my belly and saying, "I'll love you. I promise to love you."

I wanted to do the mature thing and tell Jerry I was pregnant. I didn't want anything from him, just to let him know. I expected to have a heart to heart discussion about it. When I told him, Jerry shocked me by silently moving his hand to his groin and suggestively fondling himself. Devastated by his vulgar disrespect, I said, "I don't want anything from you. I don't expect any child support. I just felt you needed to know," and left the house in tears.

I didn't tell my aunt my plan to raise the baby. She'd been pressuring me to call the home for women giving up their babies for adoption. She wanted me to get information, find out what arrangements they could make for me. I did want to do the right thing. And I wanted to please my family, do something where they would say: Now there's a smart girl. So even though I didn't want to, I called the home to ask questions.

The woman on the phone listened, told me they could help me. She explained how the program worked. It sounded like a place that would help me through this, that I would be taken care of when I decided to go there. But the idea of going to a strange place, of meeting new people, most of them other pregnant girls about to give up their babies, that was scary. I walked around numb, uncertain.

Things went on like this for another month. One day, back at my aunt's house, I was loading wood into the wood box and I started to bleed heavily. I called the midwife.

"You're probably miscarrying," she said. "I am sorry. If you were going to keep this child, I'd have you come in and let me check you out to make sure you're okay, and then put you to bed. But since you're not going to keep it, go ahead and do whatever you would normally do. You will probably lose the baby."

I was devastated. I wanted to hear from someone: "I'm sorry, Nancy. How do you feel about this?" The only one in the family who said anything was my aunt. "Well, it's all for the best," she told me. "You were going to give it away anyway."

After the miscarriage, I really got into my drunken stupe. Drinking, pot, and, once, cocaine. But I didn't get the euphoria I thought other people were getting, it didn't give me any relief from the emotional pain, and the problems were still there after I sobered up. This was the second time I had tried to make it in the world and blown it. I remember thinking, *Lord, you finally have my undivided attention. Now what?* Margaret Bailey wrote a prayer, and where I got this I couldn't tell you. It says,

> "God, give me the sympathy and the sense
> and help me keep my courage high.
> God give me calm and confidence,
> and please, a twinkle in my eye."

I had the twinkle all right. Probably because I was drunk or stoned all the time. I looked around for options. I did not want to ask my mother or my older sister for help because I didn't feel either of them had room in their lives for me just then. So when my father's other sister and her husband asked if I wanted to move to Arizona and live with them, I was thrilled to be asked. Another new beginning.

I worked for my uncle at his travel agency. Started off as a receptionist, then moved into helping some of the other gals, and even took on finishing up details on one trip by myself. Uncle Bob got stressed out over his work and wanted to make sure everything was done right. One night he woke me up to ask if I got a package off on time. One day on my way home I was just bitch, bitch, bitch, bitch, bitching about something. My aunt was with me. She looked at me and said, "You've got fifteen minutes of my time. Bitch what you can. Then I'm done." For some reason that just hit me as very cool, somebody actually listening to what I had to say.

They were Baptist too, but their church scared the liver out of me. I was used to this eight-person church and their church had over two thousand people and a choir of two hundred and fifty.

The first Sunday I went, the church was doing a dedication to mothers. And here I was, crying, in this great big huge church, and nobody understanding why. Never felt so uncomfortable. I don't like big crowds anyway. Aunt Betty thought it would be better if I found my own church. She suggested one down the road. I said I'd think about it.

After ten months of staying with them, I got the job at the nursing home and moved into a two-bedroom apartment with two women coworkers. I took the couch.

So now we're back to when I met Randy, the maintenance man at the nursing home. He was twenty-nine, slender, dark hair, mustache, and drove an older model pick-up. I was still looking for a man to love me, and the easiest way I knew to make that happen was to sleep with him. Randy expected sex on demand. I knew the attention he gave me was not good attention, but it seemed better than nothing.

I couldn't take the Pill. We had high blood pressure in my family. I had a diaphragm, but it wasn't always convenient to use. And I was so in the moment and concerned about being loved that I didn't ask Randy to use anything. Pregnancy still felt like such a remote possibility, especially after miscarrying, that I figured I'd deal with it if it happened.

After a couple of months, I missed a period and started throwing up. I went to the doctor and had a test, but had to wait over Thanksgiving vacation for the results. My mom had sent a plane ticket for me to come home for the holiday. On Monday, while I waited at the airport for my return flight to Arizona, I called my doctor from a pay phone. He confirmed that I was pregnant. I felt a glow all the way back to Arizona. I was both afraid and excited about telling Randy. I was hoping he would ask me to marry him, then I would have a family of my own.

When I got back, we went out to Denny's, and I told him. He said it wasn't his child. I was so pissed that I wanted to flip that Grand Slam breakfast on him and stab him with my fork. "Excuse me," I informed him, "but I have not slept with anybody else since we've been together. And you've been with me practically twenty-four hours a day." We argued, and finally he said, "Well, maybe it could be mine." We talked about what to do and decided we'd take it one day at a time and not rush into anything.

A few nights later Randy took me out to this rinky-dink country-Western bar. We danced, then went to a table, where he got down on one knee and asked me to marry him. I said yes.

My next thought was, *Stupid! You don't want to spend the rest of your life with this man. He's going nowhere and has no values.* He couldn't support me financially, emotionally, or spiritually. But being married to him would be better than not having a man to love me, and at least I'd have help supporting myself and this baby. I had a dream of living in a little white house with a white picket fence and a swing set in the backyard, a couple of dogs, two-point-two children, and a loving husband that I would greet with a martini when he got home.

I didn't tell anyone we were engaged, not even my mom. Then I realized that if I wasn't thrilled enough to call home and tell her I was getting married, something was wrong. The truth was I was embarrassed to be engaged to this man.

When I finally got up the courage to tell people we were engaged, everyone had their own idea of what I should do. One of my roommates told me he was a jerk and I should dump him. People at work pressured me, asked me if this was what I really wanted and was Randy *the one*. My aunt thought I should talk to the people at the maternity home I was supposed to go to the first time I was pregnant. Everyone sounded *right* to me. I felt like a tug-of-war doll.

Three weeks after Randy asked me to marry him I finally admitted to myself that marriage to him wouldn't work. "I can't do this to you," I told him. "I can't do this to me." I started to cry. "And I can't do this to our child."

I think he was hurt, but he didn't put up much of a fight. We continued talking about it for three weeks. We were trying to figure out what we were going to do. In the end his attitude was more: Do what you need to. We never even said good-bye.

I was about ten weeks pregnant. What *was* I going to do? My thinking during this pregnancy was becoming different from the last one, more reality-based now. I had three options: Keep the baby, have an abortion, or give the baby up for adoption. I couldn't keep the baby. I remember thinking I wasn't emotionally stable enough to do this; I was a total wreck; I wasn't worthy. I couldn't do the abortion. I'd always felt that was my right as a woman, but I didn't have any money and, in the back of my mind, I just couldn't go through with it. So my only option was to do the adoption thing. It wasn't going to cost me anything except my spending money while I was there. The maternity home provided room, board, and medical care, found adoptive parents, made all the arrangements. And if I gave up the baby, I could build an image of myself as this mature, responsible person that people would respect and think: Look at her—now there's a brave and responsible person. I thought going to the home was what I had to do; I didn't have any other choices. Maybe I was just glossing over it, but I didn't have feelings about the decision until much later.

I called my mother and told her I was going to the home. Before she could even ask if I had considered my other options, I shut all the doors and locked them tight. I did not want her opinion, just her approval. And I definitely didn't have the courage to ask her if I could bring a baby home. Starting when I was little, I was even afraid to ask for a quarter for the ice cream truck man, so, like hell if I'm going to ask, "Oh, by the way, Mom, can I bring a baby home?" I told her that I was doing what I wanted, and she accepted that.

I quit my job at the nursing home and moved back in with my aunt and uncle in Arizona. I went back to work for Uncle Bob. Five bucks an hour under the table.

My cousin took me to a non-denominational spirit-filled church. I got good feelings out of that church. I met this lady who was in her fifties and such a *mom*. I was already pooching a little and I must have told her what I was going to do. One day she gave me a small gold ring, like a baby ring. "You need to have this. God said for me to give this to you." I wore it on a chain around my neck.

In early March of 1983, when I was four and a half months pregnant, my two aunts and my grandmother drove me to the home, a three-hour drive. I sat in the back. I felt like a complete stranger in a car full of relatives. I could hear their idle chitchat as I watched the trees and telephone poles go by. I wanted them to rescue me, to tell me I didn't have to do this. I felt like the black sheep of the family, no longer wanted and about to be left on a strange doorstep. Would I be okay? What would my new life be like? Would the girls there like me? *Dear God, help me. God, are you there? How can you let this happen to me?* It was a gut-sinking feeling.

It was afternoon when we pulled up in front of the red brick administration building. At the registration office a worker and I filled out paperwork. She said, "Your name sounds familiar." I told her I had called a year before. Turns out, she was the person I'd spoken to. She actually remembered our conversation.

At one point she opened up a phone book to the W's. "Here we don't use our own last names, for privacy purposes. So pick out a new last name, but choose one with the same initial as your real last name." For some reason I picked the name Westbury. Little Nancy Westbury.

The maternity home was a large complex taking up most of a city block. There was the administration building, a small hospital, a cafeteria and two newer apartment buildings for the girls under eighteen, and an older building that was probably one of the original dorms. Women eighteen or older stayed almost a block away in another building, and next to that building was a house that had been converted into individual apartments. I would guess the entire facility could easily have handled one hundred and fifty women. The women ranged in age from eleven to thirty-five.

My aunts and my grandma helped carry in my stuff. In the first doorway off the corridor I saw a kitchen. Several women, all hanging-out-there pregnant, sat at a table. Then it hit me—I was going to give up my baby. I didn't want to be there.

The day-resident-mother in charge when I arrived was a kind, older lady. She showed me to my room. It looked like a motel room—beige walls, twin beds with a nightstand between them, two dressers, a TV set, and a bathroom. She said it would be temporary, until they could get me settled into a regular room.

My aunts and grandmother said good-byes. I was crying and they were acting cheerful and saying, "Don't cry. Everything will be all right," "We'll miss you," "You're going to be okay," and "We'll talk on the phone." After all the trouble they had gone to just to get me there, I couldn't tell them that I was feeling abandoned. I had to prove, finally, that at age twenty-two, I was a big grown-up and I could do this.

Later, when I really looked and noticed how large the other girls were, I realized I was going to be there a long time. My due date was July 10, and it was only March. A lifetime.

The kitchen was large. Every woman prepared her own food. Sometimes a few of us would get together and make something. Beyond the kitchen area a set of stairs led up to bedrooms, and three other steps led down to the common living room. There were old sofas, big pillows, a large TV, a game room. Everything was done in beiges and browns. Doors in the living room led to a pool. From there you could see the other house, which had been made into individual apartments with their own kitchens. We could have our names put on a waiting list for one of those apartments, but most of the women wanted to stay in the main building. I wasn't much of a crowd person, and the idea of having my own digs felt more grown up. So I put my name on the list for an apartment. Within a few weeks, I moved into one.

Living at the home itself wasn't bad. At first I didn't feel welcomed by many of the girls. I remember one of them looking up at me and saying, "You don't look pregnant. How pregnant are you?" in a real sarcastic tone. Feeling defensive, my first thought was, *Fuck you*. But I didn't say anything. Once I got to know some of them, it was a little easier. We had our own jargon. For example, FOB meant "father of the baby." Someone might ask, "Have you heard from the FOB?" And we talked technical. Instead of asking, "When is the baby due?" we'd ask, "When are you going to deliver?"

Around the home, each of us had to do some sort of work, such as help in the kitchen or office. Also, there were classes. Girls under eighteen were expected to continue high school clas-

ses while they were there. For those out of high school, they offered basic continuing ed classes. The only class I was interested
in was the computer class. For about a month we met with
Donna three times a week and she taught us how to move the
cursor, words, and paragraphs around, how to delete a line. For
me it was like an advanced typing class. I grabbed hold of it real
quick. We worked on Radio Shack TRS80s. A month or so later, I
helped teach the class. With the tools I learned in the class, I developed a form letter on the computer. We typed names and ad-
dresses on form letters we sent to prospective adoptive parents. I
also worked at TelMed, a telephone medical information tape
library. I was paid five bucks an hour.

Besides the classes and assigned duties, we went to movies,
plays, and concerts with tickets that had been donated by the
community, and to the grocery store with vouchers they gave us.
Every time we went out, a bunch of us would cram into a van.
Feeling self-conscious about being with a mob of pregnant
women, I would hold my head high and walk fast. I wore a
"wedding" ring and pretended I was married and wasn't with
the others. The ring, silver with a design etched in it, was one I
bought in the summer of 1975, after my dad died. I'd worn it on
my right hand for years. When I got to the home, I switched it to
my left.

We watched a lot of television, and there was the swimming
pool. One of the most memorable times for me was seeing the
movie *Gandhi*. It was a spiritual experience for me. I walked out
of the theater feeling really good. On the way back to the home,
one gal starting cutting it down, said it was one of the stupidest
movies she'd ever seen. I thought, *What the hell am I doing here
with these people? No wonder you're all pregnant—you're idiots.*
Then I remembered, *Oh… I'm pregnant too. Whoops. Never mind.*

Being this person who didn't buck the system, it was very bold of me, but I asked if I got to meet my baby's adoptive parents. I was told no, they didn't do it that way. They asked all of us if we wanted to see the home of prospective adoptive parents. I didn't go. It felt too staged. Here you have somebody else's adoptive parents putting their best foot forward and showing their beautiful home, and a group of girls asking them to adopt their baby. When the other girls got back, they talked about how huge the home was. So I couldn't help but wonder if all their adoptive parents had big houses and my kid was going to have room to run.

The home also set up a meeting between several of the birth mothers and an adoptive couple. They seemed like nice people, probably in their mid-thirties. We asked a lot of questions. Do you intend to tell the child he is adopted? What will you tell the child about the birth mother? What kind of education do you have and what do you intend for the child? What are your interests and hobbies? They kept assuring us the child would be well taken care of. It felt as if they were trying to put on a show and supply all the right answers.

An adoptee came in to talk to us, a young man in his early twenties. We asked him what it was like to be an adoptee. Someone asked if he wanted to know who his birth mother was. When he said no, we were furious. He insisted that he was comfortable with who he was and that he had no need to know her. I thought, *Damn, I hope my kid doesn't feel that way.*

Most of the activities at the home were optional. A few weren't. We had to see a film on childbirth and go to breathing and Lamaze classes. I saw the film. It was wonderful! I was amazed that people can even get pregnant. As for the classes, I kept putting them off until later. Earlier I had asked them if I had a choice of natural childbirth and they said no, that at a certain point during labor and delivery the mother was given gas and "put out." Since I couldn't have natural childbirth, what was the point of taking the classes? Then I thought, *What are they going to do, fire me, not accept my baby?* I never went to a breathing class.

We had regular check-ups. The doctors came to us. We didn't have an assigned doctor, just whoever was on duty, and the hospital was on the grounds.

I got a great big huge butt, great big huge stomach. I'd gained fifty-four pounds. I loved being pregnant. It was a warm feeling. I loved the feel of the baby kicking. When I was out in public without the gang of preggos, I liked how people would look at me. I fantasized that they were thinking: Aw, another lucky woman starting a family.

We were assigned counselors. Mine was Mary Beth. We talked about how I was feeling physically and how I felt about my decision. I let her know right from the beginning that I was firm in my decision to give up the baby for adoption. I never explained it to her, but I knew in order to deal with the loss of a child, I would have to set it up in my mind early on that this was not my child but I was doing this for somebody else, that I was a surrogate parent. I was now thinking in terms of *the* baby, not *my* baby.

My sister Claire called me long distance every so often. I wanted to ask her for help, but pride stopped me. When I was about six months along, I called Mom and dumped some negative emotional stuff on her. A few days later I got a card from her. It had a bird on the outside. Now, I'm not a bird person. As long as they stay out of my face, I don't care. There was something probably very lovely printed on the inside of that card. What I remember was her note: "I cannot deal with your problems at this time. Love, Mom." Because I couldn't find a pen, I wrote her what I call a poison pencil letter, and I let her have it: "I don't want you to deal with my problems. I'm the one dealing with my problems. And I don't want your money. I want your support. I want you to love me. You're not my mother." I mailed it. Two or three days later she called me long distance in the middle of the day—the high rates—and apologized profusely. What I hadn't realized was that she was going through some rough stuff of her own. I accepted her apology and felt a little relieved that we'd cleared the air.

We talked on the phone every week or so, mostly polite conversation. She sent me a pillow she had cross-stitched, a Precious Moments pillow with a little girl and a basket of clothes. It said "Loads of Love."

The home was having a hard time getting Randy to sign the papers giving up his parental rights. He would tell them that he'd be somewhere, and then he wouldn't be there. So I decided to take the bus to Tucson to help find him. Rumor had it that Randy was at the Drift Inn, a skuzzy little motel with a bar and restaurant. I waited for three or four hours for him to show up, but he never did. If he didn't sign the final adoption papers, I would have to go in front of the judge to testify why he shouldn't have custody of the child.

It was hot on the 4th of July. A group of us sat on a roof landing to watch fireworks. Ally, the on-duty resident mother, was with us. A couple of days before that, I had gotten "the nesting," that enormous energy that happens a day or two before the birth and is usually spent on making sure the baby's room is ready. I was so high on that energy that I felt like I could fly if I wanted to. Whenever someone would ask for something, I'd be up and yelling, "I'll get it! I'll get it!" Everyone was teasing that it was going to be my turn next. I'd been uncomfortable all day, and when we were watching the fireworks it got worse. Ally suggested I stay in the temporary room across the hall from hers instead of in my own apartment. I agreed.

That night it seemed like every hour I had to go to the bathroom. I thought it was probably just false labor, but I couldn't get comfortable. No real pains, just an achy tummy feeling. Around dawn I decided to try walking off some of the discomfort. My next trip to the bathroom, the mucous plug came loose. I waddled over to Ally's room. She took me to the hospital building.

They did a pelvic. I was three centimeters dilated and eighty-five percent effaced. By six thirty a.m. I was being prepped—the shaving thing, the enema, setting up the Demerol IV drip. At a certain point I would be given gas and "put out."

I was lonely. I called my mother early on in the labor and told her I was in the hospital. But I didn't ask her to come and be with me, and she hadn't offered. Besides, she lived over a thousand miles away. The only comfort I got was from the nurse, Karen, who was in her early thirties and had a very kind face. She was tall and had long, brown hair, kind of a plain Jane, who would give you the shirt off her back even if it was the only one she had left. Karen stayed with me the whole time. She fussed at me a little because I hadn't taken the breathing classes. Now I understood how they would have helped and regretted not taking them. She was teaching the breathing techniques as we went along.

The contractions were still not regular. They felt like nasty cramps, a little on the annoying side. By the time the IV was put in at eight o'clock that morning, they felt a little stronger, but the baby was still up high. Fifteen minutes later, the doctor broke my water. Half an hour later, they induced me. The Demerol made me nauseated, disoriented. I asked the nurse if she could take the IV out of my body, then I threw up. By twelve thirty I wanted to push. At one o'clock I was informed that if the baby's head had not come down in an hour, I would have to have a C-section. I pushed so hard that I cried.

I was into my own world, my body, the pain. I thought sarcastically *This is not fun,* and tried to joke my way through it: "Let's quit. I'll come back tomorrow and we'll finish this up." But my body had taken over and was trying to push. Finally I had pushed the baby down far enough, and they wheeled me into the delivery room.

I remember sliding onto the table. I was feeling fuzzy. Towels were put on my legs and under my bottom. They helped me put my legs in the stirrups. I remember thinking, *Oh my god, my hoony is just hanging out for everybody to see.* Then the gas mask was put over my face. After a couple of intakes of the gas, I started to get numb. Oh, what a great feeling.

Next thing I knew I was off in another world, like I'd died and was in the middle of a laser show. Colored lights more vivid than rainbow colors came out, one right behind the other. I would go around each one, weave back and forth through the maze of swirling lights. I could hear the voices in the delivery room, but I couldn't understand what they were saying.

Then I was in the recovery room and it was two thirty that July afternoon. I said, "Have I come back to earth yet?"

"Yes," the nurse told me. "You're back down here now, and you're okay."

"What did I have?"

"You had a boy."

I was relieved the baby was a boy, because Randy and I had wanted a girl and I thought that would make it easier to give the child up. I was wrong.

I was physically and emotionally drained, and somewhat relieved that this was the beginning of it all being over. I kept
thinking of the dream I'd had while under anesthetic and how
strange it was.

A couple of hours later I was moved into a regular hospital
room. Three other women who had also just given birth were in
there. They must have been from the other complex, because I
didn't recognize them. For privacy, there were curtains we could
draw around our beds.

I was tired and hurting. Knowing I had a son was a strange
feeling in itself. Sitting in my room and knowing he was in the
nursery a couple of doors down, well, it emotionally hurt. Every
once in a while a nurse would come in and push on my belly.
That hurt. One time, when she finished pushing on me, the feeling I got from her was that this was no big deal, to stop being a
baby and get on with life. I felt like a baby machine.

I called my mother. Henry, my step-dad, answered. I told
him I'd had a boy. He asked if I was okay. Mom was just coming
in the door and saying, "What did she have? What did she
have?" I don't remember any more of our conversation.

No one from my complex came to see me, not even my social
worker or the resident mother. Most of the talk among my roommates was one-upmanshipping about the birth. "Oh, my labor
was much worse."

I didn't have a lot of information about what was happening
to my body. I was given a shot to dry up my milk. I imagined
having powdered milk in my breasts. It was probably discussed
in those classes I'd skipped.

My big question was: *What do I do now? Where do I go from
here? What's my next move?* Another new beginning. But I had no
idea where to go.

* * *

117

I was in the hospital for three days. I went back to the complex. My son would stay in the hospital nursery until he was placed in an adoptive home. We were told that we had the option of seeing our baby. On the day I was to see my son, a few of us were hanging out in the office next to the resident mother's room. I had picked out a dress to wear. It was a dark blue cotton dress with a print of little white flowers, puffy sleeves, scoop neck, a gathered waist, with a full, tea-length skirt, and a wrap-around red cloth belt. I put on make-up and did my hair all foo-foo. I even wore wedge heels. Most of the other girls wore slippers and a house jacket when they went to see their babies, and they gave me a bad time about dressing up.

"The baby's not going to know any difference what you wear."

"I'll know the difference," I told them. "I'll know what I wore."

I walked down to the hospital alone, wobbling on the heels, and was led to a small room off the nursery. The room had a rocking chair, a love seat, and a table and lamp. There was a painting of a seascape on the wall.

"He's just been fed and changed," the nurse said, "and he's in a real good mood. I'll be right back with him."

The first thing I saw when she walked in with him was a lot of wild, dark hair. Wild hair. It stood up. I sat in the rocking chair and she put him in my arms. He was wrapped in a white blanket and wore a T-shirt and diaper.

"Feel free to check for all his fingers and toes," she told me. "Make sure all his body parts are there. You can have as much time as you need."

His head was little and round, and he had a cowlick just like mine in front, and one in the back like his dad's. His eyes were dark brown, and his eyelashes went on for days. After I checked his fingers and toes, I just wanted to look at his face and talk to him. I'd had a conversation with a birth mom who said she didn't remember what her child looked like, so I thought, *I'm going to memorize this face.*

I spent an hour with him, staring at him, telling him things. I told him how much I loved him, that I'd never forget him, and that I hoped he'd be okay.

After about an hour I caught myself saying, "May God be with you," and the tears started. That's when I knew it was time to go. I don't remember how I got the nurse to come back in. I was sitting in the chair and looked up at her, my eyesight blurry with tears. She asked if I needed more time with him. "No," I told her, "I've had enough," still trying to feel confident in my decision. Slowly I handed him to her. It was real hard to hand him over knowing that could possibly be the last time I ever saw him. She looked at me with a sweet smile that said to me *Everything's going to be okay; we'll take good care of him.* I watched her— white shoes, white hose, white dress—walk out the door with him. I sat and cried.

I couldn't stay in there all day, so I went to the resident mother's room. She sat with me while I cried some more. Then I went back to my apartment, took off my clothes, crawled in bed, and lay there, dazed.

When I went to sign the relinquishment papers, I wore the same dress. I understood what I was signing, that I was relinquishing all rights to him and promising to have no further contact with him or the adoptive family until he was twenty-one. Other girls talked about how the relinquishment papers made them sound like unfit mothers. I didn't feel that way. When I read through them, I saw them as sterile, technical, legal words. I put on my businesslike attitude and sat tall in my chair, distancing myself from the reality of what I was signing.

After that, I moved into an old building in the complex that hadn't been used for a while. Five or six of us were staying in this huge, probably forty-room building that was like a college dorm. We had all "delivered." I stayed because I was waiting to go to court and testify because they had never found Randy to sign the papers.

A legal representative and a social worker from the home went to court with me. The judge and a clerk were the only others in the courtroom. The judge asked me why the biological father shouldn't take this baby.

"Judge, I don't want that child being raised in a pick-up truck."

He looked at me and said, "Good point," and slammed his gavel.

We were told we could write a letter to the adoptive parents. I did. It took me a long time, and I included a poem written by a Korean grandmother about her birth grandchild. It expressed what I felt—that I wasn't abandoning him, and I hated giving him up, but I had to so he could have a better life. I asked them to read the poem to him when he was old enough.

At six weeks, the home sent us what they called placement information, non-identifying information about the adoptive family. We called it the six-week report. I was told that this was the first child for the family who adopted my son, that they were active in their church and community. It also told me the kinds of things they liked to do. The report said that when he was presented, both parents just looked at him and she kept saying, "'He's so precious'…. She held him first, then he did. They were extremely tender and loving with him. Nancy, they expressed so much appreciation to the birth mother. They appreciated your letter so very much and were very touched by the poem. The family is eager to get him home and show him off to friends and family. The [social] worker commented, 'This is a really special couple and a couple who will be very sensitive and open with the child in discussing with him the story of his adoption.'"

If he wants to meet me, when he's twenty-one he can register with the home. I can register at any time. If we have both registered, the home will contact each of us and ask once again if we still want to meet. If we both say yes, we get to meet.

While I was still at the home, I called Whispering Pines Counseling Center. It was a Christian-based center known for intense live-in counseling. I spoke to Matt, the owner and head counselor, and told him what had been going on in my life. Being a friend of my aunt's, he offered me two weeks for the price of one. We're talking a thousand dollars a week to stay at this place. At first I thought, *Thank you, Matt, I'm a two-for-one kind of gal.* Then I thought, *Oh my god, am I that bad off?* I asked my mom to loan me the money. It was hard for me to ask, because that was admitting I was weak and not handling things on my own. But I was desperate and knew I needed the help. Then I said good-bye to the staff and some of the girls at the home.

While you were in counseling you had no access to telephones, TV, no communication from the outside world. Following more of a "let's get it done" type of therapy, counseling was one-on-one and group. I discovered that a majority of my troubles had to do with my father's death, when I was fourteen. This was the first time I actually went through all the questions and anger I had about it. Back then, my sister was at college, then got married. A year and a half after my father died, Mom met Henry. He and I got along, but I didn't feel like we bonded. Everybody had somebody but me. That's when I started what I call

121

my whoring-around period. Something a counselor said to me, a thousand dollars' worth of words, was, "God loves you." At that moment, and the way it was said, it knocked me over like a ton of bricks. I'd heard it before, but this time it really hit me, and suddenly I felt like everything was going to be okay. It knocked my socks off, and I felt that there was a purpose for me being around.

I also got the start of a backbone while I was there, and learned to stand up to people and voice my opinion. The combination of all the exercises, therapy group, and talking helped me realize I had choices, and the ability to think, and I didn't have to please other people all the time.

I'd been there a week and was running out of clean clothes. At the edge of town was an old laundromat. It was dingy, with brown walls and dirty yellow appliances. Nobody else was there. I got my quarters, put in my laundry, and thumbed through an old magazine. When I switched the laundry, I noticed a box that said "Clothes for the needy." What a clever idea, putting it in a laundromat. There were only a few things in there, and I wondered if I had anything to give.

When I was folding my clothes, my mind kept going back to the box. One of the things I had with me was the dress I wore when I went to see my son. Maybe leaving it there was something I could do to mark the separation between us, to start letting go and healing. But it was the only memento I had of my time with him, and part of me wanted to scoop that dress up and hold it tight to my bosom. If I kept it, that would be hanging onto the past. Letting the dress go meant I could start a new life for myself. I felt certain I needed to do it. My heart raced and I was short of breath. I picked up the dress and took off the red cloth belt. I would keep that. Then I folded it again and gently laid it in the box. I turned, picked up my other clothes, put them in the laundry basket, and left.

By the time my two weeks at Whispering Pines were over I was feeling pretty good about things. I moved to a place near my aunt and uncle and got a job at a dry cleaners. Didn't have a car, so I was pretty much on foot or took a bus. But what I really wanted was to go home to Oregon and get a hug from my mother. In March of 1984 I sold everything I could and used the money to get home. I was hideously delighted to round the corner of the bus station and see Mom's car.

A few days later Henry, Mom, and I sat at the kitchen table and talked about what I was going to do. I apologized for being a screw-up, for messing up so many lives, as well as my own. Henry said it was time for honesty. His exact words were "It's show-me time," meaning now that I thought I finally had my head together, it was time to prove it. Another new beginning.

I lived with Mom and Henry for a couple of months and got a job in a hamburger and ice cream shop. I went to the local community college part-time for a year and a half to study computers. During that time I ran into Jack, a guy I'd gone to high school with. We chatted for a long time, matching wit for wit. A couple of nights later, he asked if I'd like to go out with him. I was ecstatic.

As I got ready for our first date, I decided that I would not sleep with this man on the first night. I didn't even want to hold his hand. I didn't want to kiss him. And I would drink and smoke and be myself, and if he didn't like it, tough. No more games, I decided, this is it.

He came to pick me up in a '64 Buick Wildcat with the rear panel sheet metaled. An old, ugly car, but it rode beautiful. We went to a Mexican restaurant, and I smoked, I drank, I was myself. Sometimes I was scared, worried about what would happen if he didn't like me. But we had a wonderful time, spent hours talking. Our date didn't end until three in the morning.

On our second date he wanted to talk to me about something. "And I don't want you to laugh."

We were sitting in my living room on two loveseats in an L shape. He sat on one and I sat on the other.

"Okay," I said. "And I have something to tell you too. You first."

He told me he was a virgin. He was twenty-five and he was a virgin. I chuckled.

"You're laughing," he said.

"No, not laughing."

"Well, why are you chuckling?"

"Because I think it's wonderful, delightful."

We chatted a bit about that. Then I informed him that I was a birth mother. I figured if he couldn't handle it now, then see ya, I'm not going to be putting any time or energy into a relationship. When I finished telling him, he came over and sat next to me and held me. It was a wonderful, comforting, loving gesture. That's when I knew everything would be fine. He accepted me being a birth mother, and I accepted the fact that he was a virgin. And our relationship just went from there.

Two weeks later, we slept together. Three weeks after our first date, Jack asked me to marry him. Five months later, the following August, we were married.

By this time my son was three years old. Mom and I still didn't talk about him or the adoption. It seemed touchy for her, so I pretty much walked around the subject. She had been seeing a counselor, who, as it turned out, was an adoptive mother. Mom wanted to talk to her about feelings she had about me giving up the baby. She felt a door between us needed to be opened and the counselor could help do that. She asked if I wanted to go with her.

During the session we talked about the adoption and did a lot of crying. The counselor gave me a thank-you from all adoptive parents to all birth mothers. I apologized to Mom for putting her through a lot of pain and for writing the poison-pencil letter. She apologized for not being there for me. That session broke the ice, and we were finally able to build a new relationship, this time as equals.

All along I was aware that out there was a child I'd brought into the world. His birthdays were a killer. I allowed myself to be depressed. It was my day to think about him, wonder what he was doing, what he got for gifts, what kind of a cake he had. After the first birthday, the next hardest was when he turned six. He would start school that year. I wondered what kind of school clothes he got. I thought about the brand new book bag he'd probably gotten, and the brand new pencils, new ruler, new paper.

Around his seventh birthday, I started feeling lonely and sad. I knew it was connected to giving him up. Even though I knew there were other women who'd given up a child, it was like I was the only one who felt this way. Sometimes I thought I was going crazy. I'd told only a few people about it. I felt like I had this huge secret inside and it was tiring me out. I needed to find a support group where I could talk to other birth mothers and find out what it was like for them. So I went through what I thought were normal channels—called the hospital, the local help line, even the county mental health department. The closest I found was a group that dealt with adoptive rights.

At the meeting were adoptees, adoptive parents, and a couple of birth mothers. The only man there was an adoptee. I was disappointed that it was more of a search group and not a support group for birth mothers. At the next meeting Mom and I cruised through their pamphlets. I learned it could be a good idea to get in touch with the home again so it would be easier to find my birth son later. The group suggested that I write or call the home and do a medical update. Well, it had only been a few years and the only new medical information I could come up with was allergies. I figured I should wait until I got something really serious, instead of just you'll-sneeze-your-guts-out allergies, but I couldn't come up with anything else.

I spent that night at Mom's. The next morning, something kept telling me to call the home. I kept hearing, *Do it, do it now.* So I got the number, went into the kitchen where Mom was cooking breakfast, and told her I was going to call. This would be the first time I had talked to them in seven years. I shook like a leaf.

I was put in touch with a post-adoption worker. I was basically bull-shitting my way through, said I had been at the home seven years before and it was a wonderful experience. She asked how I was doing and what was going on in my life. I told her that I had joined a support group for all members of the adoption triad, knowing I had to be careful not to let her know that it was a search group. Then I had to give a reason for calling. That's when I told her that I had this medical thing.

"Okay," she said, "what is it?"

"It's allergies." It sounded so pathetic.

After I finished telling her about it, she said, "If you have a few minutes, I'd like to tell you what we've been doing lately."

"Absolutely." I was shaking. I looked over to Mother. She was busy making toast in the oven.

"If you'll write us, we'll give you an update about your son," she told me. "But only non-identifying information."

Emotion was coming all the way up from my toes. I held my hand over my mouth and started crying. What she was telling me was so wonderful! I had been feeling that something wasn't okay with him, and I was finally going to know how he was!

She said they would have new information only if they had heard from the adoptive parents, and it was possible they had not. "This is a new program," she said, "and even if they have been in contact, the whole process can take six to eight weeks because we're so far behind already."

Mother still didn't know why I was crying. She reached over and took hold of my hand. I squeezed back tightly and nodded my head to let her know I was okay and that it was good news.

I told the social worker that I was crying out of excitement and happiness and not because I was a crazy psycho-bitch from hell. She said she understood and gave me the address to write to.

When we hung up, I told Mom, and we cried together. Of course, by this time, the toast was burned.

The next day I wrote a short letter to the home requesting information. I figured it would be a couple of months before I heard from them. Three weeks later when I came home from work, Jack was sitting on the couch. He stared at me. Then I noticed a letter on the coffee table in front of him.

"You got something," he told me. "Want me to stick around or leave?"

I started shaking, worried that the reason I was hearing so soon was because they hadn't heard anything from the adoptive parents and had no new information.

"Okay," I said, "I'll go change my clothes. Then I'll read it." Like a dog who wants to play with the cat but isn't really sure it's a good idea, I wasn't sure I wanted to deal with this. I got half my clothes off before I couldn't stand it anymore and I walked back into the living room and picked up the letter. I was trying to be calm and cool, but it didn't work.

"Do you want to be alone?" Jack asked.

"Please stay."

I sat next to him on the couch. The envelope was thin, like the letter was a one-pager, so I prepared myself for no news. I opened it. The first line said something to the effect of, "It was very nice talking to you a few weeks ago. Per our telephone call..." My eyes dropped halfway down the page, and I saw, "long, wavy hair." I went into tears, big waterfall. I handed the letter to Jack and motioned to him to go ahead and read it out loud, because I was a blubbering idiot.

My son was okay and it sounded like he was happy. It was the most wonderful, warm, *relieved* feeling just to know that. I understood this to be recent information because of other things in the letter, such as, "He enjoys baseball. He enjoys soccer, and he was voted the most valuable player on his team and he slept in his uniform that night." Each year the home put on picnics for the adoptive parents, social workers, and adoption workers.* The impression I had from the letter was that his parents had gone to one of the picnics.

Once I stopped crying, I must have read that letter ten or fifteen times. At one point I practically had it memorized. Yes, this was my son. I felt proud. But who could I tell?

I called Mom. When I read the letter to her, she started crying. We cried again together. Then I called my sister. Again, we cried.

I went to the search support group and shared the letter with them. They were thrilled for me. Hearing the people at the

---

*They held separate picnics for birth mothers.

meetings acknowledge their own experiences helped me realize that I was not alone; there were others out there who'd been through this. I knew that the adoptive parents had a son, but he was also my flesh and blood.

The search group couldn't give me the rest of what I was looking for. I wanted to talk more about feelings instead of how people's searches were going. So I made an appointment with a counselor. In eight visits she discussed adoption with me only once. I stopped seeing her.

I needed help sorting out my feelings. If I needed help, I was sure other birth mothers out there needed help. So fine, if no one else was going to be first to come out of the closet, then I would put together my own support group and see what happened. I talked to Jack and Mom and my sister, got their blessings and support, and sent out public service announcements to radio and TV stations and newspapers. I didn't get any calls. I was disappointed, but I understood. Most birth mothers had been told to go home and forget, that it was over, so if she went to a meeting, she wasn't following the program.

A few months later after a second round of announcements, there was a message on my answering machine from Patricia. She was interested. We met in early spring and set our first official meeting for the first Tuesday in June. Scared the liver out of me wondering how many people would show up, or if *anybody* would show up. The lady from Boys and Girls Aid Society said she would be there. I set up a notebook and on a separate piece of paper I had a place for name and phone number and what part of the triad people belonged to, like a sign-in sheet.

When I got there, Patricia was already there. Then the woman from Boys and Girls Aid Society showed up. We waited for a while hoping somebody else would come. Nobody did. My expectations had been higher than reality called for. Still, it was a good meeting. I learned something about the Boys and Girls Aid Society and how they worked. But in the back of my mind, I was wondering where the birth mothers were.

The next month two more birth mothers came. They had seen the public service announcements. I had hoped for more, but this was okay. People showed up and were willing to keep coming back and share their stories and ideas. I soaked in other people's stories, feelings, ideas, and it broadened my horizons. It was comforting knowing I wasn't the only person out there and that my feelings were normal. Probably the biggest thrill over the years of the support group was that nobody was judgmental. I loved that.

Because of the low attendance at meetings, Patricia suggested we get an article published in the paper. We needed the publicity. Going public with my story didn't feel real until I saw it in print. After I talked to the reporter, I worried that I had said something wrong, something that would hurt somebody's feelings. Patricia called me when the article came out and I ran down to the grocery store, bought one, and sure enough, there it was, bigger than life--a picture of Patricia holding a picture of her daughter and our stories next to it. It was a thrill to see my name in print, but at the same time scary now that it was public.

My number was published in the article and my phone started ringing off the hook. I got a lot of calls from adoptive parents, all of them in support of a group for birth parents. Patricia got more calls from birth mothers.

We were gearing up for the next meeting, hoping a lot of people were going to be there. I walked into the room, and it knocked my socks off. Sixteen people! It was wonderful to see that many women come forward and say, "Yes, I'm a birth mother too," or an adoptee, or a birth nana.

One of the big shifts for me, and even though I knew it before, was when Suzanne said, "It's not just my experience as a birth mother, but this happened to my friends, my family, and the adoptive parents." For so long I had looked at it as being just my experience, just my story, forgetting that a whole lot of other people are involved in my story.

Two things still haunt me. When my birth son was about two years old, my sister told me that back when I was in the home, my mother had called them and talked to my counselor. She told the counselor that if I wanted to bring the baby home, I could, and we could live with her. The counselor had said that I had made a firm decision and she didn't think they ought to bring it up. So it was never mentioned to me. If I had known, I would have brought him home. The other thing that haunts me is that when I was young I said I wanted to have only one baby. A few years ago I had a hysterectomy because of a precancerous condition. I think about the saying: Be careful what you wish for because you just might get it.

I had started out looking for love and attention, but I had to learn how to love myself and to be more assertive. And the more I talk, the more I grieve, the more I heal, the more I learn. Being a birth mother is something that will never be over. When I left my son at the home, I left some big pieces of myself there.

Along the way, I've thought of some things I'd like to say to people involved with adoption.

First, to birth mothers or birth mothers-to-be: Ask the questions. Get the choices in front of you and look at them carefully. Make the decision that *you* think is best. Don't let anybody sway you. And ask for help!

To birth families: Don't forget to support one another.

To the spouses of birth parents: Support your spouse.

To adoptive parents: Cherish the children. Don't forget that we birth moms are out here. Be thankful every day for the fact that you have a child.

To adoptees: We love you. We miss you. Know that you're always in our hearts. Giving you up was not an easy decision (for those of us who had a chance to make the decision). Know that on your birthday we think of you.

Finally, a message to my son, who is now thirty-two: I love you. Even though I only got to see you that one time, I will never forget what you look like. Know that you are loved by me, and if we ever get a chance to meet again, which I pray to God we do, it's not going to be a reunion just between you and me, but for everyone involved. Come find me.

4

As the number of my birth mother acquaintances grew through the support group, I was surprised to meet women who were married when they relinquished. Single women could attribute part of their decision to social disapproval for having a child out of wedlock and raising a child as a single parent. Married women confronted a more complicated decision and were subject to being judged as selfish and cold. Today, the option of abortion offers another way to deal with an unwanted pregnancy, a more private, permanent way.

Evelyn's relinquishments took place in the mid-1960s, when she was in her early twenties. When I met her, in the mid-1990s, she was still questioning herself, her husband, and their choices as young marrieds excited to be engaged in the adventure of adult life but overwhelmed and uncertain when the adventure was parenthood.

Small and athletic, Evelyn had a deep voice and an easy smile. She shared with our group all she had learned about healing and searching. When she agreed to tell her story for this book, she recorded it on tape. Later, she answered questions as we walked in the park. She invited me to her country home, where she had blended her passion for the outdoors with her art. We sat in this green sanctuary surrounded by trees and her sculptures and drank tea while we talked about her decisions and healing process. She had worked hard to make sense of her choices. In her words, she walked through the flames of confusion, shame, and grief, she felt the fear, and she decided she wanted to know the truth.

ANIMA – Evelyn's Story

I was raised on a cattle ranch in Montana with my sister and three brothers. All of us kids had chores. We washed the dishes, weeded the garden, picked berries and vegetables, herded cattle, helped with irrigation, checked fences, and carted bales of hay through the muck in winter to feed the cows.

My parents wanted to farm and live the way they wanted without interference. As a family we talked about philosophy and ideas, intellectual stuff, but not about emotions. Anything physical or financial problems, those could be handled, but emotional needs were too personal, too intimate. They were supposed to be handled privately.

I was the middle child and, when I was young, the rebellious one. At age seven, I wanted to see the movie *Puss 'n' Boots*. Because my brother and sister hadn't been able to go, I wasn't allowed to go either; it wouldn't have been fair. So I stole money from my father's coin purse and went to see it anyway. When it was over, I called my parents to come pick me up.

I was a real tomboy. I played baseball and dodge ball with my brothers, rode the horse, and didn't mind getting dirty. But being reprimanded time and again took its toll, and somewhere around puberty I fell into line and tried doing what I thought people wanted me to do—be a good girl and consider what other people thought before I acted. I put myself in the role of someone who accommodates, a people-pleaser, a fit-in-and-don't-rock-the-boat person. Even though I still played baseball and rode horses, I was now also concerned with how I looked, and didn't speak up unless someone asked my opinion. I did what the popular people did. I was even a cheerleader and a flag girl in high school.

In 1960 I graduated from high school, and because all my friends were going to college, that's what I did. I lived at home and earned tuition by working at fast food places. Restless, I dropped out and moved to Sun Valley, Idaho, to work as a food server at the ski resort. I met a lot of people there and made friends. It was fun, and I began to realize that I wanted to explore the world, see what else was out there. So when some friends suggested that we go to Hawaii and work there when the ski season was over, I was game. It was just the thing for a naïve country girl filled with wanderlust.

In Hawaii I worked nights and hung around the beach with friends during the day. I was living my dream. I had freedom, independence, and adventure. And I met Michael, who was about to finish his tour in the Navy. He asked me to go dancing with him before he left for the mainland. I'd seen him around often enough to recognize that he was a nice guy—and very good looking. The next night I took off work and we went out for dinner and dancing.

Like my father, Michael talked about philosophy. I had never met another man with a lot of ideas he wanted to discuss. We talked all through dinner at a fancy hotel club. We danced to a live band on the terrace under the banyan tree. Later we went down to the beach, where we sat and talked until morning. I was charmed.

Michael would be leaving the next day. When he took me back to my apartment, there was no big scene of "I'll miss you," or "We really had a great time." He was different from guys who only wanted to get you into bed. He was careful *not* to be that way. He didn't even try to kiss me. I felt something special going on between us, but I didn't feel forward enough to ask him to write. I also didn't want to risk putting that out there and having no response. I wasn't sure if anything more would come of it after he left.

Then I got a letter from him, which bowled me over. It confirmed that he had felt something was going on too. Soon I was getting a letter almost every day. It was like a dream come true. We wrote to each other all that autumn, our letters getting more and more romantic. By winter I decided to go back to the mainland to see him and find out what there was between us, whether this was a real relationship or not. In February 1963, I went back.

Michael met me in San Francisco and we drove south to his family's home in the Los Angeles area. His parents were polite, but it was clear they were waiting to find out what he was going to do with his life and what my being there meant.

My second night there, he took me up the hill behind the house, where he had spent a lot of time, and asked me to marry him. He wanted to get married right away. I had an inkling he might ask. I wasn't sure I was ready. I'd been thinking we could be friends, have a good time together, get to know each other better.

When I was alone, I was fairly independent, but when it came to having a relationship that involved romance, intimacy, and sexuality, all the deep, primal emotions I felt about him, I reverted to the model I observed in my parents: the woman goes along with the man's decisions. I was afraid if I stood up for myself and disagreed with him, he wouldn't love me. I also believed that because we were in love, if we got married, somehow everything would work out and be happily ever after. So I said yes.

We didn't tell his parents yet. I think Michael was afraid they would interfere, maybe ask us to wait until we knew each other longer and he was through with school. Instead we drove to my parents' home, two days away, so Michael could meet them. They liked him and went out of their way to make him feel a part of the family. They could see how happy I was and were happy for me.

We returned to Southern California and bought rings. Then we drove around and found a justice of the peace to marry us. After the ceremony we took a long ride in the mountains and had dinner to celebrate. We went back to his parents' house and told them that we'd been married and were moving into an apartment, which we'd already rented. They seemed resigned. His mother congratulated us.

Michael dropped out of school and got a job as an electronic technician, something he'd learned in the Navy. He felt he should support me and that I should stay home in our small, furnished apartment. He didn't like my idea—that I go to work and support us while he finished school. He didn't want to argue about it; he was going to work and I was going to stay home.

I was shocked. What felt terribly uncomfortable was the idea that now I was married I should believe what he believed. It was like a death of the self, and after the euphoric honeymoon period, it felt claustrophobic.

Michael and I read books and discussed emerging ideas about self-sufficiency and independence. We both read the book *Atlas Shrugged* by Ayn Rand. We idolized the ideas of total self-reliance, independence, and strength, with the only acknowledgement of emotion being fantasy romanticism. Michael had embraced that philosophy, and it struck me as right too. That's the kind of world we wanted to create. We were self-reliant, didn't need anybody. We could make our own decisions and take care of our own problems. We didn't want to have to depend on anyone. In fact, that went so far that I didn't want to be dependent on Michael, and even though I hardly earned anything, we kept our money separate.

But even though we idolized Ayn Rand's writings and ideas, our inner life was the opposite of the principles she stressed. We were both twenty-one, and neither of our outer packages was the same as we were on the inside. Especially mine. I was independent in that I'd been on my own and worked, but I can see now that I also had a lot of dependencies.

So I sat at home feeling stupid, and I kept talking to Michael about my going to work. We were barely making it financially. After three months, I persuaded him. It didn't take long to find a job.

Three or four weeks after I started work, I went to the doctor. I had been vomiting in the morning. We had had unprotected sex once and realized pregnancy was possible. The doctor confirmed it. I was excited because this seemed like part of the program, the next step for us as a married couple.

When I told Michael, the news fell like a lead balloon. Silence. I'd been hoping he would be happy, but he gave off a resigned, "What I've been fearing is true." I hadn't realized how he felt. I was terribly disappointed. And mortified. I had been trying to be a good wife, and all of a sudden I wasn't okay and what had happened wasn't okay. I was living my ultimate terror — being with the man I loved, the father of my child, and he didn't want the child. I didn't want to ask him what was going on. I was afraid the answer would be that he didn't love me and wished we hadn't gotten married. So I waited it out.

I wrote to my parents about the pregnancy, and Michael said something to his parents about it, but we didn't discuss it with each other. We did move into a larger apartment. My mom sent me a blanket for the baby. But we didn't talk about clothes or the baby's room, and our parents didn't discuss it with us. No baby showers were being planned.

One night Michael did not come home from work on time. I thought of all the awful things that could have happened. I checked with his parents. I checked with his sister. I checked with the local hospital. I even called the police to find out if there were any accidents on the freeway. Then I waited. I had never felt so vulnerable, alone, and terrified.

He finally got home, near midnight. He said he had gone out for beers with one of the guys from work and lost track of time.

I was so pissed. I couldn't believe he hadn't been considerate enough to call and say he would be late.

He said he was his own person and didn't have to check in with me or answer to me, and he certainly didn't have to call and get permission. He was adamant that he didn't want to be told by his wife what to do.

That shocked me. That wasn't at all what I was thinking. All I had wanted was a phone call.

Things got worse as the pregnancy progressed. Michael would go out to bars, sometimes come home really late, and still would not let me know where he was. I was worried and confused, but when I tried to talk to him, he was defensive. We were becoming estranged. It was one of the loneliest times of my life.

When I was six months pregnant, we finally talked. Neither of us was very mature, and we knew being married didn't mean we were ready to be parents. It was a big problem. Michael didn't want to be a father yet.

It felt as if he was rejecting me and the child, that he didn't want to be a father because I somehow didn't measure up as a wife or mother. I began to fear that my life would end up being a reenactment of my mother's, raising children and being dependent on a man who was not an involved and active participant in raising them. I felt trapped just thinking about it. It seemed even more likely that I would end up being a single mother, which looked like sheer hell.

So here we were, neither of us willing to make the commitment or to force the other into parenthood. We were stuck.

Finally, he broached the idea that the child could be adopted and maybe later we would be ready to be parents. I saw it as a way to salvage the marriage, a way to deal with what we didn't know how to handle. A way out.

We made an appointment with an adoption agency in L.A. We wanted to be sure things were done properly, and this agency had a good reputation.

Michael came to pick me up from work so we could go together. We wanted to make a good impression. He had a tech job and usually dressed in shirt and pants, but this time he was dressed in a nice suit, and I wore a nice outfit. We were nervous, and except for comments on traffic on the way there, we didn't talk. One of the ways to handle what we were doing was talking about it only when we had to.

A social worker came out to the reception area to meet us and led us to her office. She sat behind her desk and we sat on the other side. I felt like a small child in need of advice and help from a parent figure, and I focused on taking my cues from her. She had us fill out forms and asked a lot of questions about our backgrounds and history. Then she asked why we were giving up the baby.

I looked at Michael and waited for him to answer. He told her something like we just weren't ready to be parents and that we were having a tough time financially. To this day I still don't know why we weren't ready. I know we told her we were afraid.

We asked questions too. We wanted to make sure that they wouldn't restrict the choice of adoptive parents based on race or religion. We believed that anyone who wanted to adopt a child and had been cleared by this agency must be wonderful and would make good parents. She promised they would find a good home, good parents, and that they had a number of families that would be good candidates. We didn't ask about their screening process. We trusted them.

We assured her that we would pay for everything, that we weren't freeloading. We'd take care of everything about the pregnancy and birth. All we needed was their help to make sure the child got a good home. We would do everything else.

Once we decided to relinquish the baby, we moved back to a smaller apartment and spent a lot of our time just watching TV and pretending everything was okay. We didn't talk to each other or make life plans.

We didn't tell his parents. But I wrote to mine and told them. Mom suggested marriage counseling. I was surprised to hear that from her, because Dad thought psychologists were people you couldn't trust and wouldn't want to get mixed up with. Michael and I both laughed. We thought it was a joke. How could anyone know something about our marriage that we didn't know? We knew everything there was to know about us. That arrogant invincibility stuff.

The baby was due in March. I would stop working in the seventh or eighth month. I didn't tell anyone at work that we were planning to have the child adopted because I felt guilty and embarrassed that we were not accepting responsibility for what is a normal thing in a marriage. I pretended we were a happy young couple having a child. They gave me a baby stroller. When I brought it home, I cried and cried and cried.

Michael and I saw the social worker a few more times. I think she wanted to make sure we knew what we were doing. Because we didn't have a real reason for not keeping our child, I think she thought we might change our minds. We took the buggy to the last meeting we were going to have with her and gave it to her, telling her that we wanted a good couple to have it. I was crying and Michael stood stiffly, his arm around me, resigned.

I wanted to say *Yes, I will raise this child*, but I was so afraid that if I did, Michael would leave me. Even if he did stay, I would have to raise the baby by myself. I felt like I could have either Michael or the baby, but not both.

The social worker looked confused, as if she was watching us do something we'd regret but couldn't help us, because we refused to make another decision.

A few weeks later labor started. Michael drove me to the hospital, but he wasn't allowed to be with me during the birth. I don't remember much about it. I was drugged during labor and given general anesthesia for delivery. I did not see the baby. The doctor didn't think I should.

When I came to the next morning, I was in a bed next to the wall at the end of a room with several beds. I was on a different floor of the hospital from the babies and other mothers. I kept to myself.

Giving up my baby was totally against anything I believed about myself. I felt guilty and ashamed. But because I'd been unconscious and never saw the baby, it was easier to deny I had feelings, easier to pretend it didn't happen. It was a coping technique that served me. Michael might have visited me once, but I don't remember for sure. We may have agreed ahead of time that he shouldn't.

The social worker we had been working with came to the hospital to talk to me and give me papers to sign. I just wanted to get it over with. As I saw it, the decision had been made and we were obligated to keep our part of the agreement. When I asked about the baby, she told me it was a girl. We didn't name her. That would have made it too real. We objectified the whole thing.

After the baby was born, Michael told his family the baby was a girl but we were giving her up for adoption. His mother was upset and called me at the hospital. She asked if we were afraid we couldn't be parents. She suggested that Michael's sister and her husband take the baby. They offered. Michael said no. He believed his family was thinking that if the child was in the family, we would eventually change our minds and everything would be okay.

I felt bad for his family. They had been the expectant grand-parents. All that time, although we didn't talk about the preg-nancy much, we'd been going over and visiting, not telling them our intentions to relinquish the baby. We didn't think that what we were doing would affect anyone else in the family. We just thought we were handling it for ourselves.

Afterwards, when we visited his parents, we never talked about it. Never. They only knew the baby had been a girl. We would not even tell them who the doctor was because Michael thought they would interfere. It was a big barrier with his fam-ily, but we all pretended everything was fine.

I thought if we relinquished our child, our relationship would get better. It didn't. Eventually I decided that if Michael and I couldn't raise a child together, and if things weren't great be-tween us, maybe I didn't want to live with him anymore. I knew I could live in Idaho for six months and get a divorce. We had an extra car, an old Chevy my mom and dad had given us. I would drive it to Idaho, and I knew people there, so I thought I could find work. If I left and divorced Michael, then I could be free of it all and start over. I wouldn't have to deal with the aftermath or work on a relationship. I told Michael I'd be leaving as soon as I had my postpartum check-up.

What a fantasy, thinking I could go off on my own with no support and make things happen, especially without having acknowledged the loss of a child or going through the grief of not getting along with my husband. I was in Idaho only a few weeks when Michael called and told me he had found a job in San Jose. He wanted me to come. We'd be in a new place, away from family, he'd have a good job, and we could start over. I said I'd go with him. He drove up to Idaho and we packed everything into our two cars and left.

In the early 1960s, San Jose was a gorgeous small town in a rural area with a lot of orchards. And Michael had a good job there. We were hopeful. The Help Wanted ads in the newspaper were divided into a Women Wanted section and a Men Wanted section. So I looked at the jobs women could apply for. Office work was what was available, so I started taking a class in stenography.

It soon became obvious to me that things still weren't working between Michael and me, and I decided to move out and live independently. We were still married, but I lived in my own apartment, a little studio near Palo Alto, where I found a job at the College Entrance Exam Board.

I'd had a period in Idaho, but then I skipped a period for two months, so I went in for a pregnancy test. It was negative. The doctor gave me some pills to regulate my cycle. When it still didn't start, I went in and had a second test. This time it was positive.

A stab in the heart. Here we were again.

This baby must have been conceived on our first night together on an overnight in Lake Tahoe when we were on our way back to California. Contraception was a big deal. Michael didn't want me to use the Pill. It was pretty new then and he didn't think it was safe. The only other thing I knew about were condoms. They were easy to use, but we hadn't had any that night.

After I got the positive test result, I called Michael and said we had to talk. I went to his apartment, the one where we used to live together, and into the bedroom and sat on the bed. He knew I had missed a couple of periods and that it was possible I was pregnant again. When I told him the test was positive, we lay side by side on the bed and held each other while we cried.

Trapped. After the hell we went through to have our daughter adopted, we faced the same thing again. It had only been a few months since her birth and, other than Michael having a good job, nothing had really changed in our circumstances.

"We've got to have this baby adopted," I told him. As I saw it, there was no decision to make. How could we raise this child knowing that we had given up our first baby? It would have been like choosing this baby over her, and I couldn't do that to her. Someone who wanted to adopt this baby could love it better than I was capable of at the time. It had to be.

I didn't even give Michael an opening to talk about my decision. I didn't give him a chance to say we should raise this child. I don't remember even listening to what he wanted. I didn't trust him anymore. I felt he had abandoned me during the first pregnancy, those brutally long months of feeling trapped into doing something that felt wrong but unable to see any other way out. Also, I shut down my own feelings by objectifying the experience. Keeping this baby would open up that Pandora's Box of feelings.

We went down and talked to the local branch of the same agency we'd gone through the last time. It was hard telling them that we had just relinquished a child in Los Angeles, but our caseworker was matter-of-fact about it.

145

I found a good doctor near where I worked and told him that I planned to relinquish the child for adoption. He had strong feelings about it. He thought that if a woman was considering giving up her child, she should hold the baby and really acknowledge that she had given birth and say good-bye, not just pretend the baby was never born. He wanted Michael to be in the delivery room if he wanted to be there, which I thought was good. I wanted him to help shoulder some of the burden.

We had some other decisions to make. Could I live away from Michael during the pregnancy or should we move in together and wait it out? Because it made no sense financially for us to live apart, we decided to live together, and, I thought, maybe we'd be able to work things out. We didn't tell our families I was pregnant again. We were ashamed that we hadn't prevented another pregnancy.

This pregnancy wasn't as traumatic. I didn't have morning sickness, so I felt better physically, and there was no tension from waiting and hoping things would turn out differently. The first time you do something is always more difficult. The second time, you know what's coming. I was hardened and knew what motions I needed to go through. In a way, that wasn't fair, because this was a different child.

I still had my secretarial job. At some point I would have to let them know so they wouldn't throw a baby shower. I waited for a time when it wouldn't seem like a big deal, then asked my boss, the office manager, if I could speak to her. Once we were alone I told her. "Michael and I have talked to an adoption agency and we're going to have the child relinquished for adoption." I kept it neutral, businesslike, without getting into the feelings. She said, "Okay. I guess you know what you're doing. If there's anything we can do for you, let me know."

There was a temporary worker there who was also pregnant. Her husband was a university student, and she talked about their plans and the things they were doing to get ready for the baby. It should have been tough for me to hear, but I tuned out and let her be the focus of office attention. In a way, maybe it made it easier because the attention was on her and her pregnancy rather than mine. They didn't say much to me about it. The other women in the office and I had a good rapport and the office manager was supportive. At one time or another most of the staff had been teachers, with a background and training in giving support. When it was time for me to stop work before the birth, they gave me a present—a lace nightgown, mint green with a gauzy white layer over it, very feminine.

Michael and I again spent a lot of time watching TV. Our apartment complex had a pool, and I swam regularly. Often I would just stand at my bedroom window and stare ahead at the space between our apartment building and the light-colored stucco building across the way, wondering what life would be like when the pregnancy was over.

Again I went into labor at night. Michael was working the night shift and came home to get me. It was a long drive. We were afraid, anxious. He stayed with me in the prep area, where I was shaved and gowned. He held my hand during labor, and I remember that it helped to kind of bite on his hand when it hurt a lot. Being in there was hard on him, made it more real for both of us.

I was given a caudal to numb me from the waist down and moved into the delivery room. Michael came too. It was a primal experience. I was crying, pushing, and the doctor was coaching me to breathe and push. Giving birth felt like a tremendous release, physically, mentally, and in every way.

The baby was a boy. I don't think Michael and I said anything to each other. I was just glad he was born, that he was healthy, and it was over. The doctor gave me medication so my breasts wouldn't swell with milk. I was put in the maternity ward, surrounded by women who had children. None of the other women knew I was giving up my baby for adoption.

Later they brought the baby in for me to feed and hold. I held my son in my arms. They gave me a bottle to feed him. He was a cute little boy with dark eyes and a mass of black hair that stuck straight out from his head. As he ate, I spoke to him and told him what a cute little boy he was. They brought him in to me a couple of more times, but because I was giving him up, holding him and being with him wasn't something I could really take in and feel good about. I could have the experience, but only in a limited way. I had second thoughts, but they were fleeting. It had already been decided and I was too naïve to realize that I was the one who could undecide it.

Then he was not brought in when all the other babies were, and I panicked. I started ringing for the nurse and asking where my child was, but no one answered the call. They just left me alone. I didn't want to raise a ruckus. I was embarrassed about putting him up for adoption. All the other women had their children. They were normal. I was going against what was accepted as being a good mother, and I didn't want to call attention to myself. I also believed that once something was set in motion, it was important not to rock the boat, so I shut myself down.

I didn't see him again.

I don't know if Michael went to the nursery to see him. I think he was afraid to. We again intellectualized it, kept what was happening in our heads. If we had acknowledged our feelings, we wouldn't have been able to do it.

"The next child we'll keep," he said. That sounded ludicrous to me. What did he mean we'll keep the next child? I thought, *If you can't keep this child, then screw it. I don't want anything to do with you.* I confused the two births, only eleven months apart, and didn't see that I was the one who had made the decision this time. It was clear to me there was no way I would be able to have a child with this man and keep it.

I got rid of the clothes from both pregnancies. It was like a final act, a resolution that I was not going to deal with this anymore. The only thing I kept was the blanket Mom had sent to me for the first baby. It had been mine when I was a baby, made for me by my grandma.

I went back to work six weeks after the baby was born. People were polite to me. I was trying to get my weight back down, get in shape again. "You know, Evelyn," my boss told me, "I would never guess you had a pregnancy recently. You look so good." She was being positive, and I took it as a compliment.

There was another married woman at work who didn't have children. She and her husband and Michael and I went out together a few times, but no one brought up the subject of our baby. Michael had said to me, "It's nobody's business. We don't need to talk about it to anybody." I took that stance too, closed the door of the closet and kept it there. I was already in denial, so it was pretty easy to keep it up. The only time the door cracked open was when someone asked if I had kids, or when I was with women who were discussing their pregnancies or growing children. Then I got a little queasy waiting for the subject to change. When they asked me if I had kids, I always said no.

It seemed like Michael and I had spent a lot of time waiting for the babies to be born, thinking everything would be okay after-

149

ward. That was a process we went through frequently — if such-and-such a thing would happen, then everything would be okay — and we never really talked things out. Relinquishing our second child became another barrier, a big wall. There wasn't a lot of texture to life, just survival-mode gray.

I worked during the day and Michael worked in the evenings, so we didn't see much of each other. When we did, we didn't talk, just existed together. I was still in love with him and kept hoping we'd have a breakthrough and things would change. Thinking it would hit him between the eyes with the fact that our relationship needed help, I moved out again. As it turned out, I found it was easier for me to handle our relationship when we each had our own place and met on weekends. By this time our life together in no way resembled my magical fantasy of marriage being two people who are close, together forever, and always worked things out.

Against Michael's wishes, I took birth control pills. He still didn't like the idea of chemicals in my body, but I was terribly fearful of becoming pregnant again. I tried almost every kind of birth control pill available, and with every one I had side effects. What I really wanted was a hysterectomy, to put an end to my struggle with the issue of having children. The way I saw it, I didn't deserve a family. I'd already screwed up two times, so I didn't have the right to have more children. And if I wasn't going to have any more children, why should I go through all the trouble of dealing with birth control pills? I considered having a tubal ligation, but that would mean I'd still have periods, like a normal woman, which was not how I saw myself anymore. Not having periods sounded great, and with a hysterectomy, I would never have to worry about getting pregnant again, which was at the top of my list of possible disasters. Michael didn't want me to have a hysterectomy and didn't understand why I wanted it. We did not talk about having more kids, and even if he had brought it up, I don't think I would have considered it. My doctor and I frequently talked about my having a hysterectomy, and after three or four years of discussions, he finally acquiesced. When I was twenty-seven years old, I had a hysterectomy.

One night I called Michael to say that I'd be over that week-end. "Don't come," he said. "I need to think and I don't want to be with you this weekend." That was the first time he'd ever said anything like that. Something was up. When he was finally ready to talk, we drove up to the mountains together. We sat down on a bluff overlooking the valley. "I've met someone else," he told me, "and I want to get married."

I couldn't believe it. This was the worst of the worst. He didn't say he was sexually involved with her, but I figured he was. He did tell me she had five kids. This was the man who hadn't been ready to be a father. In my mind he had chosen this other woman over me. I felt so ashamed and shitty about myself that I didn't even get angry.

People could file their own dissolution of marriage papers, so just to get it over with I volunteered to file the papers. At the courthouse, I started crying, and realized I couldn't do it. I told Michael he'd have to, and I would sign whatever he needed. He went and got the papers, filled them out, and we got a divorce. We had been married seven years.

I cried a lot, stumbled around. I went to school and in 1975 got a bachelor's degree in business administration. I had started dating again. When I was working on my bachelor's I started living with Jim. By then I had come to feel that it was okay to live with someone and not marry him. I think Jim was enthralled with the fact that I was older than he was, by six years. Also, he didn't want children and knew that I didn't either. When I told him I had relinquished two children for adoption, he said he didn't want to know anything about it. That was fine with me. He was an alcoholic and in denial about who he was and his past. Who better for me to be with than someone who was guarding his feelings with alcohol? In that sense, we made good partners. Jim and I lived together for eight years, until I broke off the relationship.

After I split up with Jim, I went to school again to get my AA degree in data processing. I got a job in the computer field. Most of the people in computers at the time were young and into partying. I skied, traveled, played tennis. I joined a group that rented a house in Tahoe for the winter. I made good money and lost myself in material things. I also started running and ran five marathons. Getting physically tired helped keep down my emotions.

Everything was focused on the outer world, not the inner one. I became better off financially and physically, but emotionally I was more superficial. Even the kinds of people I associated with, most of them in the computer field, didn't want to develop a relationship or go into any kind of deep feelings. They were the perfect people for me to be with at that time. Whenever anyone asked if I had children, I would tell them no. I was just a divorcée, free and clear, raking in money, running marathons, traveling. I thought I had it made, and in the yuppie world of Silicon Valley in the early '80s, I fit right in.

When we changed computer systems at work, I had to learn a lot of new things that I didn't take to, and I didn't see how I could enjoy the job anymore. I felt grumblings of something not being right. Slowly I started to realize I was becoming a person I didn't want to be. I was turning into an automaton.

Then I broke up with the man I'd been seeing. I was discouraged and unsure about what to do with my life.

A friend and I went to San Francisco with a couple of other people from work for dinner and to hit some night spots. At one place there was a gypsy fortune-teller, a palm reader. I was talking with my friends, using my hands like always, and the fortune-teller came over and took them in hers. "You talk with your hands so gracefully. Let me look at your palms." Studying them, she said, "You have two children." She could *see* that? I froze. She looked up at me and said, "Okay, we won't talk about that," and went on to report other things she saw there, none of which I remember.

Later that evening a friend came up to me and brought up the gypsy's reading. "You really kept mum when the palm reader talked. What's going on? Is it true?" That's when I told her. Then she told me about her own situation, that she wanted children but her husband did not. We talked for quite a while.

She suggested I check out the travel-study program at UC Berkeley. When I looked into it, I learned about the summer trip to Italy. That sounded fantastic. I imagined Italy as an open place, where people enjoyed themselves, a place that had good food and wonderful music. This would be a whole new experience. I signed up.

It turned out to be a major breakthrough. Twenty people went on the three-week tour of Renaissance art and architecture. They were art majors, English majors, or interested in architecture and Renaissance life, and could care less about computers. I was meeting people I usually would not run into.

The tour started in Rome. We took a bus through a countryside of vineyards and tall cypress trees, and through little hill towns. We arrived in Orvieto, where transportation was mostly on foot or by bicycle. The cobblestone streets were narrow and the cars were small. The buildings, most made of stone, had been built to last. It was so different from California, where things become obsolete so quickly. This was a place where people were open, where the language and the food were new to me, and the stories ancient and mostly having to do with religion.

We toured a large, old church that had been only partially completed, and had a huge well with a long stairway leading down. We heard the story about the siege that had taken place there and how the people survived in the church next to the well. The church had been critical to their survival. The discovery that religion could provide a safe haven for people and support them in their art and work hit me at a deep level. My father was an atheist and I had not been raised in the church. Childhood beliefs that I'd never questioned were being shaken. I felt another side of me opening, and I was in awe. This was the gateway to my spiritual and emotional journey, my awakening.

After the tour, I spent a fourth week alone just to see if I could get along by myself in a foreign country. I took the train to the northern Italian cities, then into Switzerland, and ended up in Geneva. I flew home from there.

When I got back, I saw with new eyes. Before, I had looked at life superficially, with an intellectual approach. I didn't delve into deeper feelings and spirituality. I had grown up valuing intellect and believing spirituality and emotionality were one and the same. Now I knew there was more to it than that. I wanted to explore, to understand the real nature of who I was as a human being, and how my spiritual, emotional, mental, and physical body were connected. In 1986, at the age of forty-four and after seven years of working for the same company, I took out the retirement money I had built up, and I quit.

I took some workshops and floundered a bit before I decided to go to graduate school. I didn't just want a degree; I wanted to learn whatever was necessary for me to open myself up. I needed self-growth and understanding of my feelings because, while I looked great on paper financially and career-wise, emotionally I was in chaos. My intuition was showing me the way. Fortunately I followed it and decided to study counseling psychology.

Graduate school was a time of tremendous learning and change. I attended classes and workshops, read a lot both in and out of class, and spent a lot of time alone writing in my journal about my feelings and relationships. Everything I did revolved around psychology and self-examination, because if I was ever going to be a therapist, I would have to take care of my own stuff first. I had a good framework to operate within. Living on student loans meant my energy could be put into psychological search, thinking, and feeling. I didn't have to worry about crying or feeling out of it while on the job.

I started psychotherapy. I liked my therapist and felt comfortable with her. She suggested I join her therapy group. The group met in the large study/meeting room in her renovated home. French doors led out onto a beautiful terrace. The place was homey, with couches, chairs, pictures, bookcases full of books, and a desk in the corner. There were already nine people in the group, which met for an hour and a half each week. At my first session, everyone introduced themselves to me. Then it was my turn to introduce myself.

Everyone was looking at me. My face felt hot and my hands were sweaty. This was my time of reckoning. My heart raced. Do I cop out or do I go ahead and really do some work here? Could I tell the truth? Should I tell them about my marriage, and about my struggle with self-esteem? About relinquishing two children for adoption … and the shame? I decided it was time to start being real and that this was the appropriate time and place. But I couldn't think straight. I was trying to say the words, but when

155

they came out, it was as if I was hearing myself talking. I was dissociating. "I'm Evelyn. I'm working on self-esteem issues, and shame issues. I gave up two children for adoption."

"Oh boy!" said one woman, who then slid down in her seat. "We're really going to get into it now."

Another woman who looked about my age and seemed very proper wanted to know more about what happened.

"I had a daughter and a son. They're only eleven months apart."

"Let's start slowly," said the therapist. "We'll discuss more later. For now, that's a good introduction." That was a wise thing for her to do. Groups work better if someone says things incrementally rather than dumping everything at once.

I had taken the plunge and I was glad, but I didn't feel relief. I knew this was just the beginning, and that I had taken too many steps down the path to go back to the old comfort zone. I was changing, and while I was uncomfortable and anxious, it was better than the old denial. A quote by Anais Nin comes to mind: "And the day came when the risk to remain tight in a bud was more painful than the risk it took to bloom."*

When I opened the deep freeze, I saw the fire that lay beyond it, and I knew that the only way past was to go through. These flames were made of confusion, loss, shame, and grief. As I confronted the grief, I saw it as a spiral that I came back to each time at a different level. I saw the red flames of shame that interfered with my life in every way. It felt like walking across hot coals. The shame was old, from the past, and if I spoke up and pushed through its barrier, I was able to get past it. For a while things would get less hot, less uncomfortable. Then more grief would

---

*From *The Journey to Wholeness* by Barbara Marie Brewster (Portland, OR: Four Winds Publishing, 1992).

spew up. Loss. I couldn't even remember my daughter's birth-day. I knew what month, but I didn't know the date. More con-fusion.

Confronting my shame and grief led me to bodywork. My back and neck had started to hurt a lot. I went to a body worker who did massage and deep muscle work. Massaging and hold-ing the muscles, then letting them go, helped release a lot of pain in my body. While she worked on me, feelings and images rose, as if I were in a dream state. One image was that of a hole in a dike and me putting my finger in it to hold back the water. After that session I took a long walk and cried, feeling the release of whatever it was that was being held in my muscles. It was like I had taken my finger out of the hole to free the waters behind the dike.

I started doing art and clay work as therapy. They were a way I could express and release what was happening. My art instructor had a degree in psychology and was interested in how people can release feelings through the creative process. She wanted us to express emotion in our work. One of my clay pieces was of a woman's torso. At first I gave her a head and tried to give her arms, but as I formed and worked with the clay, I cut off her head and arms. I gouged out one breast and made a slit down her side. When I put the piece in the kiln, it came out broken. The instructor helped me gather the parts and glue them back together. We put a good patina on it, gold, copper, and tur-quoise. We could still see where it had been glued. Scars. It was a powerful piece, and I named her Anima, after the Jungian in-ner female in psychology. I was finally getting in touch with my female side, acknowledging that I was a woman, that I had given birth. I acknowledged the attachment I had to my two children. "You can see that this woman has gone through trauma," my instructor said.

As I worked in therapy, I realized that one of my biggest fears was that my children had gotten stuck in the foster care system instead of being adopted. I called the adoption agency, the same agency for both. For seventy-five dollars, they said they would send me non-identifying information. I thought it was outrageous that I had to pay to find out, but I sent the money. I also asked if they would put my name, address, and permission to contact me in each of the kids' files. The social worker said she would and if the agency was contacted by the adoptive families, they would give them my information. But the agency would not initiate contact or do searches.

While I waited for the non-identifying information, I attended my first birth mother support group meeting.* Several months earlier, I had cut out an ad in the newspaper about a group forming, but I hadn't gotten up the nerve to go. I wasn't ready to acknowledge to anyone outside the therapy group that I was a birth mother. The therapy group was a safe environment. They didn't push hard and backed off when they saw me back off. But it was time to move out of the cocoon and into the world.

Two women, birth mothers who had been dealing with this issue for a long time, co-facilitated. One was also a search consultant. Her son was part of her life again, and she helped others who wanted to search. I didn't realize it at the time, but the first meeting I attended was on my daughter's birthday.

After that first session, I was compelled to go and talk with these women who had had an experience similar to mine. We met for two to three hours every week for over a year. Each week the facilitators gave us a subject to write about and discuss. We covered how we got pregnant, the situation before the pregnancy, the pregnancy itself, going through the birth, the birth

---

*Evelyn is referring to a different group, one she joined in California.

158

fathers, our families and whether they had anything to do with what happened to us, what happened to us afterward, how our lives progressed or not, whether we had told anyone, and searching. A number of women had been in a home for unwed mothers, and we talked a lot about how they had ended up there and what had gone on in the homes. I was the odd duck in that I had been married and relinquished not one but two children.

Still, these women had done a similar thing and experienced the same feelings I had. In the therapy group I had to explain what I felt. Here they knew what I was talking about. We explored different aspects of what had happened. We talked about shame. Every time I looked at it, I saw something different. I was getting a clearer picture of what had been going on in my life and my relationships at the time I relinquished my children.

We talked about searching. Did giving up my children mean I did not have the right to know they were alive and well? We discussed adoption laws, which to us seemed to primarily protect the adoptive parents and their family unit, and how adopted children seemed to be treated like property.

We talked about open adoption, which was becoming more common then, in the latter part of the 1980s. In open adoption not only could the child have a good family to grow up in, but the child and birth family did not have to give away a future with each other.

I realized no one could take away the reality that I had birthed these children, and if I was going to deal with this in its entirety, I would have to know what happened to them. They would now be in their early twenties. Were they still alive?

I didn't know what the searches would entail, or where they would lead. Searching for them meant not only leaving the horror of not knowing, but also leaving the safety of not knowing. Naturally I thought of worst-case scenarios—that they were dead or hadn't been adopted. Maybe I would find out something that would cause an emotional shock, or maybe it would be wonderful. Whatever happened, I knew I would never be the same.

I decided to look for my son first. I still lived near where he was born, so it would be easier to get to the records. The support group's search consultant showed me how to search public records. First I would have to find out his name. I looked at birth announcements in old newspapers dated just before, on, and after his date of birth and noted the births listed. Because he was adopted, his name would probably not be listed. I then went to the local courthouse and searched the microfiche files for that year's birth records in the county and city in which he had been born.

As I worked, I was scared, self-conscious, thinking that of course everyone could read my mind and know I was looking for an adoptee's birth records.* What I was doing wasn't ap-

---

*See Preface re: sealed records. Only Alaska and Kansas kept the original birth certificate open. Records were closed in other states, the first being Minnesota in 1917 and the last being Alabama in 1991. Reasons given include: to protect the adoptee's privacy and spare him or her the public stain of being either illegitimate or from poverty; to offer the birth mother privacy so that she could return to her life as if she had not given birth to this child and to spare her the public humiliation of a pregnancy out of wedlock; and to protect the privacy and ensure the integrity of the adoptive family.

Searching for birth family is seen as "breaking confidentiality" between birth and adoptive families. This understanding of closed adoption is being brought into question. Many adoptees are asserting their right to know their genetic roots, especially since these contracts were entered into without building in a way for them to address the issue when they come of age. Many birth families are asserting their right to know how their sons and daughters have fared. As the number of birth families searching increased, and as many adoptees exerted

proved of by the general public. Birth mothers weren't necessarily approved of either. So if someone asked, I was prepared to
tell them I was doing family genealogy work.

I was able to cross off names that had also been listed in the
newspaper birth announcements, and by this process of elimi-
nation, I came down to one name in the microfiche records not
listed in the newspaper. I sent away for that birth record and received the amended birth certificate, the one that listed the
adoptive parents and the child's name. My doctor's name was
listed. This was it! It had to be my son. His name was Phillip.

A sharp feeling went up my spine. It had seemed like a
dream before, like it hadn't really happened, but names on a
birth certificate were proof it had, it was real. The certificate also
listed an address and his adoptive parents' occupations.

Shortly after that I received a letter from the adoption agency
with the non-identifying information I had requested. I had
heard of many cases where the non-identifying information provided was incorrect. Even birth dates were changed. Although
California wasn't known for this practice, in certain states it was
common that the records were intentionally falsified. I checked
to see if the information the agency sent me matched the information I had on the birth certificate. It did.

The letter was like one of those glowing Christmas form letters people send telling how wonderful everything is. His adoptive father was a military officer and his adoptive mother was a
teacher. The last contact the agency had had with the family was
six months after the adoption, and at that time the baby had
been gaining weight and in good health.

---

pressure to have access to their own birth records, some states have
changed their laws to make the original birth certificate, an invaluable
search instrument, available to adoptees.

Then I received the non-identifying information for my daughter, which came from a different office. It was one page long, with passages crossed out. It looked like a copy of a social worker's report. It stated that my daughter was a cute little girl who had been in a foster home for six weeks before she was adopted, and her foster mother adored her. It said she had been adopted, but there was nothing there about the adoptive parents.

At least I now knew they *had* been adopted. But I was disappointed. The only information in the reports was about when they were babies. I wanted to know more. Now that I had my son's name from the amended birth certificate, I had to decide what to do next. I talked with my therapy group and with the women in the birth mother group, and I meditated about it.

I decided to take the next step and try to find out where he lived. I had the adoptive parents' address at the time of the adoption, so I started looking through local phone books. There was no listing for them now. Then I looked in phone books of major cities on the West Coast. The fact that Phillip had an unusual last name made it easier. It wasn't until I tried New York that I found the same last name, but a different first name. I continued with the East Coast and finally tried Boston. There it was, same first name and last name. The address was in Cambridge.

The only thing I knew of in Cambridge was Harvard, and he was the right age to be in college. I got up the nerve to call Harvard. I pretended I wanted to employ Phillip and was checking to see if he was really going to school there. Harvard couldn't find the name. One of the women in my birth mother group reminded me that MIT was also in Cambridge, so I called MIT student services and asked if Phillip was enrolled. I gave them the name and birth date, and sure enough, he was enrolled as a nuclear engineering major. My son a nuclear engineer? I called MIT again and asked when spring break was. It was the same week as my school's. I also asked to check on the address of a student because I wanted to come and visit. I gave them the address I had, and they verified it.

I had been reporting to my therapist and my groups about the quick progress I was making in the search for Phillip. I also talked about what I should do when I found him. I didn't want to write or talk on the phone. If he did want to meet me, I wanted to be there in person, to see who he had become and to let him see me. If he did not know he was adopted, it would be traumatic for him, but he was an adult now and I thought he should know the truth. And I was prepared to do whatever it took to help him. There was also a chance he knew he was adopted and wouldn't want to see me. I would let the choice be his. At least it wouldn't be just a letter or a phone call.

I flew to Boston and got a hotel in Cambridge. I planned to call him from there. Thinking back on it, I see that it was gutsy, and scary. Fools rush in where angels fear to tread. But I was compelled.

I arrived late in the day in the middle of the week and decided to wait until the next afternoon before calling. I went over to MIT and looked up his picture in the school annual. He didn't look as I had imagined. He was too clean-cut to be my son. I saw a lot of Michael in him, but he resembled me a little too, which surprised me.

When I called the next afternoon, a woman answered the phone.

"I'm calling to speak with Phillip. Is he there?"

"He's at school right now," she said. "I'm Jacqueline, his girlfriend. Do you want to leave a message?"

"I'm a relative of his and I'm in town visiting. I'm staying at the Quality Inn. Can you ask him to call me when he gets home?"

"Sure."

I left my name and number.

He called a couple of hours later. I had a speech prepared.

"My name is Evelyn Bach. I relinquished a child for adoption on February 5, 1966. I believe you may be my son. I'm here in town if you'd like to meet me."

Sounding uncertain, he said, "I've got some papers to write for school, and I'm not sure when I'm going to be free."

I had practiced with the birth mother group how to handle different scenarios. I knew he might hesitate, and I was ready. I didn't want to come in and insist that he know me. I wanted it to be his choice.

"I'm going to be here for a week," I told him. "Why don't you think it over, and if you decide you want to meet me, give me a call?"

There seemed to be a sigh of relief from him. "Well, how about dinner tonight?"

We made the plans and he said he would come pick me up. Of course I couldn't decide what to wear. I had brought a dress and jeans. I changed a couple of times before I decided I wanted him to know me for who I was, so I put my jeans back on, along with a nice sweater. I tried to read. I combed my hair. I tidied up the room. I got out my camera, the family pictures I was going to show him, and the family chart I'd made for him, and set them on the table.

He was right on time. I opened the door to a tall, dark-haired young man dressed in a nice wool coat and pants, and cardigan sweater.

"Hi," he said, smiling. "I'm, Phillip." He looked me in the eye. He looked so self-assured and preppy. He was tall like his birth father and had his coloring and hair.

"Hi, I'm Evelyn. Come in." Trembling, I resisted the urge to hug him. I didn't want to push him or do anything to offend him. In the birth mother group we had talked about how I needed to be cautious about what I said and did when we first met because that first meeting would color what happened later. I was acutely aware that I could blow it here.

He sat on one of the chairs and noticed the pictures I had left out on the table. He grasped the picture of Michael and stared at it. I explained that that was his birth father. He seemed excited — here was someone who looked like him.

"He's got a good head of hair in this picture," said Phillip. "Does he still have his hair?"

"As far as I know. I haven't seen him in a long time."

"Just want to know if I'm going to be bald or not."

We laughed. He had big hands like my father and brothers, and I could see some of myself in him. For some reason I had the idea that he would look like Michael and not at all like me. It was extraordinary to see our resemblances. I felt an immediate knowing of him, and that surprised me.

We went out to dinner, and talked and talked and talked. Even though he hadn't thought of searching for us, he was interested in knowing about us. I told him about his birth and what had happened. I told him that he had an older sister, and about his birth father and that we were divorced. It was so hard to admit how screwed-up I had made things. I couldn't control my tears, and I worried that he would think me an hysterical, emotional wreck.

His reaction wasn't like that though. He listened quietly. He seemed okay with what he was hearing, and wanted to know more. After dinner he walked me back to the motel and I showed him the chart of the family and talked about where I grew up. We talked until one or two in the morning. At one point in the evening Phillip said, "I know we're related, because you think like I do." That hit me in the heart. It was validation.

We didn't make arrangements to meet again. I left it up to him, telling him that I was going to be there for a while.

"I'd like to give you a hug good-bye," I said.

"Sure."

The last time I had hugged him was just after he was born. How strange to hug this great big guy.

The next day I didn't want to sit around hoping he would call, so I went out and toured the town. When I got back to my motel room mid-afternoon, I had several messages from Phillip and Jacqueline inviting me for dinner that night.

We had a wonderful spaghetti dinner in their little studio apartment. Again, it was like Phillip and I already had a sense of each other, a built-in familiarity.

A couple of days after I got home, I checked my answering machine for messages. "Hi, Evelyn, it's Phillip. My parents want to talk to you," and then he'd hung up. My first reaction was, Whoa, they may be pissed. Shortly afterward, the phone rang, and I picked it up. It was Tom and Laura, Phillip's parents.

"We thought we'd better try to get back to you soon. We overheard Phillip leaving the message. It probably came across as abrupt, and we thought you might be feeling worried about us and unsure what was going on."

"Well, it did sound a little ominous."

They were cordial, told me that they were happy I had found Phillip, glad he had someone else in his life. Phillip got on the phone too, and we all talked for quite a while. I learned that after Jacqueline gave Phillip my first message about being a relative, he had called them and asked if they knew anyone by the name of Evelyn Bach. No, they didn't. When he and Jacqueline went home for spring break, Phillip had planned to tell them about meeting me. When Tom and Laura picked him up from the airport, he was still figuring out when and how to tell them. But right off they asked, "Hey, Phillip, what about the Evelyn Bach relative? What happened?" They hadn't recognized my name because the adoption papers listed my married name and I was now using my maiden name. It had never crossed their minds that it was me. Once they got it all straightened out, they said, "Well, we should call her and say hello!"

A few days later I received from them some pictures of different phases of Phillip's life, and Phillip sent me his adoptive family tree. That was tough to look at. For me it drew attention to his separation from our own family. I had not put his name on the family tree I had given him. I wasn't sure how he'd feel about it.

I was ready to get the rest of the skeletons out of my closet and make some changes. I hadn't talked with Michael since we'd divorced eighteen years before, but on the chance he still worked at the same place, I called. He was there. I said I needed to tell him something that affected us both. He agreed to come.

When we met, I told him that I had found Phillip and was going to search for our daughter as well. He didn't like the idea. As we talked, he seemed reluctant to talk about his own life. Eventually he did tell me that he had remarried again, and that he and his third wife had two children together, an older daughter and a younger son. It was almost like he had recreated the same family he and I might have had. I could see why he was reluctant to mention it. And here I was struggling to find the two children he and I had relinquished for adoption, and he didn't approve. He believed that the adoptions had been confidential and that we shouldn't look back.

I needed to release the anger I had about our relationship, and over several calls and in-person meetings, we argued. I have to give him credit—he didn't run away or try to avoid it, but he listened. He stood and took it. He did tell me that during the first pregnancy he had been waiting for me to change my mind, to say, "No, I don't want to do this." That blew me away. I had no idea he felt that way. I had believed I was supposed to do what my husband wanted, and I knew he was upset and said he didn't want to raise our child. If we had been able to talk as it got closer to the birth, we might have made a different decision. But once we had made our decision, neither of us talked about it. It was like we had been stuck in the ocean without wind for the sails.

I went on to search for our daughter, who was then twenty-three. I started to search for her the same way I had for Phillip, three months before, by using the microfiche files in the local courthouse. Because she had been born in a small town outside LA, I didn't know what local paper to look through, so I decided to use the microfiche to find all the names for her birth date for that city and county and see what happened. At the courthouse I asked for the microfiche, thinking it didn't necessarily matter where in the alphabet I started. First I would look to see if she was listed under her birth name. Since we hadn't named her, she would only have had our last name, "Baby Girl Ortega." I asked the clerk to give me the records for *O* and *P*, but she mistakenly gave me the "N's" and "O's." I found her original birth certificate under "Ortega," the one that listed Michael and me as parents, and looked at the way the record was coded. I would try to find her amended birth certificate, which would list her new name, by looking for the corresponding code on the amended birth certificate that matched the date and city. I thought I'd start with the *A's*, but the clerk wasn't around to get the records for me. So I looked through the microfiche she had already given me, the *N's*. There was only one listing there for 1965—Julia Nichol. When I finally got the other microfiche cards and started looking further into the alphabet, I couldn't find any other names, only Julia Nichol. I thought, *Gee, maybe this is it.*

When I got home I called a friend who did searches and told her I'd found only one name, but it was the right city and county. I asked her how I could find out if this was my daughter.

"Let me make a phone call," she said, "and see what I can find out. Give me the information."

She called me back that evening. "You are lucky, lucky, lucky!" she said. "Bingo! That is your daughter."

It was like the last piece falling into place. What a high! I was ready to take the next step. Then I had a moment of caution and asked her, "How do you know? How can you be sure?"

"Don't ask. I can't tell you. Just trust me, it's her."

I believed her, but I wanted to send away for her birth certificate for verification. When I got the amended certificate, I saw my doctor's name on it. It was her. Julia. The certificate also showed the names of the adoptive parents and their address at the time. When I looked in the phone book, I found a listing for them.

I didn't know what to do next. They lived in Southern California, only a few hours away by car. Again, for a couple of weeks I meditated about it and sounded out other people. In the end I decided to call the number. I expected her mother would probably answer, and if she said Julia wasn't there, I would talk with her.

"Is Julia there?"

"This is Julia."

My thoughts went out the window. I had written down what I was going to say to her mother, not to Julia. I hesitated.

Then I started telling her that I had relinquished a child for adoption who was born on March 14, 1965 and I thought that she might be my birth daughter, if that was her birth date.

"Hang on a minute. Let me go to another phone."

I waited while she switched phones.

"I knew it was you when I heard your voice," she said.

The connection was there, and just like with Phillip, I felt I knew her. We talked for a long time. I asked if it was okay to visit. She told me that she lived somewhere else and just happened to be visiting her adoptive mom that day. She gave me her own phone number, then suggested a time and place for us to meet.

A couple of days later I drove down, checked into the motel, and waited for her. At the knock, I opened the door, and there she was. Smiling. She looked just like me, only with dark hair. We were both near tears. We hugged tight. It felt so natural, and my body tingled with joy.

"I'm so glad I found you," I said.

"Yes," she agreed.

I invited her into the room, where I had the family pictures and chart laid out. Julia told me about her childhood and that when she was seventeen her adoptive father had died, which devastated her. She had brought an album of her adoptive family, her parents and two adopted brothers. She gave me a picture of herself at two years old.

We drove in her old Mercedes to Santa Monica, had dinner, and walked on the beach. It was wonderful. She pointed out some of the places that she loved, many of which had been my mother's stomping grounds when she was young. When we got back to the motel room, we realized that we had forgotten to ask someone to take a picture of us together. So, looking into the mirror, we took the picture ourselves. I didn't get another chance to see her that trip.

For some reason, I thought my son and daughter wouldn't resemble me, so seeing myself in each of them was a major revelation. And I felt something that I'd never felt for anyone before—unconditional love. I would love them no matter what. It was like being in love, and even if I never got to see them again, I would love them forever.

Only a few months later I flew to Boston to see Phillip again. Laura and Tom, his adoptive parents, drove up to meet me. At their invitation, I rode back with them to their home in Virginia and stayed a couple of days. They wanted me to see where Phillip had grown up. During the car ride I told them the story about how I came to give up my children for adoption and my path to healing and searching for them. Telling the story, especially after just finding Phillip and Julia, moved me deeply. They listened intently and seemed amazed by it all.

Phillip and I have a good relationship and talk on the phone often. One time we took a car trip together and he showed me places where he lived when he was young. We visited New York and where he used to live on Long Island. We had a good time together, talking, becoming friends. One Christmas he came out and visited me, and on another I was invited to join him and his adoptive family. I was touched to be considered part of their extended family. When Phillip and Jacqueline got married, I was included in the wedding. Laura introduced me to the guests, saying that Phillip was their adoptive son and I was his birth mother. I felt so included, and I bonded with Laura and Tom as well as with Phillip.

171

Julia's mother had a different reaction. Julia had told her mother about my finding her, and her mother was unsure about it. Having had such a good experience with Phillip's parents, I took the chance and wrote Julia's mother a letter explaining who I was and that I had met Julia. I wanted to show that I was friendly and supportive of her relationship with Julia, not a threat. Writing that letter must have been the wrong thing to do, because I got a letter back, very cold, saying that Julia was a loved and cherished child. "She is our child and you have broken confidentiality by contacting us. Please don't ever contact me again." I haven't communicated with her since.

Because her adoptive mother doesn't approve of my finding Julia, Julia feels disloyal when she contacts me. So I leave it open with her. I don't want to interfere with her and her adoptive mother, so I let Julia initiate and direct all our communication. When I do get to talk with her, it's like we were never apart.

Graduation with my master's degree was really a graduation for so many things besides school, and I planned a celebration and family reunion. This was a coming out to my family in the sense of being open and inviting them to participate in building a relationship with Julia and Phillip. No one in my family had met them yet.

Julia and a friend of hers were coming in from Southern California. Phillip and Jacqueline were coming from back east. His adoptive parents and sister, extended family to me now, would be there. I had asked my parents and siblings to come. My mother wanted to, but my dad was having trouble with his leg, and, even though he could be quite gregarious, he didn't necessarily like a lot of social activity. My brother Eric and my sister-in-law offered to drive Mom and Dad down. It was uncomfortable for Dad, but he agreed to come. It was a major show of support from them all.

Julia arrived when I was out with my dad, and I got back in time to see my two children together on the beach, riding the ocean waves. My family, together. I had walked through the fires of shame and loss, I had found my children, and I had brought them into the circle of our family. It was a completion of a cycle of the journey.

Later that evening, after dinner, Mom and Dad had gone to bed and the rest of us played charades. It was all pretty silly, with both Julia and Phillip joking and singing and talking in different accents. They were enjoying each other's company. Just to be able to watch them was wonderful. I saw similarities in their mannerisms and gestures. Phillip can dress up and look nice, but his basic demeanor is informal, like Julia's. I marveled that they shared abilities in music and language.

We all went to the aquarium together. We also drove by where Phillip's adoptive family had lived when they adopted him. Everyone was acting pretty normal, which I thought was exceptional considering the emotional impact of it all.

All of us being together was wonderful, but sometimes my feelings were intense, overwhelming, and it was hard to be in my body. I dissociated, put the feelings aside until I was ready again.

I was glad my mom and dad came down and actually experienced my family, the family I was trying to piece together after all these years. I had not told them about Phillip's birth until I started looking for him. They had acted surprised, but I suspect they knew there had been a second pregnancy and hadn't said anything.

My father dove right in and started talking philosophy with Phillip. Fortunately, Phillip was well educated and had a strong sense of himself, so he was a definite match for Dad. In fact, he was more than Dad had bargained for. It was fun to watch. Phillip identified with my dad and got a good flash of his genetics. Meeting my family affirmed for him that there are other people in the world like him.

I have a picture of Dad talking with Julia, and she's looking at him with amazement. This was her grandfather. I had not heard her talk about a grandfather and I didn't know if she'd had one who played a part in her life. Dad was not one to put on airs or engage in social chitchat. He liked to talk about important things. Julia was just like him in that way.

While all this was going on, my mother was a little standoffish. Having trouble fitting this into her world, she reverted to being proper. She was dealing with the old "What do we tell the neighbors?" issue. In the end, she put their pictures up with the pictures of her other grandchildren.

Julia told me later that after the reunion, Dad and Mom sent a letter to both Phillip and her telling them about themselves, what their philosophy was, and about settling in Montana. They wanted to make sure both she and Phillip knew about the family. She appreciated that letter.

After graduation I mailed pictures of Julia and Phillip to the rest of my relatives. I wanted them to know that I had two kids to be welcomed to the family. Out of fifteen or twenty letters, I received only a few responses. A cousin sent me a note saying that I had two beautiful children and my aunt wrote that she was happy I had found them. My older brother Larry thanked me for sending the pictures. "My children mean so much to me that I have a very hard time understanding how you did it."

Both kids have met Michael. Julia came to live with me for a time, and that's when she called him and went over there. She didn't talk to me about their meeting except to say that she would like to get to know him better. He had given her a picture of his other two children, her half-siblings. Phillip went to meet him when he was out for my graduation. Michael gave him a copy of the same picture. The first thing Phillip said when he came back from meeting Michael was, "Well, he was taller than I thought he'd be." Phillip didn't talk about it after that, just said it was okay.

Michael hadn't told his family about Phillip until after I had found him. Michael's mom asked to see me. We had lunch together and I brought pictures of Julia and Phillip for her. Now that things were out in the open, I felt I could really communicate with her. She had never heard my side of the story of why we had relinquished the children and why we had divorced. She was so happy that I had found Julia and Phillip. She wanted contact with them, but apparently Michael discouraged it. She has since met Phillip, but not Julia. Julia asked me for her address, which I gave to her, and Michael's mother has written to her. I think Julia is conflicted about meeting her. She knows this was the one person who tried to fight for her, and maybe meeting her would be too emotional just now.

Julia had strong feelings about being relinquished. When she visited me for a week, she told me she felt I had betrayed her when I relinquished her. She said she had always felt the heavy weight of my own grief and felt that somehow it was her fault, which of course it wasn't. I was distressed that she carried this burden. Had she felt in her own body the emotions and turmoil I was going through during the pregnancy? I told her the decisions were Michael's and mine, that none of it was her fault or her responsibility. I gave her the blanket that my grandma had made for me when I was a baby and that my mother had given me when I was expecting Julia. She treasures it.

175

In March 1996 Julia and her partner had a baby girl, my first grandchild. Julia wrote to me when she was pregnant and told me how she understood why I might have been afraid to be a parent, that she had had those feelings herself. She wanted to have a natural birth and liked the idea that she had Native American blood in her from Michael's side of the family. She lived in Arizona at the time and decided to give birth in a teepee with a midwife present. I wanted to be there at least in spirit. I had some cow skins, which I sent to her for the floor of the tent. I also made a quilt for the baby. I imagined the cow skins on the floor of the teepee, symbolic support, and the quilt giving her cover. Julia told me later, "Evelyn, you were there through the skins and the quilt." She also told me that she had come full circle. Giving birth to a little girl closed the wrenching gap she used to feel. I'm happy about that. In a way I guess that's true. She is now the mother.

When her daughter, Meagan, was two and a half, they were going to Montana for a friend's wedding. Julia asked if I could meet them there. This would be the first time I would meet my granddaughter.

She was gorgeous! I had a delightful time playing with her. When they were leaving, Meagan asked if I would be going with them. Julia told her, "We'll see Nana Evelyn again. She'll go with us on camping trips sometimes." I was touched that she wanted me to be part of Meagan's life.

During that visit we all had dinner at my mom's. Julia pointed out that four generations sat at that table. In a way, I felt part of it, and at the same time I felt disconnected. Because I hadn't raised her, it felt as if an important part of our heritage was truncated.

Relinquishing Phillip and Julia for adoption were the toughest things I have ever done, much tougher than running marathons or giving birth, and if I had had counseling, if anyone had talked to me about the reality of the pain and the grief, I would not have done it. Even though I found my children and have done a lot of healing, my relationship with them will always be different in that I will never be their parent. As I struggle to make peace with my choices, I wonder what Julia and Phillip would have been like had I raised them. I can't envision how I would have gotten through raising two children so close in age, and probably on my own. What I could have provided was more limited. Julia would not have had a home with music and without financial worries. Phillip would not have had the wonderful educational opportunities. My love for them would have been different, too. As a struggling mother trying to provide for two children, experiences attached to the struggle would have colored our relationship. The love I have for them now is without expectations. Julia likes to call me her godmother, and in a sense I guess I am, in that her God-given gifts came from me and from her birth father.

The searches and reunions were life-opening experiences, births. Now Julia, Phillip, and I have the long haul of building a foundation for our relationships. Maintaining contact, learning who they are, and letting them get to know who I am is hard work, especially when we're so far apart geographically.

My opportunity to be a parent is gone. When people talk about their children, I now say I have two children and they're grown. But when the conversation moves to when they were growing up, I'm at a loss. Because I haven't raised and nurtured another human being, haven't had to put another's needs before my own, a part of me is not developed, and I still feel insecure about that.

I'm still not "over" having given up my children. For me, getting past it has to do with realizing I'm not a bad person. I go out and accomplish things that give me a sense of pride, a sense of self. Getting my master's and finding my kids have helped. When shame rears its ugly head, I push through it by doing something that brings me back to the here and now until I get to a comfortable place where it doesn't interfere with my life. Then I note the situation that brought it up, so next time I can be more aware and ready to return the shame to where it belongs—in the past.

Forgiving myself is an ongoing process.

I went through the fire, looked at fear, and said: I want to know the truth. I wanted to know about my children and thought they deserved to know what happened to them. They should not have to search for the truth. We should give it to them.

Telling the truth has freed me. Before, when I lied and told people I didn't have kids, it got me off the hook of explaining, but every time a heart-pounding panic threatened to overtake me. As long as it remained hidden, part of me could pretend it hadn't happened and I wouldn't have to *feel* anything about it. Oh, but what an amazing amount of energy was tied up by staying hidden and in denial.

I feel fortunate to have been put to the test. Not only am I confident in my ability to weather a storm, but it's made me a deeper and more courageous person. I realize that we change by doing what we know is right even when we are afraid. In the process of surviving it and learning, it becomes easier to do the next time.

I have learned the value of relationships and family, feelings, and the emotional side of life. The intellectual stuff is fun, but emotional connection, talking, understanding, and feeling empathy for another person give life joy and meaning.

5

In 1991 my neighbor, Rabbi David, called and asked if I would talk to a friend of his. "I think the two of you have something in common. She's just been found by the daughter she gave up for adoption more than thirty years ago."

It was only a year and a half since Andrea had found me and I had just met Nancy. We were looking for other birth mothers to join our group. I told him yes.

"You know," said David, "I think there's a lot of shame in this whole experience."

My stomach sank. He was being terribly presumptuous. "What do you mean 'shame'?" I felt relief that she was back in my life, and sometimes still grief-stricken, angry, manipulated, embarrassed. But ashamed?

"The hiding," he said, "the secrets. You know what I mean. I think there's shame there. And I think it would help if the two of you talked."

I realized then that although I had felt it, pushed it away, walked past it, and even right through it, hearing the word "shame" spoken aloud felt like being tossed into the street naked. He was not being presumptuous; he was right.

"She's here now," he said. "Her name's Marti Daniels. Do you have time to talk with her?"

I told him to send her over.

In her late fifties, Marti was a woman of style. Her business was selling jewelry, a late-in-life career she enjoyed. Her clothes and jewelry were contemporary and tasteful. While she told her story, I couldn't help but admire her unadorned honesty. She admitted to being uncer-

179

tain about her feelings for the daughter she'd relinquished. She admitted to being upset about being found. She was frank about her feelings, her faults, and her regrets.

In 1960, the baby boom era, when birth control was less reliable and abortion was illegal, Marti found herself trapped by both her biology and the social expectation of large families. She felt left with no choice but adoption, in secret. She agreed to tell her story so birth mothers like her would know they were not alone, and to present another side to what she calls the happy reunion stories.

EXPOSED – Marti's Story

Paul and I were married in the 1950s, when I was nineteen and he was twenty-nine. I was a recorder for the telegraph company and Paul was a disc jockey at a radio station. We usually worked until late in the evening, then met to go out to dinner and often to parties with show-biz types Paul knew. I thought life was one big party, except when a bout of depression or my migraines came back. The headaches had plagued me since I was fifteen.

When I was twenty-two, I quit my job to stay home and take care of our first child, Rachel. A year later our son, Larry, was born. Even though we used birth control, I never had a planned pregnancy. I should have been a brood mare: I conceived easily, my migraines stopped when I was pregnant, and I had easy deliveries. But the adjustment from working life to housewife was difficult. I missed the outside world, and the migraines and depression grew worse. I was sure the migraines were emotionally based and that there was a secret, magic answer someplace, so I started therapy.

Then Paul lost his job and we were having money problems. When he landed another broadcasting job in a small town in upstate New York, I didn't want to go. I didn't do well in small towns. Besides, I had lived in the New York City area through high school and all of my family was there. It was home. But women generally weren't assertive in those days, so I was uprooted from my beloved city to this little spot on the map. I went kicking and screaming. Then I was depressed.

A few months after we moved, I took the kids to New York and I called Paul and told him that I wasn't coming back. I wanted to end the marriage. He convinced me that we had a lot going for us and that I should come and work things out. I cried, went back, and got pregnant again.

So here I was in a troubled marriage and with two small kids I dearly loved but hadn't planned on, living away from my family in a town I hated, and severely depressed. How could I take on more responsibility when I was barely making it? I was terrified. I'd sit in the bathroom, and sometimes the closet, and cry. I even considered suicide.

"I can't have this baby," I told Paul, "because it will take either my life or my sanity."

"Whatever you want to do," he said, "I'll support your decision."

I thought that was pretty remarkable, especially considering we were having such a difficult time.

"I want to have an abortion," I said.

But in 1959 abortion was illegal. Someone had told Paul that in a town two hours away we might find someone who would do it. So Paul took the day off work and we went to find the place. We drove up one street and down another, and I looked, and he looked, and finally, we looked at each other. "What are we looking for," I asked, "somebody with a sign that says Abortions Done Here?" Realizing it was futile, we turned around and went home, only to find out that Paul had been fired.

Now we worried about having enough money for food, rent, and living expenses. Paul knocked on doors to try to find work, and I was still trying to think of a way out of the pregnancy.

Paul heard of a doctor who could help, so I went to see this man, thinking he would offer to do an abortion. He told me not to worry, that he'd find a suitable couple who wanted to adopt a baby. That wasn't the help I was looking for, but it was the only way out. I wanted to be sure it would be kept secret, though, because family is terribly important in our Jewish culture and giving up a child was considered unnatural.

"Don't worry," the doctor reassured me. "The baby will be placed outside the area." He explained that the family would also be a match to us in all the important ways, which I took to mean economically, educationally, and religiously.

Paul and I talked about it. "Whatever you want to do," he said again. "If you want to give this baby up, I'll stand by you."

"Fine," I said, feeling flat, detached. "That's what I'm going to do."

Within six weeks of being fired, Paul found another job as a disc jockey with a different radio station in town. The population was 24,000 and there was only one TV station, so the morning radio disc jockeys were local personalities. Paul became quite the local celebrity. Everyone knew I was pregnant, and several people—the radio station, my neighbors, and some other friends and women from my exercise class—wanted to give me a baby shower. I would put them off with comments like, "I'm in this tiny place and I don't have any room right now, so let's wait until after the baby's born and I'll see what I really need," or, "Let's wait until after the baby's born, because I know my family's sending me a lot of things."

Back then I didn't even know how to drive. A friend drove me to my exercise class. Sometimes we'd even play volleyball, and here I was with a tummy bigger than the volleyball, but I didn't feel pregnant. I had no emotional attachment to what was growing inside me. None. I felt like I was playing a part in a play. I must have been an incredible actress, except I didn't feel the emotion that a good actress can feel.

Labor and delivery were easy. I didn't even have anesthesia. Only the doctor and the nurse were in the room, and although I had decided ahead of time that I wouldn't see the baby, it took me by surprise when the doctor put a towel over my eyes before he delivered the baby. I didn't even ask if it was a boy or a girl. He showed me the placenta, though, I guess so I could see that I'd done something. The only thing I knew about the baby was that it was small but healthy. It was June 14, 1960. I didn't mark in my mind that it was a significant date for me. It was a day I was away from home, that was all. No big deal. I came home the next day, which back then was soon after childbirth. I was bleeding and a bit tired, but feeling okay.

Paul and I had agreed to tell people that the baby didn't make it. Paul told the kids the baby had died, and I made up this wild story, a combination of truth and fiction, that I told so many times I almost believed it. I told people the baby had been badly malformed, that the doctor had put a towel over my eyes so I wouldn't see it, and I didn't even know whether it was a girl or a boy. My neighbors were sympathetic, and I acted stoic. The kids asked, "How come you're not crying, Mommy?" I explained that I had never held or fed the baby, that I hadn't nurtured this baby, so I didn't have that connection. My mother, step-dad, and sister didn't discuss it with me, which was typical of them. My mother was a simple woman and didn't talk about such things. Paul's mother, widowed then, decided maybe it was for the best since the baby was deformed. No one even asked if we were having services. While I tried not to be cold about it, I did not feel the loss of the baby. I felt relief.

There were still details to handle. A lawyer and a social worker came to the house a few days later. They were really very sweet. They asked a lot of questions and I gave them detailed information about our families—where my father was born, what his occupation was, when he died, where my parents had lived, where my mother had been born. I figured the baby would want to know at some point, but mostly I gave the information because it was what I was supposed to do. The attorney then took me into another room from Paul. He wanted to know if Paul was the dad, and if he was not, was this a Caucasian baby. I didn't feel insulted or indignant about it. I just wondered why he was asking because of course Paul was the dad.

After I'd returned from the hospital, Rachel, six years old at the time, got very sick. She had had measles a week or two before the baby was born and had developed a form of meningitis. She had to be hospitalized, and my attention turned totally to her. When someone asked if I was grieving for the baby, I explained that I was grieving for Rachel, whom I'd known and taken care of. Fortunately, Rachel's hospital stay was short.

About a year later I decided that this was an okay place to live, so we bought a house on the other side of town. We were pretty active socially and went to a lot of parties. It turned out that we were moving in the same social circle as the attorney who had handled the adoption. The first time I saw him at a party, I was terrified. This man knew my secret, but he was always professional and never brought it up. I never felt that he sat in judgment of us.

There was one other person who knew besides the doctor and nurse, the attorney, and the social worker. We had a dear friend with whom we had an incredible level of trust. She was easy to talk to and I could tell her things I wouldn't even tell Paul, and in those days I told Paul almost everything. She was wonderful, supportive. I'm still not sure why I told her, but it probably helped me feel a little less burdened.

When both kids started school, I went back to work. Paul wanted me to stay home and be the full-time mom and house-wife, but I pushed back. I wanted to get out and be with other people and have money of my own, and I promised that I'd be home when the kids were home. I started working part-time for the state. Then I got a job working for a real estate company. I worked as a secretary and ran the front office. I enjoyed the work.

I hadn't yet figured out why, but I still had bouts of depres-sion and migraine headaches, so Paul arranged for me to see a psychiatrist. For three years I was in individual counseling and group counseling. Although I talked about the third pregnancy and the interesting delivery with the towel over my face, I never told the psychiatrist that I had given up the baby.

I was such a nebbish, so dependent on Paul. He tried to teach me how to drive, but that was awful. Then a woman in my ther-apy group said she'd teach me, and we got to be friends. Alt-hough I still had headaches, I was no longer stuck, dependent, and waiting for someone to take me from here to there.

Learning to drive was a transforming experience. Freeing. It changed my identity. We bought a little car, not a very reliable one, but I could drive around and do things. I used to tell the kids—they were teenagers by this time—that as soon as I got a good car, we'd take a trip. And we did when I got a '65 Oldsmo-bile convertible. Up until then, before I went anywhere, I would ask Paul if it was okay and whether he'd mind. This time I didn't ask permission. I told him I was going to drive to New York City with the kids. I had never driven that far in my life, and it was an incredible adventure, thrilling, not scary. Less than twenty miles from home, we picked up two guys, one with a guitar. It was a real '60s scene. We dropped them off and entered the city during rush hour. Driving in the city was terrifying to me, but I did it. While we were there I took our son, Larry, to see a Yankees game, and Rachel went shopping with my sister. I took them both to see *Hair*, and we went to see a comedy act in a nightclub, where the kids had hot chocolate. We had a wonderful time. I felt like a different person.

My work changed. I advanced from being a secretary to being a real estate agent. It was challenging and I did well. But by the late 1980s, after many years at it, I no longer liked the pressure of meeting sales quotas. I wanted to do something different. That's when I met with Beth, a career counselor who had a reputation for being a wise adviser, and in the course of this career counseling, I told her my secret.

"I have lived with this for so long," I confessed, "that I really don't think about it except when Paul brings it up. Now I'm worried because adoptees are beginning to have these reunions with their birth mothers. I don't want to be one of those 'reunions.' I feel awful that there's this person out there someplace and that I don't want that person in my life. And I worry that people are going to think badly of me for having given up a baby. If I'd had the choice, I'd have had an abortion."

"Remember, you gave life," Beth told me. "You didn't have an abortion, so you did give life."

It was not a soothing thought. I didn't feel responsible for a generous choice. Many times over the years when Paul would see someone about the age the baby would have been, he'd say, "I wonder where our kid is. I wonder what he's doing. I wonder what he looks like." I'd tell him, "Look, don't talk to me about it.

It never happened. Besides, I think it was a girl." I don't know why I thought it was a girl, probably because the doctor said it was a small baby. But I never looked into the faces of young girls about that age. I didn't even remember the date of her birth, although I could have figured it out by going backwards in time to how old Rachel and Larry were.

I entered a period when life was really good. I embarked on a new career selling gift items, and it was taking off. I traveled a lot, still sold real estate on the side, and was involved in many community activities, including being one of the founders of the local Jewish community. In January of 1991 at a meeting of the Religious Practices Committee, the rabbi mentioned a woman who had just learned that she was Jewish and who wanted him to teach her about Judaism.

"What do you mean she just learned she was Jewish?" I asked.

"Well," he explained, "she was adopted as an infant and just found out her biological parents were Jewish."

I panicked. Was this the child we'd put up for adoption? I kept my cool, though, and continued to play the role I'd been playing all those years. I asked him how she had found out, but he didn't know. I tried to forget it. I didn't even mention it to Paul when I got home.

I didn't forget, though. The following Friday night I forced myself to go to services. When I walked in, I felt total relief, because there stood this tall woman, who was fortyish, too old to be mine. Even though I couldn't remember exactly when the baby had been born, I knew it had to be sometime after 1959, because we moved in '59, and that's what I marked by. This was a nice woman, and I welcomed her and talked with her. I asked her how she found out that her birth parents were Jewish. She said that the records were sealed, so she did it illegally.

I felt as if my heart stopped. Somehow I smiled and asked, "Gee, how could you do that?" She explained that she worked for the police department and had access to records that other people didn't. I believed then that anyone could get the information if they really wanted to, and that terrified me.

It was Saturday, April 13, 1991. Paul and I went out and returned late that morning to a message on our answering machine from a long-time friend who was buying some property through me. I returned his call.

"Are you ready for this?" Tim asked.

"Yeah. What?" I said, wondering if he was going to tell me that he'd changed his mind and feeling irritated about losing the commission.

"We ran into this young woman a few nights ago at Le Bistro," he started to explain. "Her name's Christy. She's here at our house, and she has a letter—"

I thought, *So?*

"—that I'm going to read to you," he told me.

The first sentence, I knew I was busted. This was the moment I had lived in fear of. The letter was what is known as a non-identifying letter. It started with, "You were born on June 14, 1960, at Memorial Hospital."

I was sitting on the couch and Paul was standing in front of me. He mouthed the question, "What?" and I wrote, "Adopted." He asked, "How old?" I wrote, "Thirty-one. Girl."

He was getting excited and I was gesturing to him to be quiet, and the guy on the phone was reading this letter telling me that the adopted woman's birth grandfather was a cabinet-maker born in Europe and died at forty-six of a brain hemorrhage, that her birth mother's brother was an accomplished musician who had a mental illness, that her birth mother was born in New York and her birth father was born in California and that they had two children, and the reason for the adoption was the mother's emotional state at the time.

As he read, I laughed and made little comments like, "God, this is bizarre!" and "Wow!" Talk about an act—I should have gotten an Oscar. Inside, I was dying. I really wanted to die. He finished the letter.

"That is really bizarre," I said. "What a bunch of coincidences!"

"And you know what, Marti?" he said. "She even looks like Rachel."

I started laughing. "Tim, what are you trying to tell me?"

"Well," he said, "I should have known you wouldn't give away a baby." He sounded sincere.

I just kind of laughed.

"She's right here. You want to talk to her?" he asked.

"Sure, why not?" I answered. I did *not* want to talk to her. I wanted the whole situation to go away, to be what it was an hour before.

"Hi," she said in a timid voice, "I hope I'm not upsetting you."

"No! Me? Why? Nothing to be upset about," I told her.

"I'm doing this search, and it's really important for me to find out who I am," she explained.

I thought, *Give me a break! You have all that information in the letter.* But what I said was, "Well, that sounds reasonable to me. I can certainly understand that."

Then she started telling me about herself. "I'm five-foot-five—"

"You're too tall," I interrupted. Now why did I say that? If I hadn't given up a baby for adoption, why would I say that? She

189

picked up on it. I was busy laughing and making jokes, thinking I was being funny, but what I was really being was revealing.

So she told me that she had straight brown hair, was divorced, and had two little boys, ages five and eight. She was a bartender and waitress. She told me where she worked and that she'd be working there later that day. I was thinking that I didn't want to know all this, but I continued to chitchat with her, being flip but friendly. Then she told me that on Monday she was going down to get a copy of her original birth certificate.

"How do you do that?" I asked. "I thought you said you couldn't get your records."

"I'm telling a lie that I need it for something," and she made up a story.

I was shaken, but I still played the role. I finally asked, "What if you find these people and they don't want to acknowledge you? Have you thought about that?"

"Yes, I've thought about that," she said, "and I'm prepared. I think I'm a fairly happy person and I'll be able to handle it."

"Well, Christy," I said, "you sound like a lovely young woman." Then I added, falsely, "I hope you get what you're looking for." I told her that maybe one of these days Paul and I would stop in where she worked for one of those great margaritas. We said good-bye and hung up. I slumped back against the couch, limp. Paul looked at me.

"My life is over," I told him. "I just can't do this. I don't know what I'm going to do."

I had always taken responsibility for having given up Christy; it wasn't Paul's decision. Now I worried about what people were going to think. I wasn't who I told people I was. I had done something so unlike what they knew of me—I'd given up a child. My kids thought their younger sibling died! I was worried that people would judge me and that my kids would hate me. I thought, I could lie to Christy all I wanted to but if she got the birth certificate that said we were her parents, there would be nothing I could do.

Paul suggested I call the attorney who had handled the adoption. I did.

"I'm sorry for calling you at home on a Saturday morning, but I really need to talk to you about something that's happened." I told him about the phone call and then confided, "I'm terrified and don't know what to do. She's going to get confirming information on Monday. How can I stop her?"

"I don't know of a way you can stop her legally," he said. "I don't like these searches. They can be devastating. Disruptive. They don't always turn out 'happily ever after.' It's the chance you take."

I thanked him and hung up.

"I can't believe we're starring in this soap opera," said Paul, shaking his head.

I decided to call Beth, the career counselor I'd told six years before. "Remember the secret I shared with you? I just got a phone call from her. I need to talk to somebody. Can I come and see you?"

"Come right ahead," she said.

I also arranged to visit another friend, a woman who had given up a child in an open adoption, but most of her friends didn't know about it.

They both thought it was wonderful. Each asked me what was the worst that could happen.

"That my kids are going to hate me," I said.

"How do you know?"

"I don't know, but they will. I lied to them."

Beth said, "It may be wonderful."

"It's not going to be wonderful. People are going to think of me as a monster who gave up a child. Women don't do that."

"Yes they do. Just remember, you gave life," said Beth.

"It was an act of love," said my other friend.

"Bullshit," I said through my tears. "It was an act of desperation. It was not an act of love. I didn't feel any love. I felt fear and desperation."

The other problem was that Christy lived in the same town. She hadn't been placed out of the area as the doctor had promised. I was sure she would tell people that we were her birth parents and I wouldn't have any choice as to whether or not I went public.

Lovingly and tenderly, my friends convinced me that I had to face the situation. I dried my tears, turned around, went home, and said to Paul, "Okay, let's go."

Visibly nervous, he looked at me. I was cold, controlled, numb. My mind and body felt mechanical. We drove to the restaurant where Christy worked. On the way there Paul asked, "What are you going to say to her?"

"I don't know."

"Are you going to tell her it's us?"

"I don't know."

"Well, what are you going to say?"

"I don't know."

We went over and over it during the eight miles to the restaurant. When we got there and were standing outside the place, Paul was so nervous. "How am I going to know which one she is?"

"Just relax, you'll know," I said. "It's okay." I wanted him to be quiet and not bug me. I couldn't deal with his nervousness; I had enough turmoil of my own.

I stood at the door, hesitating. Then, I took a deep breath and marched right in and up to where she was standing behind the bar, and with a big smile, I said, "Hi, you must be Christy. I'm Marti and this is Paul, and we thought you could fix us a margarita." She looked like me. I could see that *she* was nervous.

"This is Marti's show," Paul told her while she mixed the drinks. I understood he meant that whatever I was going to say, he'd back me up, but I thought Christy would think it was a confirmation that we were her birth parents.

We walked around and visited with friends of ours who were there. Then, a while later, I went up to Christy and said, "Hey, if you have a couple of minutes, we'd like to talk to you." I still didn't know what I would tell her. I thought maybe I could cast some kind of spell on her so she wouldn't bother us anymore, or that I'd figure out between that moment and the next what I'd say, some way I could stop it from becoming public.

She was being sweet. "I'll get somebody to cover for me."

"We'll go outside," I told her. "There aren't a lot of people out there." I didn't know. Maybe I'd hit her over the head or something.

I never had control of this situation. Not over conception, although I thought I had. Not over whether or not I would carry the pregnancy to term, because abortion was illegal. Not over where she was placed for adoption, although I'd been told that she would be placed out of the area. Not over whether or not I would be reunited with her, because here she was. And not over whether or not I would go public with the story, because here we were in the same small town.

While I hadn't been able to express it to Paul yet, somewhere along the line I came to the conclusion that I had three options: First, I could tell her that no, we were not her birth parents. Second, I could tell her that yes, we were her birth parents but we didn't want her to tell anyone. Third, I could tell her yes, we were her birth parents and welcome to our family. I realized that the first two options weren't going to work, because I didn't know this person or what she would tell other people. So I decided that if I followed option three, at least I could take some measure of control and be the first to tell people. It was scary.

When I saw the patio door open from the bar, I stood, walked toward her, and just nodded my head. We hugged. I didn't feel any connection with her when we hugged; I just did what I thought was appropriate. Christy sat with us. Paul was excited. He checked out her hands and said, "Oh, you've got my fingers!" She looked like I had thirty years before, except taller. She even looks more like me than our other two kids do.

I was in shock, but I managed to join the conversation a couple of times. Christy told us about her little boys and that she was seeing a man, someone she had dated in high school. We learned that her adoptive dad had died of a heart attack when Christy was about ten, so her adoptive mom had raised her alone. I felt it was important to ask her not to tell anyone the news until we'd had the chance to tell our other children. She said she understood and wouldn't tell anyone.

Paul then invited her to breakfast the next morning. I acted agreeably enough, but I was angry with him for suggesting it. I don't like doing breakfast in the first place, much less under such difficult circumstances. When we left, Paul must have sensed something, because he offered to help with breakfast. He did most of the cooking anyhow.

The next morning Christy arrived with her two little boys, who immediately came up and hugged me. They felt like strangers. As we talked, Christy told us how she had gone about finding us and that our paths had crossed before.

First, the doctor who placed Christy, my physician, had broken his promise to us and placed her just a few blocks from where we lived at the time. Christy's adoptive mother had always suspected that the baby we "lost" was the baby they adopted. She had been in my exercise class when I was pregnant and remembered me. When Christy told her mom ten years before that she wanted to do the search, her mom felt threatened and said sarcastically, "Well, you might start with Marti Daniels." At that time we were well enough known in the community that Christy thought it was just too easy to be true and discounted the remark as defensiveness on her mother's part.

Four years after that Christy and her ex-husband were at an advertising agency in town saying hi to a friend of theirs, and they were introduced to someone else who was there—Paul. Christy felt shy as she remembered what her mom had said, and she stood a little behind her husband, reticent to come face to face with Paul. Of course Paul had no idea who she really was. Besides, he still believed the baby we'd given up had been a boy.

It was during that same period of time that Christy worked as a waitress. We had gone to that restaurant with some friends for Sunday brunch, and she had waited on us. I usually engage the waitperson in a little conversation, but apparently not that time, because I was busy with the other people. She remembered it, though. While we were eating, Christy had a discussion with one of her fellow workers about family. She had said, "I don't know about my family history. I'm adopted. For all I know, they could be my family," and she pointed to us, remembering what her mother had said a few years before.

Christy got involved in ALMA, the Adoptees Liberty Movement Association, which helps adoptees and birth parents find each other. She also requested and got the non-identifying letter from the state. While it didn't give our names or our address, it gave a lot of details about who we were. She took that letter and did some math. The letter told her that we already had a daughter and a son, ages six and five at the time of her birth. So she had gone to the library to check old yearbooks. She found pictures of Rachel and Larry. The resemblance was so strong, especially to Rachel, that she thought she was on the right track. Then she went to the courthouse and looked up voter registration information. Paul and I matched the ages listed in the letter. That's when she went to my client, Tim, and told him. She didn't know him that well, but she knew Paul had worked with him in the past and assumed we were friends. She told him she thought we were her birth parents, and then said, "And I want to send them a letter."

"Why send them a letter?" Tim asked. "Why don't you call them?"

"Yes," Tim's wife agreed, "Marti is such a nice person, that even if they're not the ones you're looking for, I'm sure she'd help you out."

So Tim had left the message on my machine.

Telling our other kids about Christy was going to be the most difficult part. Larry was still single and lived in the area. A professional athlete, he was on tour and wouldn't be home for a few weeks. Rachel was married, had one daughter and a stepson, and lived a few hours' drive away. She was working that weekend and wouldn't return until Monday night. On Monday I called her.

"Rachel, I need to come and see you. I want to talk to you about something."

"What is it? It's not a good time," she said.

"It's not something I want to talk about on the phone, and it's nothing bad," I said.

Paul yelled from the background, "Oh, it's wonderful! It's real positive!"

"What is it? Tell me," she said.

"I can't," I insisted. "Nobody's sick and we're not getting a divorce and we're not moving away. It's nothing like that. But it is something I can't discuss on the phone."

"This is a bad time," she said again.

"But this is when I need to talk to you. I'll be there tomorrow and just stay overnight. Then I'll leave."

So the next day I drove to Rachel's. After dinner she and I went outside and sat on the steps.

"Do you remember when I was pregnant and you were in the first grade?" I started.

"Yeah, the stillbirth."

"No," I said gently, "there was a baby, and I gave the baby up."

"I... I..." Rachel, the most articulate member of the family, was stuttering. She didn't seem real happy about the news, and I thought I felt disapproval from her. Once she recovered enough, she explained why it was a bad time for a visit. She told me that she'd just had her seventh miscarriage. I felt awful for her, devastated, and terribly guilty for burdening her with this just then.

"Why didn't you tell me?" Rachel asked.

"How could I tell you? I wasn't going to share it with anyone."

"You could have told me when I was older."

"No, I couldn't. I was going to take this secret to my grave."

I tried to explain why I had given up Christy, the situation and my state of mind at the time. I felt I was making excuses, as if I were justifying, which I was. I shouldn't have had to, but I felt as if I did. I resented Christy for putting me in that position.

"She wants to meet you," I said. "Your dad's real excited. He's thrilled."

"How do you feel about it?"

"I don't know what I feel about it."

I was feeling a lot of things, but mostly about Rachel, not Christy. It was much like Christy's birth, when I was feeling for Rachel, who was sick, and not for Christy, who I didn't know and was going someplace else. Here I was doing the same thing again.

After I got home, we were on the phone every day, Rachel, Paul and I, about how we could arrange for Rachel and Christy to meet.

"I don't want to meet her there for the first time," Rachel said. "Can you bring her here to some place neutral? Maybe a restaurant?"

I didn't really understand why Rachel made this request, but we talked to Christy and found out what day she could go, and together we drove to meet Rachel. Paul was thrilled. I was controlled. I thought Christy was nice, and if I met her as another person, I'd like her, but I was going along so I could help Rachel through it.

We got to the restaurant before Rachel did. I sat facing the door. Paul was at my side, and Christy's back was to the door, so Paul and I saw Rachel come in first. When Christy turned and Rachel looked at her, Rachel's mouth fell open. Christy's resemblance to both Rachel and me was incredibly strong. Paul enjoyed the reaction of the two young women meeting, talking. There was pretty good chatter, maybe a little strained on Christy's part.

"I wish you could have grown up with us," Rachel said after a while.

What a sweet thing for her to say!

* * *

About two weeks after Christy found us, I went to a gift show in New York City for my business. I was glad to be getting away. A friend of mine came along. I did the show and tried to forget about the situation at home, and I pretty much did. When the show was over, I was tired, drained. My friend was going to Philadelphia, and I was supposed to return home. But I wanted to stay in New York for a few more days. I could make calls, do some business, relax. I didn't want to go home. I called Paul.

"So when are you coming back?" he asked.

"Maybe Tuesday," I said. This was a Wednesday night.

"No, you have to come now. Larry will be back tomorrow about midnight, and people are beginning to talk. We have to tell him."

"Then you tell him. You handle it."

But my friend persuaded me to go and take care of my family. I called Paul back and told him I'd be back the next night.

I still dragged my feet, not leaving until mid-afternoon the next day. I had spent the morning with my niece, then I started the long drive home. Physically and emotionally exhausted, I had a hard time staying awake while I drove into the mountains. I started to doze off and drive off the road, when I felt someone poke me on the shoulder. I looked over and said out loud, "Oh, thanks." I looked again, and nobody was there. I figured maybe that was God's way of saying, "You have to go home and finish this." So I did. I got there about midnight.

"Call Larry," Paul said, "he just got in."

"I don't want to talk to him."

But I did. "Hi. I just got home," I said. "I hear you just got home, too. We have something we want to talk to you about. Are you busy tomorrow morning?"

"What is it?" he asked.

199

We went through the same thing I had with Rachel about, "Not over the phone," and "It's nothing bad," and all the things it wasn't about, and Paul did his lines about its being "wonderful," and "real positive."

The following morning we went over to Larry's. He stood in front of me as I sat on the sofa and broke the news.

"Oh, what a shame," he said.

What did that mean? Did that mean, what a shame I was such a bad person? Had I just lost his love and respect?

He wanted to know the same thing Rachel did: "Why didn't you tell us?"

Once again, I tried to explain the situation and my reasons for giving her up.

We talked for a while, and then he asked, "When do I get to meet her?" From the way he asked, I knew he had accepted the situation, and that I hadn't lost him.

"She's working at Le Bistro. She's working tonight."

"I'll go there and have a drink," he decided.

"We want to go too," Paul said. "Part of the kick is seeing your reactions when you meet."

It wasn't going to be a kick for me to see them meet. For me it was a gut thing. I needed to protect my relationship with Larry.

"No wonder you had so many problems," Larry said. He looked at me, and I saw love in his eyes.

So we made arrangements for them to meet. Larry told us later that he played golf that day and found himself smiling about it a lot. He and Christy hit it off well. Rachel said she thought it was interesting that the men in our family accepted the situation so easily. We agreed: Life doesn't spring from their bodies.

After Christy found me, I felt I was playing a role once again, that I had to keep up the pretense of being fine when I wasn't. It was awful. There were so many difficult moments. A month after she found us, Paul and I were invited to a picnic of about a hundred people. We brought Christy with us to introduce her. I think the reason I had agreed to bring Christy was so that *I* could be the one to open my closet door and present my skeletons. In retrospect, I hated that we brought her to that picnic. People thought it was so wonderful and were reveling in it, which irritated me, because no one seemed to realize that it certainly wasn't wonderful for me. I think the picnic was difficult for Christy, too. Here she was, being welcomed into our circle of friends, the people she might have known had she grown up in our family. She seemed guarded, and at one point she was so overwhelmed she cried.

I found myself telling people, even casual acquaintances, about the adoption, because I wanted them to hear it from me first. Sometimes I would say it like, "Boy, do I have an Oprah Winfrey story for you." Most people were wonderful. Women would cry, "Oh, I love a happy ending!" But once in a while I would tell someone who would get quiet and look away, apparently uncomfortable, and I would get a sick feeling in my stomach and think, "Well, that was someone I shouldn't have told."

About six weeks after Christy found me, I went into therapy again, this time with Joan, a therapist who knew about adoption. She had worked in Los Angeles for the county with adoptees, adoptive parents, and birth parents.

"Married Jewish women don't do what I did," I told her.

"Yes they do," said Joan.

"No, they don't."

We argued back and forth, and she finally said emphatically, "Marti, you've lived in a small town too long. They do. They just don't talk about it."

That was a revelation to me. I really thought I was the only one.

Paul had gone with me the first time I went to see Joan. Christy came with me a couple of times, too. I also felt I wanted to make things easier for Christy's adoptive mom, Harriet, so I brought her with me once in the hope it would help us both get in touch with what we were feeling.

Before I had gone to New York City on my business trip, I had called Harriet and asked to meet with her. It was important to me that she know I was no threat to her. She was nervous, and I tried to reassure her. "You're her mom," I told her. "I was just the vehicle that brought her into this world. But she's not mine, she's yours. And you did a wonderful job of raising her." Neither of us was very in touch with our feelings and our joint therapy session was uncomfortable for both of us. We were different kinds of people with different interests, and the only thing we had in common was this young woman. My relationship with Christy was different from hers—she was the mom, I wasn't. But I realized I couldn't help Harriet deal with this reunion. I had my own problems to straighten out.

I was in therapy for several months. It was tough. I had a lot of resentment and anger about being found that I was trying to work through. Even with Joan's help, I didn't know how. It was hard getting in touch with my feelings. Really hard. I was mostly pissed off. Christy's relationship with Larry was strong. Her relationship with Rachel was developing slowly, but in a positive direction. Yet when she made appointments to meet with Paul and me, she was usually late and often missed them altogether. I felt as though by finding me she had ripped open my life, and then left me dangling while she went off to play with her new siblings.

A little over a year after Christy's first call I was sitting in the living room, really depressed, feeling dreadful about the state of my life, and I decided to call the SOB doctor who had handled Christy's birth and adoption to read him the riot act. He had told us that the baby was being placed out of the area. He knew that was important to me. I told him that I thought placing her within blocks of where we lived was unethical and unconscionable. He knew who my husband was and that we'd become this visible family in town.

The doctor was apologetic. "Well, I didn't know."

"What do you mean you didn't know? You knew who we were and where we lived, and you knew the adoptive parents and where they lived."

"The young woman came to me three years ago to get information about her birth parents," he said, "and I wouldn't give her any."

"That's not the point. If she wanted to find us and you had given her to a family in Timbuktu, she would have found us, but it would have been different; it wouldn't have been as traumatic. But to put her in this small town where we lived was wrong. Had I known, I would have moved."

"I'm so sorry," he said. "So sorry. I don't know what I can do."

"Well, you can pay for my therapy," I said half-jokingly.

"What?"

"You handled a lot of adoptions, so this is not the last call like this you're going to get. What you can do for me is have the women call me, because we need all the support we can get." And I hung up.

I thought when I called him it would release a lot of anger and I'd feel better. It didn't. I was still devastated. It just went on and on.

About a year and a half after Christy found us, I started experiencing pain in my side and ended up in the hospital for twelve days, throwing up, going through test after test. They couldn't find anything wrong. I didn't realize it until I got home and started putting it together, but the pain began about the same time I started feeling things I'd never felt before about Christy and giving her up for adoption and being found.

Feelings of caring and love for her surfaced. I began to feel remorse and guilt for the way it was all handled. That was something that bothered Rachel—she knew me as emotional and caring, and I hadn't been about this. Giving up Christy had been the right thing to do, what I had to do to survive. What I felt now was new, and I realized that this whole illness had probably been due to the sudden eruption of deeply repressed feelings.

I invited Christy to the house. We sat side-by-side on the couch. I turned to her and said, "I'd like to reintroduce myself to you. That person you've known for the last year and half was not really me. I'm not that detached and controlled. I do care about you. I love you, and I'm sorry for the way I handled things."

We hugged and cried. This hug felt good.

Now that I was getting in touch with my feelings, I wanted her to feel in touch with hers. "If you have any resentment," I told her, "I certainly understand, because my giving you up was the ultimate rejection."

"I had a good childhood. I don't have any negative feelings about your giving me up. If they're there, I'm not aware of them."

I didn't quite believe her, but I hoped that she would come to her own feelings in her own time and that I would be able to handle the flak that would follow.

Things are better now. Not good, but better. I don't know if it'll ever be good, but I'm not fighting it like I was. There are still times I resent being found. As traumatic as the first year and a half was, it helped that at least I liked Christy. I may never feel like she's my daughter, but we're friends.

Adoptees and birth parents who search should be careful. Many people have unrealistic expectations and set themselves up for major disappointment. They expect the loving, happily-ever-after reunion, and it doesn't always work that way. There are birth parents who have made another life for themselves and don't want a relationship. There are also adoptees found by birth parents, many trying to expiate their guilt, and the adoptees wish the birth parents would leave them alone, let them live the life they've created with their adoptive family. Reunions are so disruptive.

Lots of times after Christy first found us Paul would ask, "Aren't you glad now? Aren't you happy now?" and I'd say, "No." Am I glad and happy *yet* that she found us? Not particularly, but I'm not as upset as I was. Can I change it? No. If I could, would I? Yes.

There have been a lot of lessons in this experience. The basic one is that I have to face up to my life. Being exposed has forced me to face up to what's happened in the past and what's happening now.

Everybody thinks that because she found us we've had a happy ending to a lovely story. What do they know? It's an okay ending. Except it's not the end—I'm going to be working for the rest of my life dealing with the consequences.

6

I first met Dena, a street-smart woman with a deep heart, when she came to our support group, where we talked about how adoption had affected us. Marti had said that Jewish women didn't do what she had done—give up their babies. Yet here was Dena sitting at the same table, although her circumstances were significantly different.

She had led a difficult life of abuse and drugs. Her rebelliousness in youth had turned into strength and a fierce protectiveness for anyone who was abused. She was now in her forties, and although she was on the small side and soft spoken, she gave off a feeling of inner toughness. An attentive listener, she instilled trust. She struck me as someone I would want in my corner. Her lifelong work with drawing, painting, sculpting, collages, and masks helped her release emotions. She looked comfortable with who she was and how to make her way in the world.

At that meeting she told us that she was just starting to search for her daughter. At the next meeting, she reported that she had found her. I'd never heard of a search being completed so quickly. But then, maybe it wasn't really that quick. Her own past as a victim of abuse and as a drug user propelled her to heal herself first, then find her daughter to learn if she was okay. Maybe Dena would say it was many years of surviving and preparing before she could look for her daughter.

Last I heard from her, she was living in southern Arizona, riding motorcycles and making art.

WOUNDED REBEL – Dena's Story

My mother told me she got pregnant to get back at my father and that she bled the whole pregnancy. It must have been scary. When I was born, in 1951, I was three months preemie. The staff at the hospital told my parents to concentrate on the two healthy children they had at home and not get too attached to me because I probably wouldn't live. For the first two weeks of my life they didn't even know whether I was a boy or a girl. I was in the hospital for a month. My dad was working three jobs. They lived in a little two-bedroom apartment and were real poor, and now here were thousands of dollars in medical bills. So the whole thing started off sick and it progressed. I believe our relationship was torn.

By the time I was a teenager, my parents owned the two largest restaurants in town and were fairly well-to-do and prominent in the community. My older brother and sister had moved out by then. My sister did everything right—she married and started a family, and lived not too far from Mom and Dad. My brother, the family brain, left to get his college education. My little brother, twelve years younger than me, was like an only child and mostly raised by hired help because when he was two Mom went to work managing one of the restaurants.

My dad was a workaholic and seldom home, and when he was, he and my mother didn't get along. They yelled and screamed at each other a lot. My mother ended up with complete responsibility for the day-to-day care of the children. She told me that her own parents should never have had children because they were too into themselves and poor at being parents. Looking back, I see that my mother's own parenting skills were zero. There was no consistency at home. The rules changed, often, and I didn't know what to expect from one time to the next. Sometimes a dirty pan left in the sink meant nothing and sometimes it would send her into a screaming rage. She would throw things at me. She came into my room at one o'clock in the morning and told me we had to rearrange my furniture. She was controlling, and no one wanted to cross her. But I was probably more difficult than the others to raise because I didn't care what anybody said, I did what I wanted to do. It was a toxic mix.

My drug use began when I was eleven. Our doctor prescribed diet pills to help me lose weight. All during high school I used amphetamines, as well as my mom's prescription sleeping pills.

When I was sixteen, I met Earl. He was a year older than me, and wild. With Earl and other friends, I started smoking pot and found it to be a great release. We spent a lot of time at parties getting stoned. I felt like I fit in there. And I had this image I thought I had to uphold and I dressed in the full gear of the '60s—wild clothes, big earrings, moccasins.

My parents decided I needed to get a job, which I thought was kind of unfair. My mom's philosophy was that if you have it hard, then you'll understand and appreciate what it is to have. They stopped giving me money for clothes. Then my mom stopped giving me bus money to get to school. It was a couple of miles away, and I walked, but I got in trouble because I was always late. I told my mom and dad that if they didn't give me bus money and clothes, I would quit school. They tried using reverse psychology and told me to go ahead and quit, probably thinking I wouldn't. But I did. Then Earl and I started hanging out together all the time.

He took me away from my house, away from my environment, and I didn't have to deal with that unless I went home to sleep. He was the first man I ever had sex with. I have trouble calling him a man now. But at the time I thought he was a great guy. I was sixteen, what did I know?

I remember my dad wrote me a letter and slipped it under my door when I was asleep. I don't know what he knew about what I was doing, or what my mom told him, but he was best friends with the chief of police and the police usually knew where I was. The letter said that the people I was hanging out with were the scum of the earth and he was afraid I was doing drugs and he needed to talk to me. He was right about the drugs. By that time I was doing a lot of them—pot, speed, LSD. I was even stoned when I went to meet with him. At our meeting he said he wanted me to see a psychiatrist. I agreed just so he'd stop talking.

That didn't work out really well. I saw the psychiatrist once a week for a couple of months. Things got more intense at my house. My mother was physically violent with me. I'd be walking by and something would fly at me—a pan, wooden hanger, stuff like that.

I ran away with Earl to New York City, a couple of hours away, and hung out in the Village. It was kind of neat, kind of fun, different. Back then you could find a place to sleep for two dollars a night. We were gone for about a week. When we got back, police were at the bus station. I just knew they were looking for me, so I told Earl I'd handle stuff. I was afraid of what they would do to him because I was jailbait. He took off. I went to a pay phone and called my mom, told her I was back and okay, and she should call off the cops. I also told her that if she bothered me or asked me a lot of questions, I'd leave again. It was quiet at home for a while.

Soon after that I discovered I was pregnant. No one had ever explained sex to me, and it wasn't until I got pregnant that I realized how I, as a human being, got on this planet. I knew I didn't want to tell my mom when we were alone. So, I told both of my parents that I needed to talk to them together about something very important.

When the time came to talk, my dad was downstairs waiting, but my mother stood upstairs and refused to come down. I finally said to my dad, "It doesn't look like she's going to come down, so I might as well tell you: I'm pregnant. I need your signature so Earl and I can get married."

My mom yelled from the top of the stairs, "I've known this was going to happen since you were twelve years old!"

I was devastated by that remark, and she kept yelling and getting louder. Finally I couldn't stand to listen anymore and I walked out to be with Earl and to mellow out. I was still smoking pot. I'd stopped doing other drugs when I found out I was pregnant.

When I got home that night, my dad was on the couch in the den, where we had a large bar and kept decanters of alcohol. He didn't usually drink, but that night he was passed out on the couch with a bottle of Johnny Walker beside him. I felt so sad. My mom was upstairs asleep.

Within a week or two, they agreed to sign for me to get married, which I needed because I was only sixteen. I still feel it was a great mistake on their part. I don't care how much war I put out about it.

Earl must have been eighteen at this point and didn't need a signature. He and I got married by a justice of the peace and moved in with his parents.

They lived in a government project apartment. Their lifestyle was totally different from what I was used to. My parents were up here, with all this social stuff happening, and his parents were way on the other end of the scale, never went out, just watched TV. But I thought I was in love. It felt like caring.

Two weeks after we moved into his parents' house, Earl started hitting me. He'd never done anything like that before. He started by beating me on my back. His family didn't see what was going on, and the bruises were covered by my clothes. Earl was still doing drugs, and he would threaten to kill himself by doing heroin if I ever left him. I was terrified that he really would. I felt trapped.

Earl robbed a store. He also sold drugs—pot, bennies, amphetamines, LSD. Somebody evidently knew exactly where he kept the drugs and told the police, because the police came to the apartment and went through the boxes and took everything. But we were lucky—they didn't arrest us for possession or sale, or even write it up, probably because they knew who my dad was.

I was about three and a half months pregnant when my mother came to meet me on the street somewhere. She told me that she thought that Earl was terrible to me, that I needed to stop being with him, and the only way out was to get an abortion. I was repulsed she could even bring that up. "There's no way I'm going to do that," I told her. As I look back now, I see she was trying to be helpful.

My dad knew everybody in town, so he called the woman in charge of government apartments and got us in one. It was the nicest one, big compared to the others in the projects. Some nights my friends from high school came over. Having my own place and having my friends over was like playing grown-up.

I started doing bookkeeping at one of my dad's restaurants. That helped with money. After Earl was fired from his job because he had stolen from them, my dad got him a job as an apprentice plumber.

Earl was hitting me a lot by then. Never on my face, but all over my body. He fit into the abusive pattern—he would stop, be very sorry and promise he would never do it again, then the abuse would get worse. I was scared of him, but I was having a baby, and staying with him was the only way I saw to take care of the baby. I'm not sure how aware I was that I was going to have this being. Mostly, I was doing everything by rote—*Now here's the crib, and isn't that cute, and these little clothes are so cute.*

When I started my ninth month of pregnancy, he beat me bad. This time he got me in the face. When I called the doctor and told him I thought I needed stitches, he told me to get right to the hospital and he'd meet me there. Earl walked with me the two blocks to the hospital and was in the room when the doctor came in. The doctor must have suspected before then that Earl had been beating me, but we had never talked about it. This time, the doctor screamed at him to get out of the room. He sewed me up, bandaged my eye, and told me that I should leave Earl. The doctor knew my family because his father was a close friend of my parents, and after I left, he called my parents to tell them what had happened.

Earl took me back to his parents' house. His dad was upset about what had happened. Then my parents showed up. Earl and his family said nothing, but sat in the living room and watched us talking at the door.

"Dena, you have to leave," my father said.

"What am I going to do?" I said. "How am I going to take care of this baby? I need to take care of this baby."

And between them they said: Don't worry about it. We'll take care of it. Everything will be okay. Things will work out.

By that time I had had more than enough, so I went with my mom and dad. I don't remember Earl trying to stop me. He was probably afraid because there was somebody bigger in the room.

I stayed at my parents' for a couple of days. I was afraid, really afraid, that Earl would get nuts and come after me, hurt someone else, or kill himself. My mom and dad were nervous too. Apparently they had already arranged for me to go to Kansas City and stay with my aunt and uncle. My parents promised that as soon as I returned with the baby, they'd set us up in an apartment. So I agreed to go.

* * *

The plane ride was horrible. I was seventeen, about to have a baby, trying to escape from an abusive man, still sore from the beating, and going to a strange place to stay with people I didn't know. I couldn't stop crying. This young guy in an army uniform was sitting in front of me, and he kept trying to say sweet things to help.

My aunt met me at the airport. I had never met her before, but she was kind to me. My uncle, my dad's brother, was a physician and would be my doctor. They had two kids—a daughter two years older than I was and a son two years younger. To make room for me, the son agreed to give up his room and sleep in the den.

My aunt and uncle introduced me to a social worker friend of theirs. She started doing therapy with me at the house a few times a week. Right away she talked about adoption. "It's the only chance that baby has for a good life, Dena," she said. "You'd be doing the most unselfish thing you could possibly do." I was bombarded by talk of giving up the baby for adoption. It was railroaded into me that it was the only thing that was right for the baby. Those were the words given to me: "The only chance that baby has for an okay life."

Then my parents withdrew their offer to set up the baby and me in an apartment back home. I was warned that the baby might be in jeopardy if I brought it back to where Earl was. They said none of us knew what he would do.

My uncle and the social worker told me the adoptive parents would be Jewish and well-to-do, able to provide anything the baby desired. I remember thinking all of a sudden that adoption *was* the only thing I could do. It seemed right to me.

I'd been at my aunt and uncle's two weeks when my cousin, who had a little sports car, came in and said, "If you go over a lot bumps you'll have the baby. Do you want to go over some bumps?" I said, "Sure." When we got back to the house, I was so hungry I had to have a sandwich—roast beef with a lot of horse-radish on it.

"God, Dena, you're going to make yourself sick," my cousin said.

"I'll be fine."

I ate the sandwich and went up to the bedroom. At nine o'clock I started having little pains. I thought, *This is interesting*. The pains grew stronger, but I didn't want to bother anyone, and my uncle was out delivering another baby. The pains kept com-ing. I remember realizing that this whole situation was real, not at all like a dream anymore. And I felt scared and alone.

Then I felt the presence of my Grandma Rose, my father's mother. She had died when I was five or six. That eased my fears for the rest of the night. At seven or eight in the morning, I heard my uncle come home and I went down to talk to him.

"I'm having these pains," I told him.

"It's probably false labor," he said. "You're not due for an-other week or two yet. Your aunt will take you to the office this afternoon."

I went back to my room. The pains kept coming. My uncle had told my aunt what was going on, and she checked on me often and told everyone else to leave me alone. At two o'clock she drove me to my uncle's office, forty minutes away.

"Yes, it's labor," my uncle said. He broke my water bag. "Go back to the house now, and in a couple of hours your aunt will take you to the hospital."

We went back to the house. I remember being in the room and just walking and crying, holding myself when a pain came. My cousin walked by and tried to say something sweet through the door. My aunt yelled at her to leave me alone. My mother

215

called. I told her how scared I was. "It's just going to happen, Dena," she said. "It's natural." There was no comfort for me in that.

At five that evening it was finally time to go to the hospital. My uncle advised me that because I was married, it was illegal for me to give up a baby for adoption, and if Earl wanted to, he could take the baby. Also, my uncle was not supposed to be treating a family member. "Remember, Dena," he had said, "we're not related and you're not married," and he gave me a new last name.

My aunt stayed in the labor room with me much of the time. I was in heavy labor now and kept asking my uncle to come in and check me. He'd check to see how dilated I was, then tell me it wasn't time yet.

"When?" I asked.

"Soon, Dena, soon."

They gave me a drug to mellow me out, but I was getting pretty pissed off and decided that this was a bunch of garbage and I was going to leave.

"I'm not going to do this. I've had enough!"

"Where you going?" my aunt asked.

"I'm going home! He's going to hurt!" I meant Earl.

Laughing, she said, "Dena, you can't go."

Anyone who knew me knew I tolerated no one telling me what I could and couldn't do. I got up to leave. People came in and tied me down and gave me another drug to settle me down. My uncle came in and reassured me that the baby would be born soon. Then he and my aunt went to visit somebody they knew down the hall.

I felt it first, then I saw blood between my legs. I had no idea you bled during childbirth, and I freaked out. I screamed at the top of my lungs, "Uncle Seymour! I'm bleeding to death in here and nobody cares! Nobody cares!" At that point, I didn't care who knew he was my uncle.

He came and checked me. "Okay, Dena, it's time."

"Nope," I told him, "I've changed my mind. I'm not ready yet. No, no, no!" I struggled as they tried to get me on the gurney to wheel me into the delivery room.

The next thing I remember is seeing my grandmother again. She was so real and her presence comforting. Then my eyes opened. My uncle was there and he asked me how I was.

"I just saw Grandma Rose."

He jumped back as if I'd struck him. She was his mother, and she had died years before.

"You had a baby girl," he said.

"How much does she weigh?" I asked.

"Six pounds, seven ounces. And I've sewed you up just like a virgin. No one will ever know you've had a baby."

I slept.

My daughter was born on March 20, 1969. My uncle and aunt, my cousins, my parents, and my older sister and brother knew she was alive. Everyone else we knew would be told that the baby was stillborn. That way, at least Earl wouldn't go looking for her.

The next day, I was thinking of the name I had picked out for this baby when I was five months pregnant—Jennifer Rose. I'd written it hundreds of times, and it made me realize that this baby was mine and I couldn't give her up. This adoption could not happen. I decided to leave the hospital and take her with me. I was on the second floor, and I knew that if the only way to get out of there was to jump out the window, then that was what I would do. Just then, my uncle came to see how I was.

"I'm doing fine," I said. "I'm taking the baby and jumping out the window."

My uncle had penetrating blue eyes that could reel you in. He looked at me. He knew I was bleeding and in pain from the birth, and I still had a bandage over my eye from Earl's beating. "Fine," he said. "Jump. Say you jumped and took her. And say you lived when you hit the ground, where are you going to go with a little baby?"

I couldn't answer. There was nowhere for us to go and no one willing to help me keep my baby. I was defeated.

My room was diagonally across from the nursery. About the third day, I was feeling a little better, so I got up and walked around. I opened the door to my room. I had noticed the nursery windows before, but the blinds were always closed. This time the blinds were open, and I ran over there. There were babies, ten or fifteen of them. I zeroed in on one with dark skin like Earl's and I knew she was mine.

Then this huge lady, a nurse, saw me standing there and said, "Come on," trying to get me away from the window. I kept saying, "That's my baby. That one's my baby."

She said, "Come on, let's go weigh you," and put her arm around me and guided me away.

"That's got to be my baby. Tell me that's my baby. Tell me."

She couldn't say yes, she couldn't say no, but she kind of smiled, so I knew I was right. She managed to pull me over to the scale. I weighed 140 pounds.

I was in the hospital another day or two and I checked the nursery blinds several times. They were always closed.

Two women I'd never met brought me papers to sign giving away all legal rights to my baby. I cried and cried, and I signed.

My memories of the weeks following the birth are sketchy. A week after the birth my mother came out and took me to the county offices downtown to sign more papers. She was angry that my dad wasn't involved and she had to take care of my business by herself. She took me back to my aunt and uncle's, stayed maybe another day, and left. I stayed with my aunt and uncle.

My uncle and the social worker told me the adoption was illegal because I was still married, which meant Earl still had parental rights and if he found her, he could take her. That really scared me. I was told to tell people that the baby was stillborn.

Since before I went into labor, the social worker had been coming to see me every other day. We would meet in the finished basement, where my uncle kept oil paints and an easel. Painting was an outlet for me, and I would paint while we talked. I remember painting a picture of a clown. It started out as a happy clown, but by the time I finished the paint was a quarter-inch thick and the clown was extremely sad. The social worker talked to me about how I was feeling. She was a good friend of my aunt and uncle, and I thought she was my friend, kind of.

I hadn't been feeling good about my decision. A few weeks after the baby was born, the social worker showed me an article my parents had sent about Earl being arrested for heroin use. She and my family were trying to say, "Look, look what a good decision you made. Look what's happening." I just hated him more. How could he have done that? And I was even more scared for what could have happened to the baby, and glad neither of us was back there.

I got a job as a waitress and my uncle prescribed diet pills to help me lose weight. They were supposed to be non-addicting.

They were addicting. It was a great escape for me for years. When you take enough amphetamines, you don't feel very much. So I lost weight and needed clothes that fit. My mom refused to send any, and my aunt was livid. "Of course you're sending her some clothes!"

My mother sent my old high school clothes. When my aunt opened the box, she said, "What is this? She's got to buy you some new clothes. You deserve new stuff."

That was the first time I ever heard that I *deserved*. It was my first inkling of self-worth. So my aunt got my parents to send money, and I got new clothes. I realized that my aunt was a powerful woman, and she was fair. Things here were not like they were at home. I knew what I was supposed to do here, I did it, and everything ran smoothly. In my house there was always yelling, but not here. It was just more rational. My aunt wanted me to stay, but after four months I went back to live with my parents. My uncle gave me about a thousand "non-addicting" diet pills to take back with me. He told me to let him know if I ran out of them and needed more.

My parents gave me a job as a waitress at my dad's restaurant. I decided I was going to try to straighten my life out. People would come up to me and ask about the baby, and I would tell them that the baby was stillborn. It was like a knife turning in my heart every time. I was denying her existence and living a lie, and all the while I missed her and wanted her.

One day I was carrying a cup of hot coffee to a customer when I heard, "How ya doin', darlin'?" I froze, then looked up, and, sure enough, there was Earl.

My hand began to shake so hard the coffee was spilling out of the cup. My boss, a bully of a manager, picked up on what was happening and threw Earl out, threatening to harm him if he ever came back. That was the last time I saw Earl.

I was trying to keep myself straight and, except for the diet pills, I was off drugs, so when my cousin from Kansas City and her boyfriend were going to Woodstock and asked me if I wanted to go with them, I said no, because I knew there would be a lot of drugs there. Then there was a big pop festival near our home, a mini-Woodstock. I planned to stay away from that one, too, because I knew I would start smoking and doing other stuff. My brother's friend came up from North Carolina, and my brother said, "You have to go with him." I was intimidated by my older brother, so I agreed to go. It was there that I started using again—pot, hash, crank.

Soon after that, my mom started in with her "you're a worthless piece of crap" talk. She would say things like, "Who's ever going to want you? You've already had a child."

It wasn't good for my mom and me to be in that house together, so when my dad saw an ad in the paper for a live-in job at a state institution about an hour and a half away, he called and told me about it—a government job that would also provide a place for me to live. I applied and got the job.

This institution was for mentally handicapped people, kids and adults. Most of them were there from birth to when they died. Some weren't even mentally handicapped, but physically impaired. It was a dumping ground. I was an aide there.

The state paid well, gave paid holidays and time and a half. It cost me only sixteen dollars a month to live there. They cleaned my room twice a week better than I could have, and they gave me fresh towels and three meals a day. It was great.

But my mother's words *Who's going to ever want you?* rang in the back of my mind. I would think, *No one will ever want me.*

Through an old high school friend, I met Ted. We dated a while and partied a lot. I introduced him to drugs. Less than a year after starting work at the institution, I quit. I wanted to be closer to the partying. Ted and I moved in together. I also went back to school and got my GED, which gave me a little self-esteem.

I thought I'd show my mother that someone would want me. Not only was Ted Jewish, but he was a European Jew, which was better than being an American Jew as far as I was concerned. They had more weight. And he knew about me giving up the baby. A year after we met, Ted and I were married by a rabbi. His parents refused to come because we weren't having a big hoopla wedding, and my dad didn't come because he was working. My mother came. She loved Ted, thought he was wonderful. *She* should have married him.

I had used up the diet pills my uncle had given me, and I called him and told him I was still fat and needed more. At the time I was down to ninety pounds. My aunt and uncle came out for a visit. When we met, my uncle looked me over and said, "I don't think you need any more diet pills."

"Oh yes I do," I said. "I'm still about ten pounds overweight."

"No way, Dena."

So I did crank for a while. Anything to cover up the pain.

Around this time a friend called and told me that there was a story in the paper about Earl being arrested for molesting a kid. I was sickened, but at least my daughter was away from him.

After Ted and I had been together for about three years, I got pregnant. I still smoked cigarettes, but I got straight and wasn't doing any drugs. I ate, though, and got huge. The doctor who took care of me for most of my first pregnancy until I left town took care of me during this pregnancy, too. He was sweet. I told him the first baby was stillborn.

This pregnancy meant everything to me because I knew I would keep this baby. Almost five years to the day after my first baby was born, Reuben was born, and some of the pain from losing my daughter was eased.

Things were tough at home. Ted controlled all our money and had trouble parting with it for necessities. He wanted "stuff." Stuff made him feel good. We had a nice apartment and nice things, but no food in the refrigerator. I had to ask for the two dollars for diapers, beg for money for food. I kept thinking something was wrong with this picture. I didn't like living this way. We went to a marriage counselor, but it didn't help. Finally he came home with a Lincoln Continental. He had signed my name to the car loan. I didn't even have a driver's license. Why would I sign for a Lincoln Continental? The payments cost more than our rent, and we were already in debt. I thought the way we were living was just too sick.

One thing was definite—no one would ever take Reuben away from me. He was about a year old, and by that time I had heard about welfare, so I applied for assistance. It took about six weeks for me to settle into a new place—a basement apartment in a nice house. The welfare program required me to get job training. That's how I ended up in nursing school. I dropped Reuben off at daycare and went to school. It was the mid '70s, and I was twenty-three and a single mom before it was commonplace.

It was a struggle, but I always made sure that Reuben had what he needed. I didn't have a winter coat, though. Waiting for the bus in the middle of a snowstorm one day, I couldn't stop shivering. Something in me snapped and I knew I needed help. I broke down and called my parents. They lived about six blocks away.

"Look, I just need a coat," I told my mom.

She said no. Her philosophy was that hardship would make me appreciate what it is to *have*.

Then Reuben got sick. He had an infection, then an allergic reaction to the medicine and had to be admitted to the hospital. They treated him and sent us back home. He still had a high fever. Someone from the nursing school called to find out why I wasn't there, and I told them what was going on. The welfare program offered to pay for a daycare provider who was also an RN so I could go to school, but I didn't feel good about taking him to somebody else's house when he was so sick. If I were in the same situation today, I would take them up on their offer, but I was still a new mom. I managed to keep a B+ average, but I missed too many days of school to finish the program. They didn't take me off welfare, but they told me I'd have to go back in September to finish.

It had been over a year since I'd split with Ted. He saw Reuben only a few times. Ted, his mother, his sister, and his girlfriend were unhappy with how I was raising Reuben. They said I didn't dress him okay and I didn't feed him. They were calling the agency that handled child abuse. At that time when the agency got a phone tip—they would say it was anonymous, but they knew who it was—they would have to go investigate. So they started investigating me, coming over once and sometimes twice a day. Raising a child alone was hard enough without the added pressure of others' expectations of how I should be doing it. There was never a time when Reuben's well-being wasn't okay. My well-being wasn't okay, but his always was.

In August, a guy I knew offered to help Reuben and me move to the West Coast. I took him up on it. We went to the central California coast. I lived with him for a couple of months, then he became physically abusive.

I went to a psychiatrist, told him what was happening. He wanted to call my parents to see if they'd help me out. I said, "Don't call them. It's not going to do any good." He tried anyway, when I was in the office. I watched as he spoke to my mother. He told her that it wasn't good for us here and that Reuben and I should come home, that we needed help. I watched him shake his head in disbelief as he listened to her. There would be no help from my parents. The psychiatrist gave me tranquilizers.

I split up with the abusive guy and moved to Sacramento. I started doing drugs again. It took away the pain, the emptiness I felt in my heart.

I couldn't even remember the exact date of my baby girl's birth anymore. Every March, though, I would get depressed and stay that way for the entire month. There was no way I could get out of feeling it then.

I was surviving through odd jobs, selling drugs, and sometimes welfare. Reuben was in preschool. Somehow I kept him okay. But when he was four and a half, I decided I needed to get straight. I knew I would die if I kept going like this, and I needed to be alive for him. It was my utmost priority to keep Reuben safe and never wound him.

I knew we had to leave where we were living, because drugs were too easy to get there. A friend of mine had a cabin in the woods several hours north. She said she'd help me out if I moved there. So Reuben and I moved there.

It was a wonderful thing for me to mellow out and come off drugs. And I kept telling myself that if I ever did drugs again, it would kill me. Whenever the urge to take drugs hit me, I fed on this thought, and it stopped me from giving in.

I did any kind of work I could get—maid work, production work. Food stamps helped. Art was always important to me. I drew, carved stone, and made wire and clay sculptures and masks. It was a way of releasing things. Sometimes I sold something I made.

I've always been right-on with Reuben, real open about feelings, and as soon as I knew he wouldn't be afraid that I might give him away, I told him that he had a sister. I explained that I'd had to give her up and it was the hardest thing I had ever done. "I don't know where she is. Someone else is raising her." He didn't seem threatened. He seemed more worried about me.

I had a couple of relationships that were pretty abusive. It makes sense to me now, looking at how I grew up, that I would always find myself in an abusive relationship. Finally, after living alone for two years and without abuse, I met Ray. He was not abusive, and I was looking for a father figure for Reuben. We got married in 1983, when Reuben was almost nine.

Of course, I told Ray about my daughter. She was never a secret to anyone who entered my world as a friend. He knew it was important to me to find her, but I felt it wouldn't be right for me to look for her until she was at least eighteen. When she was eighteen, Ray brought it up. I decided that I wasn't good enough yet. I had to be superwoman. I needed to have my shit together before I met her. I told Ray, "I'll do it in my own time."

In my early thirties, I tried to establish a new relationship with my mom. I'd been gone for so long and we had both changed, both grown. We never talked about the abuse, but I no longer allowed myself to be abused. If she said something unkind, I wouldn't let it bother me. She had started seeing me as an okay person. As mother and daughter our relationship had been dysfunctional, but as peers we were friends.

One day, when my daughter was about nineteen, my mom sent me a paper about the Carson City registry.* In all those years, she and I had never discussed my daughter. I called her, and she said, "I just thought you would want to have that. You know, the adoption thing." That's all we said about that, but I knew Mom wanted me to find her, that she knew how tough it had been.

I didn't fill out the papers and register then. It wasn't time yet. I still wasn't superwoman enough. But I did call my aunt and asked her questions about the adoption. She suggested I call their social worker friend who had helped me when I was pregnant and just after. The social worker had just found her own son, who was in his forties, and she might be able to help me. Hearing that, I felt betrayed, ripped off. During all those talks we'd had, the social worker had never disclosed that she'd been through this herself. Why hadn't she shared that with me? There had to be pain. That's what I believe. Whether you acknowledge it or not is another thing, but to just give away a baby and act like, "Oh, it's okay, I'm fine forever-after," you're bullshitting. I was angry. She never told me how hard the path was going to be, not even an inkling of it.

I told my aunt that I wouldn't be calling the social worker. She asked if I still wanted to search. I told her I'd get back to her about that.

* * *

---

* International Soundex Reunion Registry in Carson City, Nevada, was a mutual-consent reunion registry for next of kin separated by adoption, divorce, foster care, abandonment, crisis, etc. It was considered *the* place to go to start a search when official channels were not open.

My mom sent me another article, this one about ALMA.* Then she got real sick. Cancer. We became close, and in the last year of her life, we talked on the phone every day. Even though she never talked about it, ever, I knew in my heart that she wanted me to find my daughter.

I was working in a home for abused children ages ten to eighteen, taking care of them, watching over them, playing with them. I liked my job a lot. It was when I started working there that I realized how abused I'd been, and I had work to do on myself. I took a couple of psychology classes and started seeing a counselor. I looked into my past and my relationships, and saw patterns. By the time I was forty, I had become someone who had gained a lot of self-worth and power, power that came with knowing who I was.

At this point Ray and I were having trouble. I had changed a lot and we were no longer on the same wavelength. We decided to divorce.

In my work with abused children, I came across stories that were hideous and I recognized that the abuse could happen to any-one, which made me frightened for my daughter. I had to start looking for her. I needed to know that she wasn't abused. So in November of 1993, I decided that I was as superwoman as I was ever going to be, and that I might never be financially secure. This was just going to have to be good enough. So I signed up with two reunion registries, and called around and found some people who would show me how to search.

In October, November, trying to start the search, to think of which way to go—the names on the birth certificate were wrong,

---

* The Adoptees Liberty Movement Association, an adoptee rights or-ganization and reunion registry.

everything was wrong—made me want to go back to bed emotionally. This was going to be hard.

In January of 1994, two months after I first started looking into searching, I got this heavy intuitive message, a thought that overpowered me: *Now is the time to start looking, and don't stop, no matter how tired or how worn out you get!* It was followed by another message: *You're a grandmother.* The message was so strong I couldn't ignore it. The next morning I called my aunt and told her I had to look for my daughter now, that I was really serious this time and I was not going to stop until I found out something.

"I was waiting for this," she said. She sounded excited and was happy to help.

The hospital where my baby had been born had been closed down and we couldn't find out where they had put the records. My uncle had died by this time, and even if he hadn't, my medical records had been kept by the doctor who signed everything, not by my uncle. My aunt said she'd try to find that doctor's records.

On January 26 my aunt called to tell me that the doctor had died many years before and his records had been destroyed. Another message ran across my brain. It felt as strong as the first one. The message assured me: *Don't worry. It's going to be easy.* My first reaction was: How can it be easy—my real name wasn't on any papers? But this serene feeling and repeated messages of how easy it was going to be kept me peaceful.

"Okay then," I said to my aunt, "we need to try to find the lawyer's name."

Neither of us could remember his name, but she had a couple of ideas about how to find out.

Two days later when I was coming home from work, Reuben, eighteen now, told me to call my aunt. I figured she hadn't been able to find the lawyer.

"Are you sitting down?" she asked.

"Yeah," I said, bracing myself for bad news.

"I just talked to your daughter."

It felt like a bolt of lightning hit me. My heart started pounding. I began to cry.

"How is she?"

"She's fine. Her name is Rochelle. She's got a child and she's married."

I couldn't stop crying.

"Dena, *she* found *you*. She called me today. Her mother had given her some papers, and apparently your real name *was* on something. I asked her a couple of questions just to make sure she was the one. She is."

"This is amazing!"

"I know. And she wants you to call her. But, Dena, compose yourself first."

I agreed and took down the phone number she gave me.

I ran in to tell Reuben. He and his girlfriend were in the living room. I grabbed him and pulled him aside to tell him. I was literally jumping up and down with joy. He was jazzed, especially to see how happy I was.

Then I tried to compose myself, but I soon realized that there was no composing, that I could wait forever and never be composed about this. So I called her.

"Hi. Is this Rochelle?"

"Yes," she said.

"I'm Dena Meyer."

"Oh my god!"

"I was looking for you, too!" I was crying and talking at the same time. "I wanted to know that you were okay."

She was fine. An intelligent, rational, warm, caring human being. I liked this person. For someone twenty-three years old, she had her life pretty together, much more than I did at that age. It was amazing to me that I was speaking to her. The only vision I had of her was as she had been in the bassinet in the hospital nursery, and even though she was in her twenties, I still thought of her as my baby.

I thought she would hate me for giving her up. She said she didn't, but I couldn't get that through my head. She said she always had the feeling that I cared for her, and after she had her own baby she began to understand how hard it must have been for me to give her up. She talked a lot about her son, Tyler, who was eighteen months old. My baby had a baby!

She had started looking for me in November, the same time I checked into searching for her. She was getting nowhere. Then on January 28 her adoptive mother was going through the safe deposit box and she came across Rochelle's adoption papers. Apparently I had used my real name on one. She gave Rochelle the papers. That same day Rochelle checked with Directory Assistance and found two people with that last name. My aunt was the second one she called.

I told her how I had started searching for her and about the messages that it was going to be easy and how protected I felt. It had only been two weeks from the time I called my aunt to start the search in earnest until Rochelle and I had our first phone conversation. I was convinced something more than the two of us was at work here. Where had those messages come from?

We spoke for over an hour and a half that first time. It was the most beautiful conversation I ever had. After I hung up, I wrote down her phone number in my address book under the name "My Baby."

She was real to me now, and I wanted to share the good news with my family. Except when my mother gave me the reunion registry information, we'd never talked about Rochelle. My sister was happy for me. She realized how much it meant to me. I left a message with my sister-in-law, telling my older brother the news, but he never called me back about it. I didn't know it until then, but my younger brother had never known about Rochelle. He was shocked, but happy. When I started looking into searching for her, I had told my dad, so he wasn't surprised when I called him. He was happy for me, but afraid that I would do something irrational, like pack up and move to where she was living.

Rochelle and I had so much to talk about that we spoke on the phone every day. I asked if she wanted to meet me in person. She did. That was all the encouragement I needed. I made a plane reservation.

I was so excited that I couldn't eat and I was awake for days. I worked at the shelter for adolescents in that shape and then realized it was a mistake. It was always my intention to never say anything to a teenager that would be wounding but, being pretty raw just then, I was having a hard time honoring that intention. So the third day I called my boss and told him what had happened and that I wasn't functioning well and needed to go home. He told me I could leave as soon as a replacement came in. Then I made an appointment to talk to him the next day.

When we met the next day, I explained that I needed to take time off to meet my daughter, that I had been waiting twenty-three years. He told me that I had no vacation time coming, and if I had already waited twenty-three years to meet her, I could wait a while longer.

I couldn't believe that. I had an especially difficult time with the fact that he, the director of a shelter for abused teenagers, refused the request of a woman who finally had a chance to heal her teenage wounds. I wanted to hit him. I said, "You do what you have to do. I'd like to work here, but I am going to see her."

"Then you'll have to resign," he said.

"If that's what you want, that's what I'll have to do."

"I want it in writing."

I said okay, although I had no intention of giving him a written resignation. We left it at that.

Two days later a friend from work called when they were in the middle of a staff meeting.

"Don't resign," my friend said. "I don't have time to explain what's going on. Just don't do anything yet."

Later she called to tell me that at the meeting the thirteen other employees talked about what had happened to me and how wonderful it was. My boss watched in amazement as my co-workers, not knowing he'd asked me to resign, took up a collection for my trip—one hundred and fifty dollars. After the meeting, he called me back to his office and asked me to forget our previous conversation, that I could have the time off. Once again, I felt protected.

A little less than two weeks before Rochelle found me, a friend gave me an article from the local newspaper about a support group of birth parents. I had never talked to anyone about how it felt to give a baby up. The counselor and I had talked about it in terms of abandonment issues, but we never really got into the nitty-gritty of how I felt as a result of losing her, not like I did with the other women in the support group.

Within less than a month, I had gone from not talking about it and having trouble searching to being found and talking to Rochelle on the phone every day, talking to my family, talking to the support group, telling the people at work, and making arrangements to go and see her—and I felt so peaceful about the whole thing. I could visualize the black hole that had been in my chest all those years starting to close. It was pretty remarkable, and I was convinced something not of this world was operating here.

Rochelle and I had exchanged pictures, but I didn't need a picture to recognize her. When I got off the plane, from the side and back I saw this short little person with dark hair. She turned around, and I knew it was her. We hugged and I started crying.

I kept repeating, "I just can't believe this is happening!"

"Dena," said Rochelle, holding up the baby, "I want you to meet your grandson, Tyler."

It was all so amazing!

Her adoptive grandparents were there, and she introduced me to them. They were sweet. Her grandfather said, "Thank you for the beautiful blessing you've given me." I started crying again. Rochelle had explained to me what a loving and guiding presence he'd been in her life, and here he was, thanking me when I thought I should be thanking him.

She then showed me a sign she'd made and had intended to hold up for me to see as I got off the plane, but because I got off the plane so quickly, she hadn't had time. The sign read, *It's a girl, Rochelle Marie, born March 20, 1969* with her birth height and weight. The sign was acknowledgment of the link between us. Rochelle and I kept holding on to each other as we walked through the airport, and it wasn't until we had to grab my luggage off the conveyor belt that we let go.

We drove to her house, where I met her husband, Greg, who was just getting home from work. Rochelle had made lasagna and baked a cake that said, "Welcome, Dena." I stayed there for the first couple of days. We talked most of the time. I told her everything that had happened, including information about her birth father. It was a lot for her to absorb.

The next day her adoptive parents came over to meet me. I started to cry when I met her mother. I was thankful to this woman for being Rochelle's mother and for having given her the adoption papers that led her to me. Rochelle's adoptive father shook my hand. He was quiet. They were probably in shock that she had found me so quickly and they still hadn't had time to adjust to the idea that I was there.

On Sunday my father and stepmother came out to meet Rochelle. They stayed with my aunt. I was going to stay with her for a few days too, so Rochelle dropped me off there. That's when she and my father first met. He asked her about her family and about how she was. He seemed concerned about whether giving her up had been the right thing. "We can't do anything to change the past," he told her, "but you have what you have now."

The next night Rochelle's adoptive grandparents invited everyone over to their house for dinner. We were all there—Rochelle, her husband and son, her adoptive parents and grandparents, me, my father and stepmother, my aunt. Having all of us in the same place was strange, and I was nervous. I did not want to have a serious or emotional discussion with anyone except Rochelle. But the two grandfathers kept the conversation light, talking mostly about their travels. The brightest moment of the evening for me was when Rochelle and I did the dishes together. We could feel the deep bond between us and were happy just to be together.

After I went home, Rochelle and I talked on the phone a few times a week. We made a pact that we would never lie to each other, and if one of us thought the truth would be too painful for the other to hear, we could choose to not tell it, but we would *never* lie. Even with our pact in place, I had trouble believing it when she told me that she didn't hate me for having given her up, but after a lot of discussion, I finally believed her. She and her adoptive parents were under the impression that I was fifteen when she was born. Her parents had explained to her that I was too young and unable to care for her, so out of love I'd given her up to people who could. Rochelle said she had always understood and accepted that. To her, I had served as a fantasy mom during her teenage years, when anyone but her own parents would have been great. Her only fear happened when she was looking for me—what if I had another family and I hadn't told them about her? While she regrets the time that's been lost with Reuben and me, she says she wouldn't trade the life she has.

That first year after our reunion was intense. Lots of pain, memories I had pushed back and forgotten, all came to the surface. Often I would be doing something, absorbed in what was going on, and I'd have a flashback from twenty years before and feel the intense sadness and anger that I'd never allowed myself to feel. I was angry at my parents, my aunt, my uncle. It took a while to work through. Every once in a while I still feel a little twinge of, "She was mine, and they took her," although now it's not nearly as intense. I've accepted what happened.

For years, when I thought about Earl, Rochelle's birth father, the only thing that came to mind was the word *ugly*. Now that I have her back in my life, I have a lot of anger toward him. He was so dangerous that it was unsafe for me to keep my daughter. I'd like someone to hold him so I could slowly beat him. An eye for an eye. Most of me hoped she didn't want to meet him. But I know it's her right, so I told her all I knew about him, including the fact he doesn't know she's alive. She said she has no desire to meet him.

When Rochelle's second son was born, I flew back there and spent a week with them. It was during that visit that my aunt told me she had held Rochelle in the hospital after she was born. It was comforting to me that someone in our family had held her with love. And at least I could now hold *her* baby.

The final part of my dream is that Rochelle and Reuben meet. They would like to, each being the other's vital biological link in this world. Unfortunately, we haven't had the money to send Reuben there yet. But I know that when I die, Rochelle will be his connection and that she will always keep the link.

I was seventeen when I gave Rochelle up for adoption, and it left a part of me stunted, still at that age. I have to grow that part of myself now. I have learned that there can be an end to the pain. Working with kids who were severely abused, going through counseling myself, and connecting with Rochelle all helped me get it together. I don't know if I'll ever be quite healed, but I feel totally different than I did before the reunion. I'm complete now. Having Rochelle in my life is a blessing.

7

Kate was not a member of our support group either. I met her when we looked for a preschool for our three-year-old daughter. I visited several before I found the small, child-centered environment I was looking for. Tall and slender, Kate was one of two women who operated the pre-school. I watched and listened as she guided toddlers with her soft voice and set limits for them with a stronger tone. All the kids looked engaged, relaxed. We enrolled Haley.

Whenever I dropped in, Kate was in serious eye-to-eye, heart-to-heart conversation with a child, or another was resting on her lap as she directed activities. She had a gift for understanding and communicating with children. Kate's father was an educator and her mother was an at-home mom and a favorite of neighborhood kids. This family was well equipped to welcome Kate's first child, and that was their initial plan.

But the medical and social work establishments at the time were geared toward another solution.

THE DECISION – Kate's Story

My mom was a child magnet. The kids in the neighborhood loved her. Frequently I'd come home after school and see her on the couch with her arm around a neighbor child who was crying and telling his story. It was hard to share her sometimes, but I was also proud to have her as a mom. She was a sweet and loving woman, and I thought she was the most beautiful woman in the world, a movie star.

I was born in 1950 and was the third of four kids in our family and the only girl. Every summer we camped. That's when I felt closest to my brothers and usually tagged along after my brother David. He was the one who wanted to find the top of the waterfall, build a dam, or catch a squirrel. Lee, the oldest, wanted to sit patiently on a rock and fish. Robert, my younger brother, would follow me around. I became a little mother to him.

My dad was a school administrator who believed in giving kids a lot of freedom. Sometimes he was a yeller, but his bark was worse than his bite. I was never spanked. When my siblings and I were angry with my parents, we were allowed to yell at them, and if my mom and dad felt they had been wrong, they would both come and apologize. That was a wonderful thing.

In 1963 our family moved a couple of hours away to a small California beach town. My father would be the new principal at the junior high I was to attend. I adored my dad. I would run up to people in my naïve way and proudly announce, "My dad's the principal!"

The town was one of those places where kids put one another into cliques, and once you were a part of a clique, you usually stayed in it. The in-group would hang out near the surfers. My girlfriends and I would go to a different area of the beach. We preferred to be silly, goofing around in the water, playing games, and exploring instead of trying to act sophisticated and cool.

I felt like I started to blossom when I turned seventeen. Every weekend my girlfriends and I went to dances and looked real hot. It was a heady experience to flirt with the guys and make them turn handsprings. I loved the wild craziness of it. Sometimes at a dance someone would shout, "Grunion are running!" and we'd run down to the beach without our shoes and try to catch the little, slimy fish. I wanted to be seventeen forever.

I had my first boyfriend that year. I met Jeff at a beach party my family and I went to. He was nineteen and a lifeguard, an occupation of special status in a beach town. I was delighted when he gave me attention, thinking his wanting me would make me okay in the eyes of other people.

My parents seemed embarrassed and uncomfortable talking about sex. They had told me they thought I should wait until I was married to have sex. They said that they had and were glad they did. By then I had concluded that sex was fun and acceptable, but I told them I would wait too. I thought the shame they felt around discussing sex would be transferred to shame about me, but if they didn't know what I was up to, then it wouldn't really matter. So I began to live a double life. In one I was the person that I thought it was okay to be. In the other I was the person I thought my parents would approve of. Jeff and I did have sex a few times, and thirteen months after we'd starting dating, we broke up.

This was 1966, 1967, and where I lived, girls did not use birth control. We didn't even talk about it. The Pill was still fairly new, and condoms were thought of as kind of dirty. For most of us sex was more something you got carried away with. For birth control we used the pull-out method.

Shortly after starting junior college, I met Eric. He looked like the ultimate guy—blond hair down to his well-developed shoulders, tan, mustache. I even liked the clothes he wore, the Arrow shirts, baggy pants, and work boots. He walked like a surfer, confident, tossing his hair now and then. He was just *it*, my fantasy person, and out of my league. I didn't even think he'd notice me. So when a woman friend of his mentioned that he wanted to ask me out, I was floored. All that afternoon I was giddy, smiling and giggling.

That night I went back to campus, where I knew he and his friend were doing janitorial work for their student work-loan program. They came and sat at my table and we talked, then the three of us walked their rounds together, laughing and talking as we all erased chalkboards. When we got to the acting room, Eric told me he had just seen me in the school play *Tiger at the Gates*, in which I'd played the role of Helen of Troy. I felt put on the spot. So that's who he thought I was! I had looked real hot in the play, but it had taken tons of make-up and a really sexy costume. I thought that if I wanted to keep him interested, that was the image I would have to live up to.

Becoming Eric's girlfriend meant I finally got to hang out with the in-crowd. I went to the pool hall and watched him play pool, or to the beach and watched him surf. Eric liked being idolized and I loved idolizing him. Afraid to let him know who I really was, I would talk about things I felt would earn his approval. I even worried about how he would handle it when summer came and he found out his girlfriend didn't tan.

I told him I loved him long before he told me he loved me, although I don't think we knew what our sincere feelings were. I was eighteen, he was nineteen, and as we tried to figure out who we were, we operated out of hormones, social expectations, and how we were seen.

There was a sweet side to Eric that deeply touched my heart. He lived with his sister and her husband and their two children, whom he helped take care of. One time we were sitting on the couch together and heard his little niece call from the bedroom. Eric ran down to her room, picked her up, carried her into the bathroom, and waited while she threw up. He then held her before he carried her back on his shoulders. He was gentle and loving with the kids.

After four months of being together all the time, Eric told me that he was breaking up with me, that there was someone else he wanted to date. I felt like I'd been socked in the stomach. I wasn't ready to let go. Desperate, I blatantly pursued him. I had no shame. I'd drive past the places we used to go or past his sister's house to see if he was home. When I couldn't find him, I'd drive around and look for his van. If I found him at a public place— the beach or the pool hall—I'd pop in as if by coincidence.

It was at this time my family was getting ready to move. My father was leaving his job in order to participate in a special program for educators at the University of Miami and then work on his doctorate. It would take two years, then we'd go back to California. Just finishing my freshman year at the junior college and with my part-time job at the preschool paying only a dollar an hour, I wasn't able to support myself yet. So I planned to go to Florida with my parents and younger brother. We had to sell our house, pack up everything, and leave within a month. I was taking finals, finishing up the play, and wrapping up all of the things I was involved with in order to go across the country with my family.

Then Eric asked me out again. We had been split up for about two months, but I wanted to see him one more time before we left for Miami. One part of me was just trying to get myself back in line and forget this guy, and another part was still hopelessly in love with him and wanted his arms around me again. I had a secret hope that now that he'd been away from me for a while, he'd realize what he'd lost and want me back.

We went to a drive-in movie. The mood was light and happy as we started to watch *The Yellow Submarine*. Then he suggested we move into the back of the van, where he had a mattress on plywood. It was as if I suddenly woke up and didn't like the way I was being treated, and for the first time, I stood up to him.

"You know," I said, "you think I got the better deal here. But I'm more than you ever thought I was. You don't even know me. I never even let you because I was so afraid of losing The Great Eric. I don't know why I did that," then I looked him in the eye, "because I'm every bit as good as you are."

He was a little taken aback, but he listened as I vented. Within those few minutes all the anger I felt at being dumped came out and suddenly I didn't have a big stake in having him back again. I liked the person I was at that moment, strong and confident instead of trying to impress and please him.

He was a little sheepish and a little bit like, "You don't really think that, do you?"

The tension between us broke. And he treated me nicer. We were in a lighter mood and went back to his house for coffee. I went because we were like old friends, laughing, teasing, and joking, and I wanted to give him a different impression of who I was, one where I was strong and self-assured instead of a door-mat.

We were in his room and laughing and talking. I was kind of putting him down and he was teasing me back. Then he was kissing me, and I was enjoying the physical sensations of it and the fact that he wanted me. I knew that he wouldn't stay with me, that it was over, and I felt ripped off by myself for allowing myself to get in this position. But I didn't think we would have sex—it wasn't a safe time and I could get pregnant. I guess I felt partially responsible for bringing it to that point, but I did try to stop him. I said, "This is not a safe time for me." And it bothered me that he didn't stop. I told him so and tried to stop him. I shouldn't have let it go as far as I did. I wasn't thinking. I didn't think he would pressure and go through with it, but he did. He entered me, and I was trying to get him to pull out. Afterward I shoved him off.

"You just got me pregnant!"

"Don't say that."

"I can feel it. You did. You just got me pregnant." I was pissed. "And I'm moving to Miami, and you'll never even know. I'll never tell you, and you'll always wonder." I knew it was a dig, and the fact it affected him gave me power.

He drove me home. When he dropped me off, I wanted to feel as if I had the upper hand. I gave him a quick good-bye hug, got out of the truck, and tried to sound casual as I said, "See ya," shut the door, and left.

A week or so later I started getting sick to my stomach. A few weeks later, when my period was a little over a week late, I went to a doctor. "I'm almost convinced you're not pregnant," said the doctor. "The cervix changes almost immediately, and there is no change here. I'm going to give you four birth control pills. Take them. They should bring on your period."

I told my mom that I hadn't been feeling well and was going to see a doctor. When I got back, she asked me what the doctor had said. "Oh, he said it was just stress—school, finals, the move. He gave me these pills," I said, showing her the four pills. "They're a mild tranquilizer to help me relax." I didn't know birth control pills looked identifiable. My mother must have recognized them, but she didn't say anything. I took them as he directed, but no period.

Flying to Miami was my first time on a plane. I felt nauseated. Maybe it was air sickness? Mom kept watching me, but didn't say anything.

When we got to Miami, we lived in a motel while we looked for a house to rent. It was unbelievably hot, with a damp, muggy smell that was foreign to me, and I was so sick. One time when my dad and brother were going out, my dad asked if anything sounded good to eat.

"How about some lime sherbet?" I said.

They brought me back a pint of it, then went off to swim in the motel pool. I ate the sherbet, and then just heaved it all. When I came back and sat on the bed, my mom came over, sat down next to me, and put her arm around me. And I think I just said, "You think I'm pregnant, don't you?"

"No!" she said. I could hear the loyalty and trust in her tone. Then with a worried *But I know better* voice, she asked, "Are you?"

"I don't know."

"Could you be?"

"Yes. I went to the doctor."

"You told me that. What did he say?"

"He said he was almost sure I'm not pregnant."

"Who's the father?"

"Eric."

Eric had come to our house only a couple of times. He hadn't been comfortable around my parents, and they had not been comfortable with him. They recognized him as someone who ran with a faster crowd.

"Well," she said, "we'll have to get you another doctor some way. I'm not going to tell Dad yet, because we're not sure."

"Okay."

"In the meantime, don't eat lime sherbet. Don't eat any citrus. Don't drink coffee. Eat soda crackers first thing in the morning, before you eat anything else." She knew about morning sickness. She'd had it from conception to birth with all four of her pregnancies.

The next morning when we went to eat breakfast on the college campus, I started to take orange juice, and she shook her head no very slightly, giving me the signal to put it back because it would make me sick. On the things that were okay to eat, she'd nod her head. She was very loving.

I knew life would never be the same. Here I was, nineteen, and either I wasn't pregnant and life would go on as it was before but I'd be a lot more careful, or I was pregnant and was going to have to deal with I-had-no-idea-what. It was too big to even look at and I kept trying to wish it away. After a couple more days of getting feedback from Mom about what was happening to my body, we were certain. We didn't need the doctor to tell us. I was having classic morning sickness, my breasts were tender—I was an exact mirror of her when she was pregnant.

My mom and dad had been going out and meeting people he'd be taking classes with, a lot of couples, many of them with kids, some even my own age. My dad started making plans for me and told people what a great babysitter I was. "Kate," my mom said, "I've got to tell him. We can't have him starting to set you up with jobs or for dates with their sons. You're going to have to decide what you want to do. But I just can't keep it from him." That night they were going to a big party. She suggested that she tell him on the way there, so he wouldn't make arrangements with people for something I wouldn't be comfortable with. I agreed.

I stayed home with my younger brother, Robert, now thirteen, and watched TV with him. I paced back and forth. "Dad's finding out now," I thought. "He knows now. He knows." My brother and I went to bed on the mattresses we'd set up on the living room floor so we could sleep in front of the box fan. I lay tossing and turning, listening for their car to pull in and wondering what he was going to think, what he was going to say. Then I heard them coming up the stairs. I closed my eyes and pretended to be asleep. I didn't want to see him disappointed in me.

Then my dad did the most wonderful thing. He came in, knelt down on the mattress, and gently hugged me. Very quietly he said, "It'll be nice to have a little one around the house." Then he kissed me on the cheek and left.

I lay there and silently cried. This wasn't at all how I had thought it would be. I had thought that if you got pregnant before you were married, you were sent away to have the baby, you gave the baby up for adoption, then you came home. That's what happened to classmates who'd gotten pregnant. But here I had a mother who was being supportive, loving, and helpful, and a father who said it would be nice to have a little one around the house. It blew me away, and for the first time I stopped to feel what was happening inside of me. I was going to have a baby, and I could keep my baby!

We told my younger brother, Robert. He was happy but a little worried about me, and maybe a little embarrassed knowing that his sister was sexually active. I wrote to each of my older brothers about the pregnancy, and they both sent letters of support.

Financially things were tight. The big risk of this whole venture for my father was the financial one. We would have no money coming in for a couple of years while Dad finished the program and then completed his doctorate. We planned to live on what little savings we had, which on a principal's salary wasn't much, and on the proceeds from the sale of our house, which also was not much.

We left student housing and rented a furnished house. For some reason the owner had taken the legs off all of her furniture, so everything sat down low, a challenge for our tall family. There was a beautiful aquarium and I had my own bedroom and my own bathroom. The bedroom had bunk beds, and we piled the extra mattresses on top of each other to make it easier for me to get in and out of bed as the pregnancy progressed.

We went to the university medical center to get me checked out. Dr. Schuling, the doctor who examined me, was an intern and looked about sixteen. As expected, the pregnancy test was positive. They told me that I was healthy and everything was fine. When Dr. Schuling found out I was not married, he left the room and came back with somebody else. They said they were sorry, but they didn't realize what was going on and he was not qualified to be my physician, but since Dr. Schuling had done the initial exam, he would stay with me during my prenatal care and as long as the pregnancy was going normally. They wanted me to meet with Dr. Donovan over at the hospital at least once and said he would be my resident doctor. At the birth, they would both be there. Then Dr. Schuling asked what I was planning to do.

"I'm planning to have a baby," I told him.

"And you're going to keep the baby?" he asked.

"Yes. My parents are fine with it "

On my next visit they wanted me to talk to a psychiatrist and a social worker. Neither my parents nor I had asked to see anyone else. I think we were being plugged into a system. These were people who were experienced in dealing with this situation and whose job was to guide us to choices that would be best for me and best for the baby.

The psychiatrist came in and asked me questions that seemed totally unrelated and crazy. I didn't understand why he was asking them.

"Tell me what 'still waters run deep' means," he asked.

I didn't know.

"If you could have one wish," he asked, "what would it be?"

"World peace," I answered. This was during the Vietnam War, and that was what came to mind. I didn't even think to wish I wasn't pregnant.

"What is meant by the expression, 'People in glass houses shouldn't throw stones'?"

"Well, if you throw a stone you might break your house."

At nineteen, I had no grasp of these abstract ideas. Afterward I talked to my parents about it. My dad said the psychiatrist was trying to find out if I had any hidden feelings of anger or was upset about being pregnant and if I wished I wasn't pregnant. "Not since you guys are okay with it," I told him.

After the psychiatrist talked to me, he talked to each of my parents separately. When Mom came out from talking with him, I could see she'd been crying. I was surprised and wondered what was going on. I realized that on some level this was hurting her. Maybe it wasn't really okay with my parents.

Then they had me talk with the social worker. "Hi, I'm Mrs. Lund," she said. "I'm a social worker and I want to talk with you about your situation. How are you feeling about all of this?"

"I'm doing okay."

"Tell me about yourself." She presented herself as a cool, with-it kind of person, and I got the sense that she wanted to be a friend. I felt warmed by her attention.

I began talking to her about what my life had been like, about school, and about our move. I told her about how kind and loving my parents were being about the pregnancy. I also confessed guilt that I'd had sex before this, but my parents believed this was the first time.

"It's okay," she said. "You're old enough to make your own decisions, and you certainly don't have to tell your parents about everything you do." Then she asked me what I was planning to do about my situation.

"Well, I'm going to have a baby and I'm going to keep it. My parents are fine with it, and I really want to keep the baby."

"Okay. We're going to talk some more. This is a big decision and you shouldn't make it that lightly. I want you to think about this from all perspectives." She said we'd meet again.

Physically, being pregnant was like being in a foreign land, so much about my body was different. My nails were growing long, my breasts were larger, my hair became glossy and pretty, and my skin cleared up. I hadn't started to show yet, so I still had a good figure. I don't think I'd ever looked so good, and I was feeling fairly good about myself.

Nausea bothered me, and I begged for medication just so I could keep food down. Dr. Schuling gave me something to help with it. Later, when I met Dr. Donovan, he got upset that I'd been taking that medication and he took me off it immediately. That scared me. Now I was worried that the baby might have something wrong because I had taken that medication.

I met with Mrs. Lund, the social worker, two or three more times. She said she was aware that right now I wanted to keep the baby, but young women often found things they had not thought about came to mind during pregnancy. She thought I would probably need to have more time to think about what I really wanted to do. In the meantime, she said, she would like me to meet with people who could handle things if I did decide to give up the baby. She wanted me to meet with Mrs. Krueger of Children's Home Society.

Mrs. Krueger was a short, heavyset woman in her late fifties, a sweet and kind grandmotherly type who also had a sense of efficiency about her, a sense of "this has been done before and you can trust me." She talked about how the Children's Home Society placed babies and selected suitable parents. If I made the

251

decision to place the baby, they would ask me lots of questions to find out what I wanted and they would get physical descriptions of family members so they could to try to match the baby with a family that looked similar. She introduced me to the person in charge of placing babies. They introduced me to some of the other girls and said they wanted me to go to their meetings.

My parents drove me to the meetings, where the staff explained to the women there what was going to happen during the pregnancy and birth. One woman in the group was menopausal and pregnant and planned to give her baby up for adoption. But most of the women were young.

One time Paula, one of the other pregnant women, and I were both in the bathroom, and we started talking.

"I can't keep my baby," she told me. "It's absolutely not an option. My mother would never let me come home. And I have no place else to go and no money." Paula started to cry. "What about you? What are you going to do?" she asked.

"Oh, I'm keeping my baby." Then I said, "You know, you could too. There's a way, I'm sure."

"No, not for me. It's impossible. I'm not even going to consider it. I'm giving it up for adoption."

I felt sad for her and lucky for me, happy I didn't have to make that decision.

The social worker and I talked a few times. She encouraged me to look at what it would mean in my life to keep the baby. Slowly I began to realize that I really hadn't made a decision. I had been more like a little kid who says, "I get to keep the puppy." When she asked me to think about what it would mean to my parents, that got to me. Everything was put into a different light when I thought about more than just myself. It started to feel selfish to keep the baby when I thought about what it would mean for my parents. The caretaker part of me was worried about what people could say about them, even more than what they would say about me.

Dad believed it was important to give kids a lot of say in what was happening in their world. The conservative old guard in our town had been in an uproar over his methods at the junior high school. I had heard public criticism of my father's ideas. He took a lot of flak from outraged parents and was frequently bashed in the newspaper. Now here was this liberal man with a daughter "in trouble." To go back there with a baby would be like giving them ammunition to say, "See what liberal gets you—a pregnant daughter." But we were three thousand miles away from home. I could have the baby and give it up for adoption, and no one there would ever have to find out.

"It's just so easy that nobody knows," I said to my parents. "It really bothers me to think of what some people will say."

"Oh, we don't care what they think anyway," my dad said. He was used to dealing with flak.

I talked about it with my mother, who shared some of my concerns for him, but she seemed more concerned for me. She suggested telling everyone back home that the baby was hers and she would raise the child as hers. "I'm not too old," she said. "I could have gotten pregnant again. We could just say I thought I was in menopause. How would you feel about it if we did that?" She wanted to both keep this child and protect us from public backlash.

"I don't think I could handle hearing my own child call you mom. It'd tear me up," I said. "What will we tell the child? Would it grow up thinking I'm its sister? I don't think I could handle the pretending and lying."

Meanwhile, over the course of months the social worker was asking questions like: How are you going to raise this child? How are you going to support yourself? Who's going to support you? Are you going to put this on your parents? Do they have to take care of it? It's your thing. You did it. Is it fair to ask your parents to pay the expenses for and raise your child? You can't get a job. If you do get a job, who's going to baby-sit the baby? Your mother's going to have to do that? Is that fair to ask of your mother? If you go back to school, who's going to take care of the baby?

I had no answers.

My parents tried as hard as they could not to sway me. They believed the decision was mine, and they would accept whatever I decided.

Mrs. Lund asked if it was an option for me to marry the father.

"No," I said.

"And that is because?"

"Because he doesn't love me. And I don't think I love him in the way I want to love the man I would spend the rest of my life with. It just feels like a poor reason to get married. So no, that's not an option. He wouldn't marry me anyway."

Part of me fantasized he would, though. I imagined Eric showing up and being so completely taken with how gorgeous I looked and with my beautiful belly that he would want the baby. Or that he'd see the baby after it was born and fall in love with it and with me and we would live happily ever after. But I didn't really believe it would happen.

I had written him a letter telling him I was pregnant. I said that I hadn't decided yet if I was going to raise the baby or not. "I don't expect anything," I wrote, "but I thought you had a right to know."

A couple of weeks later he sent me a letter in a handmade envelope on which he had drawn flowers using different color inks. It was something he had taken time and care with, giving a part of himself. It was so sweet, and when I saw it, it touched the fantasy part of me: *He wants me! He wants to keep the baby!* But in the letter he said that he was not ready to be a father, that he didn't know what he could offer and he was sorry I was going through this. He also said that he didn't have any money and could not offer financial support.

Things were looking pretty doom-and-gloom to me. Either the baby and I would be destitute or we'd have to live with my parents, putting a tremendous burden on them. There was no mention of foster care or financial help if I kept the baby. But if I gave the baby up for adoption, all medical expenses would be paid for. Then I could pick up my life again, too. Was I really ready to settle down and be a mother? There was a message that I was immature, unready to raise a child, didn't have my life together, and was living with my parents, who had just taken a big financial risk. So wouldn't the child have a better life if he or she had two mature parents ready to have a baby, and financially able to take care of all its needs?

In a way the waiting was a sweet time for us as a family. We visited tourist places and we got tons of books at the library. I read a book a day. Mom was home and the two of us spent a lot of time together. My brother Robert would laugh when I had a book propped on my belly and the baby had hiccups and the book would bounce up and down. He'd put his hand on my stomach and feel the baby kick. He helped me up out of the low chairs when I got big. During that time, the baby was acknowledged as family. Now and then we went into a store and looked at baby clothes or toys. Or we'd see a baby on TV and we'd all ooh and aah. There was a lot of want for this baby. My mom wanted it. My father wanted it. My brother wanted it. And I wanted it. We all *really* wanted it.

The decision weighed on my mind. I'd try to picture the baby and wished I could see through my belly. I talked to it. I lay on my bed and put my foot against the wall and rocked to soothe myself and felt like I was rocking the baby. I'd fall asleep rocking. Although everyone was telling me the decision was mine, I got the feeling that I was missing something, not seeing what was expected of me. I had the same dream over and over again. It changed in location and setting, but it had the same basic plot. I would be in some crowded, congested area, like my high school or college campus, and I was supposed to get somewhere—a class or a job. But I couldn't open my eyes completely and my vision was hazy. I tried to make my way through the crowds of people, but I couldn't see clearly where I was going. I was supposed to perform before people, but when I got there I didn't know what I was supposed to say or do. In one dream I was supposed to perform in a play, but I couldn't remember any of my lines. Another time I was supposed to recite a lecture, but I couldn't even remember what the class was about. As soon as I made the decision, the dreams stopped.

I got a letter from a high school friend of mine. She too was pregnant and had been sending me letters telling me about her pregnancy. She was a month farther along than I was, so from her letters I could see what was ahead for me. She was isolated, too, living with an aunt, and planning to give the baby up for adoption. Here I was on the other side of the country, also pregnant and isolated. I didn't tell her about my pregnancy. I felt disloyal, but we wanted to keep it quiet until I made a decision. Another part of it was the shame. In high school we had talked about all the girls who went away and had their babies and then came back. Part of me was afraid of being one of those girls talked about behind everybody's back.

After her baby was born, she wrote and told me it was a girl and said, "I held her."

Until then I thought that if I gave the baby up, they would take it from me and I'd never even know if I had a boy or a girl. I would never get to hold it, never know if it was healthy. Carrying something in my body for nine months and having this incredible love for it, talking to it, singing to it, rubbing it, feeling it, rocking it, and then to have it taken away and never have an image of what that baby looked like or who it was—that would be excruciating. I thought the only way I would be able to see my baby was if I decided to raise it myself. When I read that she had seen and held her baby, and then relinquished her for adoption, that became a whole new option for me. When I asked the Children's Home Society about it, they told me yes, I could see and hold the baby.

"All right, then," I told Mrs. Krueger, "I'm going to do that. And I'd like to nurse it, because I'd like it to have colostrum."

They were not real keen on that. "Well, that could be really difficult for you."

"But it's important for the baby," I said.

So I would have the baby, and hold it and nurse it, then I would lovingly give it to someone who would be a better family for the baby, and it would be a better thing for my family. I felt tremendous relief when I made that decision.

Because I'd been careless, I had put everyone through a lot. I hadn't wanted to put this burden on my parents. This way I could take full responsibility and all the negatives would be gone. It would not cost them any money, they would not have to take care of me, they would not have to take care of the baby, no one would ever have to know, my father would not have to take any heat back home, and we could all pick up life where we'd left off.

We still hadn't told anyone back home or any other relatives besides my brothers that I was pregnant. Now, since I had decided to give up the baby for adoption, we would continue to keep it a secret. That way we wouldn't hurt my grandmother. Nana, my mom's mom, was very family oriented, and my giving up the baby would have meant she would lose her first great-grandchild. That would be just too devastating for her. Nana could never know. To be certain she wouldn't find out, we couldn't tell anyone.

I was given questionnaires to fill out. Mrs. Krueger of Children's Home Society asked questions about Eric and me. She asked if there was anything I did not want in a parent, whether I had any strong beliefs or feelings about any type of person. I told her that I didn't want the child to be raised in an orthodox religion. At the time I said orthodox, but I meant fundamentalist. I talked about how I would discipline a child. I had read Haim Ginott's book about communicating with your children without shame. I liked the way he talked to kids, honoring their feelings.

At the end of January 1970, only a week after I'd made the decision, my water broke. We called the doctor. He told me to go into the hospital. So I took a shower and my parents drove me to the hospital, where I was put in a wheelchair and taken to the maternity ward. My parents weren't allowed to come with me.

Through the meetings I'd attended at Children's Home Society I had gotten a little information about what to expect, but everything was unusual. Except for my own birth, I had been in a hospital only one other time, and that was to see Dr. Donovan, the physician who would handle the delivery.

They prepped me and put me in the labor room, where there were two beds, but I had the room to myself. They laid me down on a bed, flat on my back, with a pillow for my head. I was not allowed to get out of bed. If I had to go to the bathroom, I had to wait for someone to bring me a bedpan. They gave me a button to push for a nurse.

Labor didn't start, so they wanted to induce it. The doctor on staff, with his stocky build and crew cut, had an attitude like a marine sergeant. "Hello," he said, then he asked something about my husband.

"I'm not married."

His attitude shifted from open and smiling to stern and walled-off. He radiated anger. He inserted an IV in my hand and missed the vein and pushed it in pretty hard. It was painful. Each time he asked if something hurt, he had a smile on his face. I felt like he was enjoying my pain. When he examined me internally, it was always with a great deal of force. I was afraid of this man.

They gave me Demerol through the IV and came in to check on me once in a while. My labor did not progress. I would start to have contractions, or at least what I thought were contractions except it was mostly excruciating pain in my lower back, but when he would walk in, it would stop. "You're *still* not doing anything?" he'd ask, as if I was doing something wrong.

All day I lay in bed, dreading it every time the doctor would come in the room. He was belittling to my regular doctor, the intern Dr. Schuling, as well. Then Dr. Donovan came in. When the staff doctor saw him, the change in him was like night to day. He started smiling and laughing, turned into a real sugar-coated guy. He came up and caressed my shoulder, "Well our girl's just doing a great job here." When he left the room, I looked at Dr. Donovan and said, "Keep him out of here or I can't do this. The contractions seem to start and he comes in and they stop. I can't do this if that man comes in anymore." They sent him away and Dr. Donovan sat in a chair by my bed. Then Dr. Schuling came and stayed with me the rest of the night.

Finally contractions started. I was still on my back and having back pain. I don't know why to this day no one had me roll on my side or sit up. It was like I was sick. Finally I had two whomping hard contractions. Dr. Donovan gave me a cervical block. Then I didn't feel anything.

"You stopped it!" I said.

"No, it's still happening," he said.

I lay there, looking around, not feeling any contractions, and they put me on a gurney and wheeled me down to the delivery room. Stainless steel, boxes on the walls, metal doors and cabinets—it all looked so sterile, so cold. They put my legs up in padded stirrups and then put blankets around them. The blankets felt good. Then they put another blanket over my raised legs, cutting off my view of the bottom half of my body. It was like a tent with the doctor and nurses all sitting on one side of it while I was on the other, unable to see what was happening. They gave me a gas mask and told me if I needed to I could breathe into it. Then I felt some pressure. I think it was the baby's head coming out. I put my hand down toward it, and someone quickly grabbed my wrist and strapped down my hands. The next real pain was the feeling of a needle. They had given me an episiotomy and were stitching it up. I could feel the needle going in and I complained.

"Breathe into the mask," Dr. Donovan told me.

"I can't. I'm strapped down."

"Unstrap her arms!" he said.

They did, and I breathed into the mask. The gas made me sick to my stomach. Someone brought a wastebasket for me, and I threw up into it. Then I heard a cry over on the side of the room. "What's that?" I asked. "What's that sound? Is that a baby?"

"Yes. Your baby was born."

"What did I have?"

"It's a boy."

"I want to see him."

Then I felt someone give me a shot. "That will dry up your milk," she said.

"I want to see him. I want to see the baby."

"We're cleaning him up."

"Can I see the baby?"

There was a quiet in the room.

"Please can I see the baby?" I asked again.

A nurse brought him over to me. He had a white blanket wrapped around him. His face was red, he had dark hair, and his eyes were closed. I felt like I was doing something wrong by asking to see him, and I didn't want to impose myself on anyone, so I touched his head for a brief moment and let go. Then they took him away.

I was wheeled into the recovery room. The nurse came in and took a washcloth and wiped it all over my face. There was no gentleness in it, no personal touch. I felt like a little kid getting her dirty face cleaned. She lifted my gown and with both hands pressed down hard on my abdomen. I didn't expect her to do that. And it hurt. I felt like the wind had been knocked out of me. She threw the cover back over me and said, "You're going to be here for a while," and left.

They let my mom come into the recovery room. She looked at me, gave me a hug, and cried. "Poor honey," she said.

"It was pretty hard," I told her.

She wanted to stay with me, but because there was another patient there, they sent Mom away after about two minutes.

Then they moved me again. I think they didn't want me around other patients who had had babies, so they gave me a private room. They gave me a heat light under the bed for the stitches, which felt good, and some Tucks or something. They finally brought me the most horrible meal, an awful tasting meatloaf, and I couldn't eat it. I hadn't eaten in over a day. I slept very little. All I could think about was how uncomfortable I was and how awful the experience had been. I wanted to see the baby again. When I asked, they told me he was in intensive care. They said so much time had elapsed from the time my water broke until he was born that they were afraid he'd been exposed to infection. They wanted to test him to make sure everything was okay. It was just precautionary, they told me. I wanted to nurse him, but they had given me a shot to dry up the milk. When I asked why, they said because they knew the baby was going into intensive care.

I was worried, frightened, and crying, when this sweet young woman, a volunteer worker, came in. "What's the matter, honey?" she asked.

"I want to see my baby and I can't because he's in intensive care."

"Well you go on down there and see him," she encouraged me. "You can look through the window and see him."

Then I told her that I was giving him up for adoption.

"You know, you don't have to do that," she told me. "Nobody can make you give up your baby! You keep that baby!" She was emphatic. I was surprised by that.

"You don't understand," I said, "I'm not crying because I'm giving up the baby. I'm crying because I just want to hold him."

"Okay," she said, "but you know, nobody can make you give up your baby. If you want to keep him, you keep him."

After the months of indecision, I had finally made this choice, and I didn't want anybody to get me thinking again. It would be too much to go back into all that confusion. "I don't want to talk about it," I told her, and she left.

Then my parents came to visit me. I had asked them to bring me food, and they did—a Whopper, a chocolate shake, and French fries. I was so grateful.

I went to see him in intensive care the next day. There was a tiny window six inches wide that I could look through. He wasn't in with the other babies. He was in a little room by himself. They were poking a needle into his heel and squeezing blood out of it. I had such a strong desire to hold him, but they told me I couldn't. It seemed like everything had an explanation: "No, you can't see him because your water broke and you didn't give birth quickly enough," and, "You can't hold him because we have to make sure everything is okay," and, "You can't nurse him because we have to do tests on him," and, "You're sad because you have post-partum depression."

Mrs. Lund, the social worker, came to see how I was doing. Then I got a visit from Mrs. Krueger of the Children's Home Society. I told her that I was upset I couldn't hold the baby.

"You can hold him," she said. "You can come to the Children's Home Society and we'll have a room there where you can hold him."

I felt better about it then, not quite so bereft.

I left after five days. I'm not sure how long the baby was in the hospital. I think around seven to ten days. I had the impression that, because he was being given up for adoption, they kept him there while they were getting a foster home ready for him. They kept reassuring me he was okay. I tried to trust that he was being taken care of. I felt like he wasn't mine anymore and I had no more rights.

When he was two weeks old, my parents, my brother Robert, and I all went to the Children's Home Society to see him. While we waited, I saw a woman in a room holding a baby over her shoulder and slowly walking the floor with him. I could just see the baby's face over her shoulder. It was him. He looked like a picture of my oldest brother when he was born. He had lots of dark hair. His eyes were large and dark baby blue. Tiny chin. Perfect features. Very, very, very beautiful baby. The woman must have been the foster mother.

They took us into a room and then they brought him in and handed him to me. I was overwhelmed with love. I also felt awkward. I didn't know quite how to hold his body so he was comfortable and I thought I should know. I'd thought he'd just kind of melt into my arms like he had melted into me when he was in my belly. Instead, holding him felt strange.

I asked my mom to hold him. She had the knowingness of what to do with a baby and he seemed more relaxed and secure in her arms. We all clustered around while she had him on her knees, holding his head cupped in her hands. Of course we had to open the blanket and look at him. It was good to see all of him.

"He's beautiful," my father said. "Kate, you can feel really proud of what a good job you did. He's a healthy baby."

That was wonderful to hear. While I knew I had given him the best start I knew how to give, they had kept him in intensive care so long, and I worried that maybe the medicine I'd taken for the nausea, or my not having given birth quickly enough, had hurt him.

Robert took a turn at holding him. Robert was grinning, but it was awkward for him too, and pretty soon he passed him on. Dad laughed and smiled when he held him. Then he took a couple of pictures of my mother holding him on her knees and me sitting next to them.

When the head of the Children's Home Society came in to see how we were doing, we all got teary. They had told me I could see him, and now I had. I knew it was time to live up to my part of the bargain.

Mrs. Krueger took me into her office and talked to me. She told me he was being adopted by a couple in their late twenties to early thirties who already had other children. She wouldn't tell me how many other children, just "at least one adopted child and at least one natural child." She said they would be able to care for him well financially. They didn't live in Miami, had a boat, liked to go camping, and went to church but were not fundamentalist in their beliefs. She thought it was a good match as far as physical attributes in my family and theirs. She reassured me that he would be well taken care of.

Then I gave her the book *Between Parent and Child,* by Ginott. "Would you give the parents this? Would you let them know that this is how I would have wanted him to be raised, and maybe if they haven't read it, they'll read it and it'll have an effect on how they see him."

She said she would.

At that point I just wanted to get out of there. I didn't want to deal with anything else and I didn't want to break down. As we went over to the courthouse, I kept thinking, *I hope he knows I love him. I hope he can remember somehow, that some part of him deep down inside will know.* I tried to focus on what my father had said, that I'd done a good job.

We had to wait a while in the courtroom before they called my name. Then the judge asked me if anyone had coerced me, threatened me, or forced me to make this decision.

"No," I answered.

Did I realize the decision I was making? Was it of my own free will?

"Yes."

They may have asked me about the birth father, but I'd already told the Children's Home Society that he had said he couldn't help me or support me or the baby. They gave me a paper to sign, and I did. That was it.

No one told me what would come next. I thought I'd just resume my life. I felt relief that it was over, that I'd finally made the decision, and I believed I had done the right thing and gotten everybody off the hook. It had taken almost a year out of my life, but now we could go back to normal.

I wrote to Eric and told him everything I could about the baby, what he weighed, what he looked like, and what I knew about the family he was being placed with. I remember that he'd written back, although I can't remember now what he said, something to the effect that he was sorry I had to go through it and thanking me for letting him know.

About three weeks after the baby was born, we got a call from the Children's Home Society. They told us that Paula, the woman I had first talked to in the bathroom at the home and later befriended during the pregnancy, had changed her mind and decided she was going to raise her child. The foster home parents where she had been staying during her pregnancy had three kids of their own and they didn't want her there with the baby. So Paula and her baby had no place to go. Because we'd become friends and spent time together during our pregnancies, Children's Home Society thought of us as a place for her and the baby to stay while she figured out what she was going to do. But they and my parents were concerned that maybe her coming into our household with her baby would upset me. My parents asked me how I felt about it. I was feeling sure of my own decision and that I was a stronger person for having done this difficult thing and could handle anything now.

Paula slept in my room, and we put the bassinet between our beds. She was physically and emotionally overwhelmed. The birth had been physically tough, she was terrified of facing her mother and everyone at home, and she didn't know what to do with a baby. People were upset with her for changing her mind, but I thought she was brave to stand her ground.

Mom and I helped take care of the baby. We held her, fed her, and changed her. I would get up with the baby at night and walk the floor with her. She was so cute and funny looking, with squinty little eyes and great big fat cheeks, and I loved holding her. It was hard, too, in that she cried a lot, and I could see it wasn't easy to have a newborn. It gave me the chance to see what it might have been like for me.

My mom had been worried that having Paula and the baby in the house would put me into a tailspin depression, so it was a great relief to her that I handled it okay. All of us enjoyed having the baby there. It was healing. Certainly the thought went through my mind that this bassinet could have been holding my own baby, but such thoughts were fleeting. I didn't let myself dwell on them.

Paula ended up marrying a young man—not the father of the baby—who was in love with her and wanted to marry her. About a year later I heard from her. She said she was doing okay.

I got back out into the world by getting a job as a cashier in a restaurant. I was low and melancholy. I didn't want my parents to worry, so I tried to put on a good front, but I was not as okay as I let on. My brothers sent me little greetings and cards. Family support got me through.

Then, after a year in Miami, my dad finished the program and wanted to continue for his doctorate. But we all were so unhappy in Miami. It just wasn't our kind of place, and we wanted to leave. He checked out several other schools and it came down to two: one in Maine and one in Oregon. As a family we decided to go to Oregon so we could be closer to the rest of the family and our friends on the West Coast. Before we went there though, we would stop in California, where my brother David was getting married to his long-time girlfriend.

In California I saw my old girlfriends and we went to a party. I felt like I hadn't really connected with anyone at the party, so when my ride was leaving, I was ready to go. I had one foot out the door, when I heard, "I'll give you a ride."

I turned and looked. My heart jumped. It was Joseph. Sun-bleached blond hair, goatee, and incredible smile that went clear through to his blue eyes. We'd known each other in high school, but he had been in that in-crowd. As we looked at each other now, sparks flew back and forth between us. There was a feeling of deep recognition. I stepped back into the room.

Joseph was engaged to Janet, who lived in L.A. She was supposed to have come for the weekend, but didn't. She had become a born-again Christian during their relationship and wanted him to move to L.A. and sell shoes or something, and they could join her church and become really devoted church-goers. He was in a deep funk about it.

He and I talked until one in the morning. We sang Beatles' songs and Barbra Streisand songs. It felt so good, especially after the isolation I felt in Miami. I wanted to be in love and have a romantic relationship. I wanted a social life again. I wanted my life to resume. He walked me up to the door of my grand-mother's house, where we were staying, and told me he felt like he was falling in love with me. I said I felt the same way and that I never wanted to see him again, because he was engaged. So I walked in the door and shut it, thinking, Well, there's another chapter closed in my life. I was so sad.

The next day he showed up at the door. I opened it, saw who it was, and slammed it in his face. Then I opened the door again and let him in. He explained his relationship with Janet, how it had changed, and that he really was going to end it because he couldn't be a part of the life that she wanted.

He was as good as his word. He broke it off with her.

My parents were headed up to Oregon, and Joseph said he'd give me a ride up later if I wanted to stay. So I stayed with my grandparents, and Joseph and I dated. Several weeks later, Joseph, his friend Jim, and I drove up to Oregon in the camper that Joseph had built on the back of his pick-up.

Within a couple of months of returning to California, Joseph sold a house he'd remodeled, bought a motor home, and moved up to Oregon, too. My dad was very uptight about my having a close relationship with somebody. When Joseph and I wanted to go camping together, my dad was, "Well, um, I..."

"Dad, I'm on the Pill. Don't worry about it."

"Okay."

It was obvious he'd really been worried about me getting pregnant again.

Joseph and I spent most of our time together walking and talking. I felt I knew him and could trust him. Things were getting serious between us and it was time to tell Joseph about the baby. We were camping in the mountains and had just spent the day outdoors. When we got back to the motor home, we sat on the bed. He knew he wasn't the first person I'd ever been with, but I wasn't sure how he would feel about my giving up a baby.

"I need to tell you something, because our relationship is getting strong," I said, "and I feel like I don't want to have any secrets from you." We sat cross-legged, facing each other, holding hands, and I told him the whole story. I cried as I told him about it, and he listened, looking me in the eye and rubbing my fingers. When I finished, he hugged me. "How do you feel about it?" I asked.

"Well," he said, "the first thing that came to mind is it's kind of nice to know you can have kids."

"I hadn't thought about it that way."

"Do you have any feelings for Eric?"

"No. I probably have romantic feelings around the whole experience, some part of me that wants to romanticize the whole connection, but I don't feel I want to be with him."

Joseph expressed sadness that I had gone through such a difficult experience.

Over the next couple of months we started to discuss marriage. We were both only twenty-one. I still wanted to finish school and didn't feel ready to get married yet. Then Joseph was offered a job near where his parents lived that promised to pay well. His parents weren't comfortable with us living together, so we got married, then moved to California near his folks.

Now my job was to be Joseph's wife. The men worked all day and the women kept house. His mother would tell me how to keep a house clean, how to get mildew out of the grout in the shower and stains out of the kitchen sink. Was this going to be the rest of my existence, making beds, doing dishes, cleaning house? When did it become *my* responsibility?

This was also the first time I'd been away from my family, I was isolated out in the country without a California driver's license, I didn't know how to drive our stick-shift car, and I was on birth control pills that were having a negative effect on my hormones. At times I fantasized suicide.

After a year we sold the house and moved back to Oregon. I returned to school and went to work in a special education program for kindergartners. Joseph did carpentry and remodeled homes. We went through some hard times, but we made it through.

When we were both in our mid-twenties, we felt ready to have a baby. My biggest fear about it was having to undergo another experience like I'd had at the hospital. I learned about home births and found a group of doctors in my area who attended them. They worked with a midwife, who would help the woman through labor, and the doctor would come when it was time for the baby to be born. I would have more control over how things were done, and, assuming all was well, the baby would stay with me after it was born. We were also struggling financially, and it would be cheaper to have the baby at home. Another real plus.

The doctors and midwives were nutrition oriented and had me keep a journal of what I ate. I gave up all sugar and caffeine. I didn't drink or smoke anyway. I ate good food. I still had nausea and morning sickness, but I took vitamin B6 and herbs, which helped a lot. I walked, frequently hiking across town. I read everything about childbirth I could find, took Lamaze classes, and saw films about home birth. I read up on breast feeding. I felt prepared, empowered.

My water broke on the Sunday night of Thanksgiving weekend. I shook with excitement as I got into bed and breathed through my contractions. They were not coming at uniform intervals. I got up and started walking around the house, letting Joseph sleep until I really needed him. At about seven in the morning, the contractions were pretty strong and we decided to call Gwen, the midwife.

I walked around the house thinking, "Gee, I'm in labor. I'm in labor and I'm in my own house, and no one has come in with a wheelchair and I'm not lying flat on my back."

When Gwen arrived, I answered the door. "Would you like a cup of tea?"

"Sure," she said, following me into the kitchen and sitting at the table. I went to make the tea, stopping to breathe through contractions while she talked with Joseph and watched me. I made tea and gave it to them. Then I wanted to take a shower.

"Okay," she said. "Let's just see how far along you are first."

So I lay down on the couch and she checked me. "You're almost six centimeters dilated. How are those contractions?"

"They're strong. Can I take a shower?"

"Yes, but I'd make it a quick one."

So I went in and took a shower, and I had a powerful contraction. I got right out of the shower and dried off. "Better check me again," I told her.

I was seven and a half centimeters, transition. I went in and lay down on the bed. Gwen said the baby's position was not ideal and she wanted me to alternate my position for each contraction—lie on my right side for one, on my hands and knees for the next, and on my left side for the next. After several contractions, the baby turned so that it was in perfect position.

When transition got intense, I thought I'd lose control. I was panicking and couldn't keep the breathing going. Gwen put her face three inches from mine and started doing the breathing. I looked into her eyes and did the breathing with her. And Joseph was doing the breathing. We all breathed together. That helped me through the toughest time.

She had called Dr. Evans. When he got there and looked at me, he asked, "Feel like you want to push?"

"God yes!" I said.

"Then push."

With a washcloth in my mouth to bite down on, I made loud growling, grunting noises while I pushed. Our dogs, outside just under our bedroom window, started howling.

At one point I could feel my tissue tearing, and I screamed. The dogs howled again.

"God, I'm scaring the dogs," I said.

"You're scaring me!" Dr. Evans said.

Everyone was laughing and joking. There was a light-hearted, celebratory, excited feeling to it all.

I was on my side when I gave birth. The baby's head was born, eyes open and looking at Joseph. I was still breathing, trying to concentrate on the next push. After I got the shoulders out with the next push, the baby slid out sensuously.

"It's a boy?" I asked.

"Yeah," said the doctor, "he's got something hanging down there between his legs."

The baby was crying hard. Joseph tied off the cord and cut it. Then they brought the baby up to nurse.

I was famished. Joseph brought me a gigantic turkey sandwich and a pitcher of orange juice. Within an hour I was on the phone with my mom and dad. They arrived a few hours later and held their grandson. I slept with him on my chest most of the night. The next morning Joseph made a fire in the wood stove, and then sat next to it with his baby on his lap. For the next several days our son Jesse never left us.

I thought about my older son's birth and was sad it had been so different for him. I wished he could have come into the world this way. It didn't feel right that he had to go through what he did, to be taken from me and have all those things done to his body.

I turned twenty-six that year, what I call my zombie year. Jesse was a colicky baby and up most nights. I was exhausted and challenged, but it was good. I experienced a kind of love that I hadn't known existed and which grew and intensified.

When Jesse was a little over two, our second child was born. Gwen, the midwife, came and slept in our spare bedroom the night I lost my mucous plug. Labor went easy and, unlike the last time, I didn't make a sound. No yelling, no dogs howling. Total silence. I eased the baby out gently, softly, feeling every bit of her as she slowly slid out. I put my hand down and felt her head as she was emerging. It surprised me how warm her head was. She was so alive, and still connected to my body. They brought her to my chest. She was covered with vernix, which we massaged into her. Wide awake, she made soft cooing noises. Joseph was lying beside me on the bed and we both whispered to her. I started to nurse her. I was delighted, because I really wanted a girl. We named her Megan.

Jesse and my mother were downstairs during Megan's birth. They had heard the little cooing noises. Jesse asked my mother what that noise was. She said, "I thought I heard something too."

Jesse came upstairs to check. He walked in the door and came over and stroked her head while she nursed. He said, "Hmmm, she's got my booby."

When Megan was about a year old, I went back to school. I was still nursing her and I only attended part-time so I could come home and be with the kids.

The following year I found a Montessori school for Jesse that also had a toddler program for kids Megan's age. I enrolled them both and spent a lot of time helping out. I absolutely loved being with all the kids, having them on my lap and holding them. I have a special talent for understanding how kids feel and think. The woman who ran the school liked my style with kids. She suggested I take over the Tuesday-Thursday program for her and she would handle the Monday-Wednesday-Friday program. I was flattered and surprised. It opened the door to being able to be with my kids and work at the same time, so I agreed. After two years she wanted to sell the school and asked if I was interested in purchasing it. By this time I had completed all but a few methods classes and my student teaching in order to get my degree in education and I was prepared and skilled at the work. I bought the school. The administrative part of it was tedious and I was barely breaking even financially, but it was my joy, so I continued to do it.

Joseph ran our family construction business, which was going through hard times. It was a huge drama unfolding in our lives as we suffered a bankruptcy and both of our families were pulled into a financial and legal nightmare. I started taking self-help classes that facilitated examination of my life and emotional healing. It involved bringing up shadow parts of myself, looking at my belief systems, questioning them, discarding or changing the ones that didn't work, and recognizing that I didn't have to be what I was told I was. I saw how I played the stoic victim-martyr in my life's dramas, the pay-off being the good strokes I received from people who would tell me how courageous I was in the middle of all the challenges and disasters befalling us. When I started to own that I did, in fact, create the reality of my life, I began to let go of the victim mentality and take full responsibility.

Interestingly enough, during this process one of the angriest energies I got in touch with was that part of myself I disowned when I got pregnant the first time. It was the part of me that loved life, went out and took risks, partied, played, flirted, and had a great time. As I saw it, she had gotten me into trouble, so I had buried that part of myself, shoved her down thoroughly. When she came back up, she raged with anger that I'd given up my own desires in order to be what other people wanted. She was forceful, and it wasn't until I heard her and let her rage that I was able to reintegrate that part of myself back into my being.

I also saw how I only knew myself in relation to others. If I took away all my roles—wife, mother, daughter, friend, sister— who was I? I had the feeling I'd cease to exist. I felt that there was a higher purpose to our being here, a purpose beyond growing up, earning money, and raising a family. I began to search outside my indoctrination to see what else I was, the essence of who I am, the spiritual part of myself.

This work was moving me toward a new career. I was forty-five years old and had been teaching preschool for fourteen years. My work was at the point where I'd mastered it and didn't want to repeat what I'd done the year before—the learning units, the routines. It was no longer a challenge. So I sold the preschool. After a couple of years of searching for the next course my life would take, I heard about transpersonal psychology, which takes Eastern beliefs and philosophies and combines them with Western psychology. This was what I'd been doing in my emotional healing work for seven years and the field I wanted to work in.

One of the assignments in my transpersonal psychology studies was to write an autobiography. When I shared the story of relinquishing my son for adoption, it felt as if I were telling it from a place outside of myself. It was interesting that I had examined under a magnifying glass other areas of my life, but I hadn't looked at this. When some part of me would pull me over and say, "Let's look at this! Can we do this now?" I had always put it on hold. So much was going on already that I felt I didn't have enough energy left to look at it, and if I did, I might open a can of worms.

I wasn't keeping his birth a secret anymore, not since my grandmother had died several years before. I had told Jesse and Megan about him when they were teenagers. They were excited and curious. My parents and I talked about him sometimes, wondering whether he was happy and what he looked like. Every year we remembered his birthday. How it affected me each year depended on what else was going on in my life. Sometimes I'd cry in the shower so no one could hear me. I'd mention it to Joseph, often saying something as simple as, "I have a ten-year-old son today," or, "I have an eighteen-year-old son today," and he would hold me.

But where was the intense sadness I expected to feel? Sometimes I'd feel a tightness in the center of myself, a gripping, hard-to-breathe-through pain so deep that it didn't get to the surface very often, and when it did, I wouldn't dwell there. I'd deal with it more on a mental level, reminding myself of the reasons I made the decision and convincing myself I had done the right thing.

It feels as if there are two of me. One is comfortable with my decision and with people knowing. The other feels shame and guilt and is uncomfortable with people knowing. I have the feeling there's more than I've allowed myself to see, more than I'm acknowledging. To get unstuck, I've been trying to go back and re-experience emotionally that time in my life. I need to come to terms with it and fully integrate it. Then if my son should find me, there would be a place for him to fit into my life. Had he shown up when I'd been in a deeper state of denial, I don't know what it would have been like.

I recently requested and received the papers from the adoption agency that I need to sign to allow them to release information about me to him if he's been looking for me. But I haven't sent them in yet. I don't want to face the devastating disappointment of sending in the papers and finding out he hasn't contacted the agency. As long as I haven't sent them in, there's hope.

Sometimes I think about looking for him. It crosses my mind that someone who really cared would have gone out and found him by now. I feel guilty and wonder how I can justify not having looked for him. On the outer level, the main reason has been logistical—lack of finances, time, and an overwhelming feeling that I could not take it on or burden others in my life with the cost and time it would take to find him. But is it as simple as that, or is it something I'm still in denial about? I don't know. I also think looking for him would be invasive. What if he doesn't want me in his life, doesn't want to deal with all of this? I want to respect that choice. I don't want to force myself on him.

I think being relinquished by your mother has to have its effects, which certainly vary in intensity from person to person and are influenced by other events and people in your life. But how can this big thing not have had an impact on the rest of his life? At times I fear his life may have been screwed up and he feels rage about it, and by reuniting with him I might invite something into my life that would take a lot of effort on my part, his part, and my family's part to handle.

When I come from a maternal place, I feel hope that a reunion would help him. I want to tell him this whole story, to know all about me, his brother and sister, his grandparents, his aunts and uncles and cousins, and Eric and his family. I want him to be able to look me in the eye when he hears his story, feel what really happened, be able to ask anything he wants to ask. I want him to know that during the pregnancy I was aware that an incredible thing was happening, and although I worried about my parents and about how things would turn out, I never resented him. Instead, I felt great sadness that I couldn't be everything I wanted to be for him.

I know I can never be a mother to him in the way his mother is, or in the way I am to Jesse and Megan. But I have seen how parts of my children came to them through their DNA, traits and life themes that go beyond how they were raised, and I think some of what they deal with in their emotional lives is the un-healed things that were passed to them through their family heritage. Jesse and Megan can look at me, their grandparents, and their history to better understand themselves. Although en-vironment is important, my other son has attributes, strengths, and weaknesses that came from me and from Eric. It must be more difficult to go through life without being able to look at biological parents and grandparents—those who came before you and struggled with the same issues, insecurities, and ques-tions—to help put things in perspective. I think he's going to look at himself and wonder, "What did I come from? What am I dealing with that came before me?" I'd like him to know.

8

FULL CIRCLE

"Your children are not your children.
They are the sons and daughters of Life's
    longing for itself.
They come through you but not from you,
And though they are with you yet they belong
    not to you."

– Kahlil Gibran, *The Prophet*

Many of the birth mothers I have met who were involved in closed adoptions were bitter. I was too. We felt we had been coerced into adoption by societal expectations of what should constitute a family, by likely economic destitution if we did keep our children, and often by our own families. So we relinquished our children. To live with the "decision," we hung onto the belief that the adoptive family would raise the child at least as well as we could have at the time. That belief was our lifeline, and it was important for our children that we support the adoption by staying out of the way. In closed adoptions a wall was established between birth parents and adoptive parents. We never met or exchanged any information. This wall was maintained by social service agencies, lawyers, doctors, and promises of privacy, although whose privacy was being protected is debatable. Was it to protect the birth mother from being ostracized, to protect the adoptive family from intrusion from the birth family, or to protect shady practices?

In the eleven years we met, The Circle support group was open to all. It was primarily attended by birth mothers and some adoptees, but no birth fathers, and rarely adoptive parents. I still felt divided about adoptive parents, believed they wished we didn't exist so they could go on as if their adopted children had no past, no other relatives.

Then I found out that Deborah, who had a child in our daughter Haley's class, was an adoptive mom. She had placed a classified ad announcing an adoption support group. Was her group only for adoptive parents? I wondered if I should call her and ask. I was uneasy venturing onto their turf. The stereotype was that birth parents were inept, immoral, or both, and adoptive parents were the wise, capable benefactors who stepped in to rescue the children. I mustered up courage and called.

"Of course you're welcome to come," she said.

I attended the group on a Sunday afternoon. It was one of those perfect early spring days, and to the aroma of fresh-brewed coffee, a dozen of us gathered in Deborah's living room to talk about adoption. The adoptive parents there were involved in closed adoptions and a few were involved in foreign adoptions. Two couples were waiting to be chosen as adoptive parents. Deborah had given me the okay to invite another person: Dallas, an adopted man in his sixties. He had been in our group and was interested in sharing his story with this group. I was the only birth mother present, and, feeling like a misfit and life-bungler, I was nervous.

The topic that afternoon was open adoption. Carol, Jack, and Jessica—mother, father, and their eleven-year-old daughter—had been invited to the group to share their experience with it.

They talked about how they negotiated the adoption and the financial arrangements. They told about being with the birth mother for the last several weeks of the pregnancy, being present at the birth, and continued contact between their family and the birth family. They brought a book they had made about Jessica's birth and adoption. The book, with a cover designed by Jessica, was filled with pictures and stories about the birth family, the adoptive family, and their experiences.

"When did you know you were adopted?" one prospective adoptive parent asked Jessica.

Jessica was open but shy. "I guess I just always knew."

How fragile was this trusting child? I felt protective of her. I suspect we all did. No one pried further. We thanked her for sharing her book and her story with us, and she went to play with the other kids outside.

"Do you still have contact with the birth mother?" someone asked her parents.

"We see her a couple of times a year," Carol said. "In fact, she's thinking of moving here to go to school."

"How do you feel about that?" another asked.

"We're a little nervous, not sure how it'll work out living in the same small town, but we think it'll be okay."

Another adoptive parent asked why they decided to have the adoption done this way. Carol explained that when it was clear they could not have biological children, they chose open adoption because it fit with their idea of how adoption should be: that the birth mother came to her decision as freely as she could and the needs of everyone involved would be honored and respected.

Then Jack, the adoptive father, spoke. "I just can't imagine what it was like for her to carry this baby in her body for nine months, and then give her to us." He leaned forward, rested his elbows on his thighs, and buried his head in his hands.

His comment triggered something in me. I recalled the delivery room, the nurse, holding my daughter so I could see her, then untying my hand so I could touch her head. I remembered the surprise I felt as every part of me warmed with the feeling that this wonderful being and I belonged together. I remembered how abruptly the feeling numbed as the nurse took the baby away. I remembered sitting in the chair in the darkened living room, the social worker standing next to me as I read over the relinquishment papers, and the tremendous effort it took to push down the fear, anger, and confusion and just sign.

Tears were rising and I closed my eyes to shut them down. Then I stole a look at Jack. He still sat bent over, his face in his hands. Somewhere in the middle of the room, I sensed all these feelings—the letting go and the receiving, the loss and the gratitude, the shame and the guilt, the grief and the joy. Which were whose anymore? A deeper awareness of the bigger picture came to me. Our feelings were more alike than I had realized.

Dallas, the adopted man in his sixties, cleared his throat and told us that he had just found his birth mother, who was eighty-three years old. They had spoken over the phone a few times and met in person once. Their meeting had been awkward, stiff. He said, "I can't imagine what it would be like knowing both sets of parents while I grew up. I had a good family and a good life, and I always knew I was adopted, but it just wasn't talked about then. But one time, after I was an adult, I saw my name on my adoptive family's tree with the word 'adopted' beneath it. That was when I knew I was different, that I wasn't one of them." His voice choked. When he recovered, he added, "That's when I knew I had to find my birth family."

The room was quiet, then Deborah asked what I had to say. It took me a moment to collect myself. Finally, I looked at Carol and Jack. I wanted to lean on them, on their compassion. "Thank you for being so open," I said. "When I relinquished my daughter, adoptions were closed. There was no contact."

I stopped to swallow down more emotion. I was happy that things were working out so beautifully for them, and for Jessica's birth mother. This was an open adoption that was working. Why couldn't it have been that way for me? Why couldn't I have known where Andrea was and how she was doing as she grew up? Why couldn't I have seen for myself that her parents were good, caring people?

"Most birth mothers," I said, "did not come to adoption by choice. They were manipulated into the decision by families and societal pressures. This is so different. Compassionate and caring. Loving. It takes enormous courage to do it this way. Thank you."

Jack lifted his head and looked over at me. His eyes were filled with tears, as were Carol's. They tried to smile, but they looked torn. I could not guess what they were feeling.

An adoptive mother spoke. She told of taking her seven-year-old son to see his birth mother several months before. "When I saw him sitting on her lap," she said, lowering her voice to a whisper, "I wondered if I had done something terrible."

"What terrible thing did you do?" someone asked.

"I took him from her." She looked around. "Did I? Did I take him?" She began to cry. "The birth mom told me that she had been wrong, that she realized she could have raised him after all."

How sad it was to see guilt work its abuse on her.

285

"Sometimes I wake up at night," one mom said, "and I have to go check on him. I'm afraid that he's going to disappear."

They feel that too, that gut-wrenching fear of losing a child? I should not have been surprised. Many adoptive parents come to adoption through loss by miscarriage, the death of a child, or infertility.

"My son, the first child we adopted, was six when we adopted his sister," said another parent. "He went up to her birth mother when we were leaving for home and said, 'Don't worry, we'll take good care of your baby.' "

Another said, "My son worries about his birth mother, about whether or not she's okay, because he knows she was living in difficult circumstances in an impoverished country. And there's no way we can find out how she is."

I hadn't considered a child worrying about his mother. Wonder, yes; worry, no.

"We have to remember," said a mother of two, "that these children who come into our lives in adoption are powerful. They show us our weaknesses and our strengths. And we are all on this journey together. In the end, it's an incredible experience of love that we all share."

Indeed, I thought then. Of course, now I wonder if that is just too much to put on a child, but that afternoon I was learning about another side of the adoption experience. Although we had different roles in the experience, our feelings were really very similar. My uneasiness and bitterness were lifting.

And even though my birth daughter, Andrea, had been back in my life for over ten years, grief and pain over the separation from her still surfaced. Maybe that part would never be finished. It challenged me to expand my ability to accept and to see what is true *now*.

As the meeting ended and we stood, the sound of squealing laughter rose from outside. The children were still playing. In the end, this was about them, about our finding the best situations for them to thrive as happy, healthy beings.

I was struck by what an amazing and all-encompassing path adoption is. We did not need to be divided by fear. When we trust love, openness, and generosity to guide us, we give our sons and daughters the best we have to offer. The circle is then complete.

9

THE GIFT

Secrets had lived inside of me like caged animals, and I had been afraid that if I let them out, they would destroy me. When Andrea found me and I knew I had to stop hiding, I experienced these truths: That the secrets masked a deeper love, and, if I came out of hiding and did not allow shame to have its way, my sense of suffering would ease and the experiences would stretch me to greater compassion and love. I still feel sad that I bought into the shame and let it control my decisions. Events can still trigger my anger at how we treated these mothers, limited their options, shamed them, closed channels for families to know one another. When I can, I work for change in the system.

So much has changed in the last four decades. We have sex education in schools, birth control is more accessible and reliable, abortion is legal, and single motherhood has lost a lot of its stigma. Practices in adoption are changing. Gradually, open adoption is replacing closed adoption. Unfortunately, open adoption contracts are not yet legally enforceable in all states and adoptive families often shut down contact. The laws governing these contracts have yet to represent the rights of the adoptee and the original family. Also gaining a foothold is an alternative to adoption—family preservation, keeping children with their families with the help of networks that support the family as it deals with a crisis.

I want to believe the intentions were good when adoptions were closed and records sealed. But it was a social experiment whose premises—that the birth mother would forget, that the baby would not know the difference, that the family adopting would never need the kinds of information only a birth family can offer—have been proven wrong. None of us forgets the original circumstance of the birth. We carry it throughout our lives. Cutting us off from one another does not create stronger families; it disempowers us. I believe it is time the law reflects the reality of the adoptee's situation: They have two families.

Adoptees ask: Where did I come from? Who do I look like? What is my birth story? Are there ways I behave that cannot be explained by environment and nurture? What *is* my genetic blueprint? Children raised by birth families have an entire childhood to get to know the ins and outs of the family traits. Most adoptees have no such touchstones. It is time we unsealed the records, reconciled the decisions, and managed the pain out in the open. It is time we let adoptees examine and count *our* fingers and toes.

Andrea was supported by her family in looking for both me and her birth father and in wanting to know us. When she found me, *I* then had a choice to make—to let her remain a secret in my life or to embrace her presence. The opportunity to make this choice consciously and with my family's full support gave me what I needed in order to leave behind the secrets and lies. The freedom to choose, the support of both families, and clear boundaries all contributed to our successful reunion. Without these, our relationship would be stilted or, worse, emotionally destructive. I know how lucky I am that it has worked out so well.

In the end, Andrea, this daughter I did not expect, has been one of the richest experiences of my life. She brought me to myself. I see now that all the pain I felt meant I was buying into the shame, and that my sense of loss meant our connection remained strong and unceasing. Her loving presence has challenged me to live openly in the truth. She has shown me that love is not something I can control or bury because it may hurt. It is a force of its own—fierce, generous, unbounded. It is what we are. And when I know that, really *know* it, my life becomes a quiet joy.

FURTHER READINGS

Adoption Healing ... A Path to Recovery by Joe Soll (Adoption Crossroads, 2000).

Adoption Healing... A Path to Recovery for Mothers Who Lost Children to Adoption by Joe Soll and Karen Wilson Buterbaugh (Gateway Press Inc., 2003).

The Adoption Reader—Birth Mothers, Adoptive Mothers and Adopted Daughters Tell Their Stories by Susan Wadia-Ellis (Seal Press, 1995).

The Adoption Triangle by Arthur D. Sorosky, Annette Baran, and Reuben Pannor (Triadoption Publications, 2008).

The Baby Scoop Era: Unwed Mothers, Infant Adoption, and Forced Surrender, Karen Wilson-Buterbaugh (Karen Wilson-Buterbaugh, 2017).

Being Adopted, The Lifelong Search for Self by David M. Brodzinsky, Marshall D. Schechter, and Robin Marantz Henig (Anchor Books, 1993).

Birth Bond: Reunions Between Birthparents and Adoptees—What Happens After by Judith S. Gediman and Linda P. Brown (New Horizon Press, 1991).

Birthmothers: Women Who Have Relinquished Babies for Adoption Tell their Stories by Merry Jones (Chicago Review Press, 1996).

Dear Birthmother by Kathleen Silber and Phyllis Speedlin (Corona Pub Co, 3rd ed., 1991).

The Girls Who Went Away: The Hidden History of Women Who Surrendered Children for Adoption in the Decades Before <u>Roe v. Wade</u> by Ann Fessler (Penguin Books, 2006).

Hole in My Heart, Memoir and Report from the Fault Lines of Adoption by Lorraine Dusky (Leto Media, 2015).

Journey of the Adopted Self: A Quest for Wholeness by Betty Jean Lifton (Basic Books, Reprint 1995).

Lost and Found: The Adoption Experience by Betty Jean Lifton (University of Michigan Press, 2009).

The Open Adoption Experience: A Complete Guide for Adoptive and Birth Families—from Making the Decision Through the Child's Growing Years by Lois Ruskai Melina and Sharon Kaplan Roszia (William Morrow Paperbacks, 1993).

The Open-Hearted Way to Open Adoption: Helping Your Child Grow Up Whole, Lori Holden with Crystal Hass (Rowman and Littlefield, reprint edition 2015).

The Other Mother by Carol Schaefer (Create Space, 2013).

The Primal Wound by Nancy Newton Verrier (Gateway Press, 2003).

Searching… by Carol Schaefer (Create Space, 2014).

Shadow Mothers: Stories of Adoption and Reunion by Linda Back McKay (North Star Press of St. Cloud, Inc., 1998).

Strangers and Kin: The American Way of Adoption by Barbara Melosh (Harvard University Press, 2002).

Waiting to Forget: A Motherhood Lost and Found by Margaret Moorman (W.W. Norton, 1998).

Wake Up Little Susie, Single Pregnancy and Race Before Roe v. Wade by Ricki Solinger (Routeledge, 2nd ed., 2000).

ACKNOWLEDGEMENTS

When I think of the women who have journeyed with me, and especially those who share their stories here, I feel such gratitude and admiration for your strength, your courage, and your heart.

This has been a long work in progress and many times along the way I gave up. Without the encouragement of Susan Edmonds and Becky Hale, who helped me believe in myself, I am not sure this would have been completed.

As I worked, the patience and wisdom of the Talent Writers Group guided me. Thank you Dorothy Vogel, Melissa Brown, Delores de Leon, Gloria Boyd, Deborah Rothschild, Bert Anderson, and Herb Long, and double gratitude to group members Addie Greene, who also line edited, Ellen Gardner, who photographed me, and Marilyn Joy, who suggested the title.

Thank you, Yislén Barboza Hidalgo and Susan Kimler, for your thoughtful reading of the manuscript and precise grasp on what was intended.

Thank you, Chris Molé, for your cover design and its sensitive rendering of the spirit of the experience and for your book design guidance.

Thank you, John and Tressie Fodero, for being there and for supporting this project.

I wish to acknowledge my husband, Steve, my rock for more than forty years. Thanks, babe.

Finally, to Andrea, thank you for finding me and pulling me out of hiding. Our connection did not end at birth; it is an enduring bond that makes us both stronger.

Photo by Ellen Gardner

PATRICIA FLORIN lives with her husband on their organic farm in Williams, Oregon, where she writes, edits, and helps tend the farm.

Contact Patricia via: www.PatriciaFlorin.info

CPSIA information can be obtained
at www.ICGtesting.com
Printed in the USA
LVHW081503090220
646320LV00009B/805